Leading
Lesson
Study

Leading Lesson Study

A PRACTICAL GUIDE for TEACHERS and FACILITATORS

Jennifer Stepanek
Gary Appel
Melinda Leong
Michelle Turner Mangan
Mark Mitchell

A JOINT PUBLICATION

LEARNING POINT
Associates™

NWREL
Northwest Regional Educational Laboratory

CORWIN PRESS
A SAGE Publications Company
Thousand Oaks, CA 91320

For information:

Corwin Press
A Sage Publications Company
2455 Teller Road
Thousand Oaks, California 91320
www.corwinpress.com

Sage Publications Ltd.
1 Oliver's Yard
55 City Road
London EC1Y 1SP
United Kingdom

Sage Publications India Pvt. Ltd.
B-42, Panchsheel Enclave
Post Box 4109
New Delhi 110 017 India

Printed in the United States of America

Library of Congress Cataloging-in-Publication Data

Leading lesson study: A practical guide for teachers and facilitators/Jennifer Stepanek . . . [et al.].
    p. cm.
Includes bibliographical references and index.
ISBN 1-4129-3987-9 or 978-1-4129-3987-4 (cloth)
ISBN 1-4129-3988-7 or 978-1-4129-3988-1 (pbk.)
    1. Teaching—Methodology. 2. Effective teaching. I. Stepanek, Jennifer (Jennifer Lynn) II. Title.
LB1027.L37 2007
371.102—dc22   2006021823

This book is printed on acid-free paper.

15   10 9 8 7 6

Acquisitions Editor:	Rachel Livsey
Editorial Assistant:	Phyllis Cappello
Production Editor:	Beth A. Bernstein
Copy Editor:	Colleen B. Brennan
Typesetter:	C&M Digitals (P) Ltd.
Proofreader:	Anne Rogers
Indexer:	Kay Dusheck
Cover Designer:	Audrey Snodgrass
	Michael Dubowe
Graphic Designer:	Karine Hovsepian

Contents

List of Figures and Forms

Foreword

In 1997, Dr. Lynn Liptak, the principal of School No. 2 in Paterson, New Jersey, an inner city school of 720 low income mostly Latino and African American students, organized a voluntary math study group to conduct action research in our classrooms and explore ways to improve mathematics teaching and learning at our school. I was teaching 8th grade at the time and had become very interested in learning more about Japanese teaching techniques after Dr. Frank Smith of Columbia University Teachers College introduced all of Paterson's 8th grade teachers and principals to the videotaped lessons from the Trends in International Mathematics and Science Study (TIMSS), so I decided to participate in the group to learn more.

In 1998, the group was introduced to lesson study by Dr. Patsy Wang-Iverson of Research For Better Schools, whom Dr. Liptak had met at a conference. She referred us to Catherine Lewis's article, "A Lesson is Like a Swiftly Flowing River" and videotape "The Secret of Trapezes" (http://www.lessonresearch.net), which focused on Japanese lesson study in science. We became very interested in the process of lesson study and actually attempted to do lesson study. After these first unsuccessful attempts, we realized that we needed help if we were to really conduct meaningful lesson study. Dr. Liptak met Clea Fernandez and Makoto Yoshida from the Lesson Study Research Group (LSRG) at Columbia's Teacher's College and arranged for them to come to our school to give presentations on lesson study in the summer of 1999, and lesson study in the U.S. was born.

From the outset, School 2 benefited from the expertise of many knowledgeable others. The LSRG arranged for us to meet the principal and teachers from the Greenwich Japanese School (GJS) in Greenwich, Connecticut. We visited GJS on several occasions to watch research lessons with English translation provided by Dr. Yoshida and the GJS staff. Our group of 16 volunteer teachers and administrators met for two hours every Monday afternoon to conduct lesson study with the aid of the Japanese teachers. Dr. Liptak arranged for other teachers to cover our classes during these meetings. These lesson planning meetings led to the first lesson study open house in the U.S., which took place at Paterson School No. 2 on February 28, 2000.

I will never forget my initial fear when I taught my first public research lesson to a room filled with over 40 observers, including many well known lesson study experts: Catherine Lewis, Jim Stigler and Jim Hiebert, the authors of "The Teaching Gap," Clea Fernandez, Makoto Yoshida, and Patsy Wang-Iverson, as well as many Japanese teachers, my principal and my colleagues! Afterwards, we had a big and emotional party at a local restaurant. In addition to the merriment, many of us, including the Japanese teachers, shed tears, not out of shame or frustration, but out of joy, stress relief, and a myriad of hitherto untapped emotions. The most interesting thing about it was that at the party we were already planning another open house, which we held the following May, 2000! Talk about gluttons for punishment!

After our first year of lesson study, we reflected on what worked, what didn't work, and suggestions we received for improving the process. One of the things we realized was that lesson study was creating resentment among teachers who were not involved. We also realized that for lesson study to impact our entire school, all classroom teachers needed to be involved. So the following year we made a presentation to the entire staff about lesson study with testimonials from many teachers about how it was helping them to improve their teaching, understand their students, learn more content, and collaborate with their colleagues. The result was that every classroom teacher except one asked to be included in lesson study the following year. Our principal revised the school schedule to arrange weekly 80–100 minute lesson study meetings during the school day, in addition to the 40 minute weekly prep period for teachers mandated in our contract, and created a new full time position for me to facilitate the work of the lesson study groups, all without outside funding!

In addition to our lesson study work in Paterson, in 2002 a group of 10 volunteer teachers began to travel twice a month after school to conduct lesson study with the Japanese teachers at GJS. This collaboration allowed us to see first hand how Japanese teachers conduct lesson study. We brought what we learned back to the staff and, as a result, modified almost everything we were doing. We developed a schedule of meetings based on how the Japanese teachers conducted their lesson study cycle with a specific agenda for each meeting. We also began to focus more on studying content, what Japanese teachers call *kyozaikenkyu.* We also formed a Lesson Study Promotion Committee which met voluntarily once a month after school to smooth out problems, share between groups, schedule lesson study activities, and make sure we were focusing on and achieving our lesson study goal. This collaboration resulted in several lesson study open houses at both schools.

As we deepened our knowledge of lesson study, things began to change slowly at our school. Before lesson study, classes were constantly interrupted by calls from the office, visits from the nurse, teachers interrupting to ask to borrow something, and students being pulled out in the middle of mathematics classes for remediation. Teachers began to realize that a lesson is like an engaging story that should not be interrupted and even began posting signs on their doors saying, "Teaching is sacred, please do not interrupt."

Teachers also began letting their guard down and not being afraid to admit they didn't know something or ask a colleague for help. They began to organize their chalkboards intentionally and often at the end of a lesson while students were traveling to the next class, they would literally grab another teacher in the hall and say, "Come look at my blackboard. Look at the solutions my students had!" Sharing and collaboration, which had once been rare, now became commonplace.

Teachers began teaching in more powerful ways too. Instead of just explaining how to do mathematical procedures to students and then giving practice problems and assistance, they were beginning their lessons by posing mathematical problems designed to make students think and wrestle with a problem. Lessons were becoming more student centered as teachers began to encourage students to share, discuss and debate their solutions and errors. Teachers began to develop a shared vision of what good teaching looks like, and teaching began to develop greater consistency throughout the school. We also learned much mathematical content knowledge as lesson study led us to adopt a more focused and rigorous curriculum. We even spent our summers studying how Singapore and Japanese textbooks teach different topics.

Perhaps the greatest result was the transformation we saw in student learning and thinking. Students were becoming increasingly engaged in mathematics lessons. They were learning to think through problems for longer periods of time without becoming frustrated and giving up so quickly. Instead of being satisfied with one solution method, they began to seek alternative and more efficient solution methods and learn from their peers. Instead of sitting passively and listening to the teacher lecture, they were actually discussing and debating important mathematical ideas! They also began to enjoy mathematics, a subject that most of them previously disliked, and many were saying that it was their favorite subject. You could actually see the excitement they had for learning in their eyes!

The whole environment of School 2 was literally transformed through lesson study and lesson study began to spread to other subject areas. We planned research lessons in science, social studies and language arts and saw that lesson study also helped to improve teaching and learning in other subjects besides mathematics.

This is not to say that everything went smoothly. We often experienced confusion, frustration, fatigue, bruised feelings, and other problems. We learned how to do lesson study the hard way—from our mistakes. But these mistakes were overcome by the many factors that contributed to the effective implementation of lesson study at our school. We had access to a host of knowledgeable others. We had the Japanese teachers to mentor us and collaborate with us. We had a dynamic principal who not only actively promoted and supported lesson study but actually participated, attending nearly every meeting of every group, and participated as a member of a lesson study planning team. We also had enthusiastic teacher-leaders who were willing to go the extra mile to ensure its success.

Lesson study is gaining momentum rapidly in the U.S., but new lesson study groups do not have many of the advantages that we enjoyed. They will need much guidance that may not be readily available. That is why "Leading Lesson Study: A Practical Guide for Teachers and Facilitators," is such a valuable tool. In this book, you will learn from the combined wisdom of both lesson study experts and actual practitioners. Different schools have different situations and constraints. In "Leading Lesson Study," you can learn from a number of schools that, in spite of obstacles, found a way not only to conduct lesson study, but to expand and improve it. It will also help you to avoid many of the pitfalls that those of us who pioneered lesson study in the U.S. had to learn the hard way.

Lesson study is the most powerful thing that I have ever experienced as an educator. It has transformed my own personal teaching and understanding of teaching and learning as well at that of my colleagues at School 2 and empowered us to make a difference as professional educators. This book can help you to conduct lesson study in an organized, deliberate, and effective way and you, your colleagues, your school, and most importantly, your students, will reap the benefits.

—Bill Jackson
Math Facilitator, Public School No. 2
Paterson, NJ

Preface

PURPOSE OF THIS BOOK

Lesson study is a professional development practice in which teachers collaborate to develop a lesson plan, teach and observe the lesson to collect data on student learning, and use their observations to refine their lesson. It is a process that teachers engage in to learn more about effective practices that result in improved learning outcomes for students.

Interest in lesson study, which has a long history in Japan, has been growing rapidly in the United States since publication of the results of the Trends in International Mathematics and Science Study (TIMSS) video study and *The Teaching Gap* (Stigler & Hiebert, 1999). Many people have seen its potential to change teaching practice and improve student learning, but educators who are using and adapting the Japanese lesson study model face a number of challenges. It is not easy to change old models of professional development and organize schools into places where teachers can learn. Schools need materials that provide extensive examples, models, strategies, and tools in order to facilitate lesson study.

The purpose of this book is to provide a detailed account of the lesson study process. It depicts how teachers in the United States are bringing lesson study into their schools, and it will help educators envision lesson study in their own professional lives. The content is also intended to describe the substance of lesson study—not just the process, but the big ideas and habits of mind that drive the creation of professional knowledge.

The strategies, tools, and examples are designed to make lesson study a more tangible process because it is new territory for most U.S. educators. This concrete approach is not intended to be prescriptive or to define how all lesson study teams should go about their work. Instead, it is a place to start and a means of helping teachers begin to work out how to engage in lesson study for themselves. By presenting a step-by-step process, the tools that support it, and examples that bring it to life, this book is intended to help readers to gain an understanding of what it means to collaboratively plan a lesson or to engage in a discussion about student learning during the debriefing.

Teachers starting out with lesson study often find that it is more difficult than they first anticipated. As Sonal Chokshi and Clea Fernandez (2004) point out, "Lesson study is easy to learn but difficult to master" (p. 524). As a result, teams often begin with the help of technical assistance providers and university faculty. Yet many schools do not have access to specialists who can provide the necessary guidance. Even schools that start out working with a lesson study expert may find that they struggle when this support is no longer available.

INTENDED AUDIENCE

The book is designed to meet the needs of a variety of people. For those who are beginning to learn about lesson study, the book will provide a detailed walk through the process. Members of new lesson study teams will find information that will help guide them through unfamiliar territory. More experienced teams will find new routes and new perspectives on more familiar terrain. Administrators who want to get lesson study started in their schools will also find the book useful.

This resource is likely to be most helpful to people who are working with lesson study teams in the role of facilitator. There are many different people who can take on this role. Teachers who have become experienced lesson study practitioners can branch out to become facilitators for new lesson study teams. Instructional coaches and professional development providers might work with multiple teams in a school or district. When no outside facilitator is available, a member of the lesson study team can also fill this role.

OVERVIEW OF THE CONTENT

The process used to develop this book reflects the collaborative spirit of lesson study. The coauthors worked together to plan and develop the content, exchanging ideas and drafts in an iterative process. Like a lesson study team, the group benefited from the expertise that each member brought to the endeavor and were able to build on their collective ideas and experiences.

The lesson study cycle is the primary organizer for the content of the book. There are chapters devoted to each phase of the process. Additional chapters address the issues around supporting, getting started, and sustaining lesson study.

Chapter Descriptions

Chapter 1 provides an overview of lesson study and the rationale for engaging in the process. Readers can use the information in this chapter to help make the case for lesson study in their school or district.

Chapter 2 describes the supports that are necessary for lesson study, such as time for collaborative planning, administrative support, and committed teachers. The chapter also suggests how to put the necessary conditions in place and how to develop a lesson study action plan.

Chapter 3 provides tools and suggestions for sharing responsibilities, scheduling meetings, and creating the necessary group dynamics. The first phase of the lesson study process also begins here, with identifying the research theme or long-term goal.

Chapter 4 guides the lesson study team through the planning process. Strategies and tools are provided to make this phase of the lesson study cycle as concrete and explicit as possible.

Chapter 5 describes the observation and debriefing phase of lesson study. In particular, attention is given to the challenges of setting up and engaging in an effective debriefing.

Chapter 6 is intended to guide and enhance the revising and reteaching phase. Teams will find strategies and tools to help them use the information from the observation and debriefing to revise the lesson plan.

Chapter 7 will help readers to reflect on their work and to develop a research lesson report. It also provides suggestions for evaluating the lesson study process, both formatively and summatively.

Chapter 8 provides suggestions for sustaining lesson study and dealing with the coming and going of team members. It includes strategies for bringing more teachers into the process, as well as ideas about how to enhance lesson study practice over time.

Common Elements

Within the chapters, there are a number of recurring sections. The purposes of these common elements are described below.

From Our Team to Yours. Advice from the Detroit Lesson Study Group is included at the end of each chapter. This team of five teachers has created a thriving lesson study practice in their district. They share their experiences and practical advice with readers.

From the Field. Sections labeled "From the Field" are real-life examples from teachers and others involved in lesson study. These sections are intended to highlight the knowledge and advice of experienced practitioners. They also illustrate the process and substance of lesson study.

Challenges. Many of the chapters include a section devoted to "Challenges." This section is used to examine common dilemmas that lesson study teams encounter, as well as to provide some suggestions and questions that may help reframe the problems and create solutions.

Reflecting and Assessing Progress. This section includes questions that are intended to be used by lesson study teams as they complete each phase of the cycle. It is a time to identify and reflect on the learning that has occurred and to think about the team's lesson study practice. The questions are designed to make the team's work and learning more intentional and substantial.

Moving On to the Next Phase. Following the "Reflecting and Assessing Progress" questions, the chapters close with a section about the final steps of the phase. The purpose is to briefly describe the primary outcomes of the lesson study phase and to identify the artifacts that teams can gather to document their work. These artifacts will be used in Chapter 7 to create a lesson study report.

Suggestions for Readers

Readers are likely to use the book in different ways, based on their needs and their familiarity with lesson study. The following are some suggestions for different audiences.

- **For readers who are new to lesson study:** It may be helpful to begin by reading Chapter 1 and then skimming through the other chapters to get a feel for lesson study. A second, more careful reading is likely to be more meaningful with a big-picture perspective.

- **For experienced teams and other practitioners:** The most efficient way to begin may be to look through the book for the tools and examples that can be used immediately. Alternatively, a closer reading may uncover ideas for improving lesson study practice and maintaining momentum.
- **For teachers who are engaging in lesson study for the first time:** After their first reading, teams may find it helpful to refer back to specific sections of the book. Reading the appropriate chapter at the beginning of each phase of the lesson study cycle will provide perspective on the work ahead.
- **For people who are interested in launching lesson study:** Administrators and others who are interested in getting lesson study started will find the most useful information for their immediate needs in Chapter 2.

Each chapter ends with an overview of the "Key Ideas" presented within the chapter. These are intended to reinforce some of the most important points and to give readers a few ideas to think about as they continue reading.

Lesson study involves a number of concepts and terms that may be unfamiliar to readers. When an unfamiliar word or phrase appears, it may be helpful to check the Glossary. The glossary terms are highlighted the first time they appear in the text.

For the most part, the examples and tools are embedded within each chapter. The tools can be copied directly from the book, but readers are also encouraged to enhance and adapt them. There are a few longer examples that appear at the end of the book. Resource A includes three sample research lessons, and Resource B is a set of Frequently Asked Questions about the planning process. Sources for more tools, examples, and information about lesson study are listed in Resource C: Additional Resources.

For information on lesson study professional development services, visit the Web site at: www.nwrel.org, or contact Kit Peixotto at peixottk@nwrel.org or 503-275-9594 or contact Barbara Youngren at Learning Point Associates (barb.youngren@learningpt.org or by phone at 800-356-2735).

ACKNOWLEDGMENTS

We have many people to thank for the contributions they have made to this book. We are grateful to everyone who has shared their experiences and their stories with us.

First and foremost, this book would not exist without the teachers and the teams who have been paving the way for lesson study in the United States. We would like to thank all of the teams who are featured in the book—as well as the many others who have shared their work with us—for teaching us about lesson study.

In particular, we would like to thank the Detroit Lesson Study Group—Brandon Graham, Byron Timms, Vicki Vorus, Elana Webster, Jason White—and Aleatha Kimbrough and Donna Alford from Detroit Public Schools. They generously shared their experiences and their passion for lesson study and teaching. Dr. Joanne Caniglia from Eastern Michigan University was instrumental in bringing us together with this wonderful team.

We would also like to thank the following lesson study groups from Traverse City Public Schools, Michigan, whose work is included in this book: Robin Brister, Linda Egeler, Mary Jeffrey, Kathy Johnston, Abby Leppien, Karen Nelson, Kristen

Sak, and Jessica Unger, with support from Becky Sanford, Amy Savalle, Karen Smith, and Vern Wolfgram. Lesson study in Traverse City would not have been possible without the support and leadership of Eric Dreier, science coordinator (retired).

Our colleagues have also contributed to our learning about lesson study and this book. We have enjoyed and gained so much from sharing our knowledge and our questions about lesson study among the following people: Carrie Baker, Eric Blackford, Karen Draper, Claire Gates, Linda Griffin, Constanza Hazelwood, Jim Leigh, Julie Peck, Kit Peixotto, Halimah Polk, Claudette Rasmussen, Maria Torres, Joyce Tugel, Gil Valdez, Patsy Wang-Iverson, Denise Jarrett Weeks, Barbara Youngren, and Veronica Zonick.

We must acknowledge Kit Peixotto, in particular, for contributing to the initial development of the book. Kit, Claire Gates, and Julie Peck conducted an early review of this material and provided numerous helpful suggestions that improved our work.

Finally, we would like to thank Rachel Livsey, our editor at Corwin Press, for providing us with the opportunity to write this book.

Corwin Press gratefully acknowledges the contributions of the following reviewers:

Kathy DiRanna
K–12 Alliance Statewide Director
WestEd
Santa Ana, CA

Catherine Lewis
Director of Research and
Development
Mills College, Department of
Education
Oakland, CA

Lynn Liptak
Retired Principal
Paterson Public School No. 2
Paterson, NJ

Kay Luzier
Math Fusion Teacher
Palm Terrace Elementary School
Volusia County Schools
Daytona Beach, FL

Marisa Ramirez
Science Resource Teacher
San Diego City Schools
San Diego, CA

Megan Stanton-Anderson
Project Director
GEAR UP
Long Beach, CA

Patsy Wang-Iverson
Director of Special Projects
Gabriella and Paul Rosenbaum
Foundation
Bryn Mawr, PA

About the Authors

Jennifer Stepanek is a writer, editor, and researcher with the Northwest Regional Educational Laboratory (NWREL) in Portland, Oregon. She is the editor of *Northwest Teacher*, a mathematics and science education journal for teachers. Jennifer has worked with lesson study teams at a variety of sites in the Northwest to explore how teachers in the United States are adapting the Japanese model to fit their contexts and needs.

Jennifer edited and contributed to two issues of *Northwest Teacher* focused on lesson study: "Lesson Study: Teachers Learning Together" from spring 2001 and "Lesson Study: Crafting Learning Together" from spring 2003. She is also the coauthor of *An Invitation to Lesson Study* (NWREL, 2005), an electronic resource designed to help facilitators and other professional development providers introduce lesson study to others.

Jennifer's previous projects include coauthoring NWREL's It's Just Good Teaching series. This collection of research-based monographs on mathematics and science teaching addresses such topics as equity, standards-based instruction, classroom assessment, family involvement, and effective instruction for gifted students. She was the writer and editor of *Practical Inquiry*, a topical series for school administrators on critical issues in mathematics and science education.

Gary Appel is a senior associate at Learning Point Associates, where he directs lesson study activities, designs and conducts professional development services, and provides technical assistance to school districts and state education agencies. He has 30 years of K–12 experience, having served as a science teacher, environmental educator, elementary science curriculum developer, science project director, and professional developer. Gary has helped initiate science, mathematics, language arts, and social studies lesson study groups throughout the Midwest. He has made numerous lesson study presentations to national audiences, including at the American Educational Research Association annual meeting and the National Staff Development Council's annual conference.

Prior to his work at Learning Point Associates, he was a professional development coordinator for the Michigan Department of Education's Statewide Systemic Initiative, where he worked to strengthen the capacity of the state's science and mathematics professional developers to support teacher learning.

In addition, Gary served as the executive director of the award-winning Life Lab Science Program at the University of California at Santa Cruz and is a Kellogg Foundation National Fellow.

He is lead author of *Teacher to Teacher: Reshaping Instruction Through Lesson Study* (NCREL, 2002) and coauthor of *An Invitation to Lesson Study* (NWREL, 2005), *The Growing Classroom* (Dale Seymour, 2002), and *Powerful Practices in Mathematics and Science: Facilitator's Guide* (Learning Point Associates, 2005).

Melinda Leong has served as a senior program advisor in the Mathematics and Science Education Center at NWREL since 2001. During this time, she has been providing leadership in designing effective professional development in mathematics learning, teaching, and assessment for regional and national clients. Melinda is leading development and dissemination activities to support the understanding of lesson study across the Northwest. She has worked directly with lesson study teams as a team member, facilitator, and knowledgeable other. She coauthored *An Invitation to Lesson Study: A Facilitator's Guide* CD-ROM and has coordinated several lesson study conferences.

Before joining NWREL, Melinda worked with the New York City Board of Education in District 2 as a teacher and director for 11 years at the K–8 level. She was the founder and director of the Manhattan Academy of Technology in New York, a middle school focused on integrating technology into a three-year comprehensive and rigorous academic program.

Michelle Turner Mangan is a doctoral student at the University of Wisconsin–Madison, and a former evaluator at Learning Point Associates. She has led evaluations of the Northern Michigan Lesson Study Initiative and has advised on evaluation work for the Kalamazoo and Detroit Lesson Study Groups. She is also a Spencer Fellow at the University of Wisconsin–Madison, focusing her research on the evaluation aspects of lesson study. To help bridge the gap between knowledge and practice, she guest-lectured on the implementation of lesson study to a graduate class in the Department of Educational Leadership and Policy Analysis at the University of Wisconsin–Madison. Furthermore, she is a program assistant for the Consortium for Policy Research in Education at the University of Wisconsin–Madison, where she conducts research on school finance reform.

Michelle is the coauthor of *An Invitation to Lesson Study* (NWREL, 2005) and a contributor to *Teacher to Teacher: Reshaping Instruction Through Lesson Study* (NCREL, 2002), a video and facilitator guide designed to help support effective professional development opportunities for teachers. She presented a session titled Ohio Lesson Study: Taking an Alternative Route to Lesson Study in the U.S.A. at the American Educational Research Association annual meeting in April 2003 in Chicago.

Before joining Learning Point Associates, Michelle worked as an evaluator at Research for Better Schools in Philadelphia. She provided evaluation services at Paterson School No. 2 in New Jersey, a school with a vibrant lesson study team and that is a leader in the movement to implement lesson study in the United States. She also worked as a children's outpatient therapist and adult intake supervisor at a community mental health center in Philadelphia.

Mark Mitchell is a senior program associate at Learning Point Associates, where he facilitates lesson study workshops, designs and conducts professional development, and provides technical assistance to school districts and state educational agencies. He has 20 years' experience in education serving as a curriculum developer, project director, environmental educator, and technical assistance provider to school districts.

Prior to his work at Learning Point Associates, he was a regional coordinator for the Michigan Rural Systemic Initiative where he worked intensively with rural school districts to build capacity in math and science instruction.

He is coauthor (with William Stapp) of the *Field Manual for Water Quality Monitoring* (12th ed., 2000) and of the *Field Manual for Global Water Quality Monitoring* (2nd ed., 1997), both from Kendall/Hunt. He is also coauthor of *An Invitation to Lesson Study* (NWREL, 2005) and of *Powerful Practices in Mathematics and Science: Facilitator's Guide* (Learning Point Associates, 2005).

Introduction

Making the Case for Lesson Study

Teaching is a cultural activity. We learn how to teach indirectly, through years of participation in classroom life, and we are largely unaware of some of the most widespread attributes of teaching in our own culture. The fact that teaching is a cultural activity explains why teaching has been so resistant to change. But recognizing the cultural nature of teaching gives us new insights into what we need to do if we wish to improve it.

~Stigler & Hiebert (1999, p. 11)

Classroom life is full of habits and routines that pass unnoticed. They will often remain invisible until they are viewed from a different angle or in a new context.

The teacher welcomes students and begins going over a previous assignment. The class enacts the well-known call-and-response routine, with the teacher asking questions and the students answering. The teacher reads aloud from the text. There is a short quiz. Students work quietly at their desks, getting a head start on their homework.

Not every classroom looks exactly like this, and yet this scene will be familiar to most people. The young child playing school follows a similar script. The adult recalls this ritual, thinking back with fondness or with dread.

In the late 1990s, a video study of eighth-grade classrooms in Germany, Japan, and the United States was conducted as one component of the Trends in International Mathematics and Science Study (TIMSS) (Stigler, Gonzales, Kawanaka, Knoll, & Serrano, 1999). The researchers analyzed transcripts of videotaped lessons in which all distinguishing cultural details had been removed. Although the purpose of the study was to make cross-cultural comparisons of mathematics teaching, an unintended outcome was the observed commonalities among teachers from the same country that might have gone unnoticed when looking only at U.S. classrooms.

In *The Teaching Gap,* James Stigler and James Hiebert (1999) theorize that the reason teaching is so consistent—and therefore so difficult to change—is because it is a cultural activity. In other words, we are steeped in ideas about what it means to teach from the time we first enter school, if not before. As a result, teachers tend to follow cultural scripts that are consistent with what they experienced as students.

In their book, Stigler and Hiebert (1999) describe **lesson study**—a model for intensive, school-based professional development used in Japan—as a strategy for change and improvement that is appropriate for a cultural activity such as teaching. Developing new approaches requires deep thought, inquiry, and collaboration with a collective focus on teaching rather than teachers.

> *When habit swathes everything, one day follows another identical day and predictability swallows any hint of an opening possibility. . . . Once we can see our givens as contingencies, then we may have an opportunity to posit alternative ways of living and valuing and to make choices.*
>
> ~Greene (1995, p. 23)

AN OVERVIEW OF LESSON STUDY

Lesson study is a professional development practice in which teachers collaborate to develop a lesson plan, teach and observe the lesson to collect data on student learning, and use their observations to refine their lesson. It is a process that teachers engage in to learn more about effective practices that result in improved learning outcomes for students. The **lesson study process** is illustrated in Figure 1.1.

In her autobiography, Virginia Woolf (1976) noted her desire to break through the "cotton wool" of daily life—the routines and habits that prevented her from seeing and living deeply. When teachers participate in lesson study, they have an opportunity to focus their attention on the deeper substance of their work. There is little time for such concentration when teachers are caught up in the flow of teaching.

The time devoted to investigating students as they think and learn is the part of lesson study that teachers find most appealing and exciting. Lesson study teams examine how students learn and what they bring to the learning experience. Their inquiries lead them to knowledge about what stimulates students' interest and inspires them to persist through a challenging task.

When they observe, the teachers are often assigned to follow one group of children throughout the lesson. They pay close attention to the conversations students have with each other as well as the teacher's interactions with the small groups. They are also intent on capturing students' reactions to the lesson: How eager are they to investigate the topic? Japanese teachers mention watching the students to see if their eyes are shining and listening for the exclamations that students make to themselves (Lewis, 2000).

Lesson study provides a context for examining content. Teachers deepen their own understanding, gaining a sense of how different topics fit together and build on each other. They take time to examine and reflect on curricula and other teaching materials. They also work together on how to translate their own content knowledge into experiences for students.

Figure 1.1   The Lesson Study Process

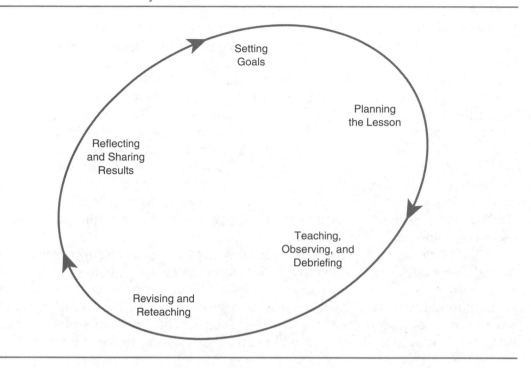

When lesson study is conducted on a schoolwide basis, improvement is continuous and happens in more than one classroom. All of the teachers in the school benefit from building on each other's knowledge and ideas. The process of learning through inquiry and discussion about classroom teaching helps teachers to build their sense of professional authority (Linn, Lewis, Tsuchida, & Songer, 2000).

School improvement efforts in the United States often fail to engage teachers as knowledgeable practitioners, instead providing mandates, incentives, or "teacher-proof" strategies and materials. Lesson study approaches teaching as intellectually demanding work rather than a set of skills to be implemented. The attention paid to each lesson honors the importance of teaching as a profoundly complex and interesting endeavor.

Lesson Study in Japan

Lesson study has a long history in Japan, where it began as a grassroots effort initiated by teachers (Fernandez, 2002). There are several different types of lesson study. It is conducted as part of teachers' preservice training, and first-year teachers continue to participate as they begin their careers (Fernandez & Yoshida, 2004; Shimizu, 2002). Research organizations conduct lesson study at the national level to explore new ideas about teaching or curriculum (Murata & Takahashi, 2002). These groups often present public research lessons at national conferences, where many educators are invited to observe and discuss the lesson. Teachers who have common professional interests—such as subject matter or career stage—form regional or cross-district lesson study groups (Murata & Takahashi, 2002; Shimizu, 2002).

Finally, individual schools conduct lesson study as one part of their school-based professional development, which is called *konaikenshu* in Japanese (Yoshida, 1999). Lesson study is used primarily in elementary schools and middle schools, and it is conducted in all subject areas—including art, physical education, and extracurricular activities (Murata & Takahashi, 2002).

It is not unusual for teachers and administrators in the United States to dismiss lesson study because of its origins in Japan. They cite the many differences between the educational systems of the two countries. Many—especially mathematics and science teachers—are weary of being unfavorably compared to Japanese teachers. Others have expressed doubts about the ability of U.S. teachers to engage in the process.

The differences between Japanese and U.S. schools cannot be denied. U.S. teachers face challenges that Japanese teachers do not. Many of the structural features that support lesson study—for example, a national curriculum—are not present in the United States. Yet lesson study can be used as a means of developing schools that are more conducive to teacher learning.

This does not require that schools emulate Japan in order to support lesson study or that the purpose of lesson study is for teachers to assume Japanese teaching styles. Schools in the United States cannot simply adopt the Japanese lesson study process without modifications. The challenge is to strike a balance between keeping the essential elements of lesson study intact—for example, collaboration and peer observation—while changing the model to fit the reality of schools in the United States.

CORE ELEMENTS OF LESSON STUDY

Understanding the lesson study process is the first step in learning about lesson study. The process is often the easiest element to grasp because it is the most concrete. Yet there are other elements that are equally important in understanding its substance. The process is the framework for developing the habits of mind and exploring the big ideas that drive the pursuit of professional knowledge. Figure 1.2 illustrates how the habits of mind and the big ideas are embedded within the framework of the lesson study process.

The Lesson Study Process

The following is a brief overview of the lesson study process. It is intended to be an initial introduction to the work of lesson study teams. The later chapters of this book portray each phase with more detail and depth.

Setting Goals

Teachers identify a **research theme**—a broad, **long-term goal**—to guide the **lesson study cycle** and focus their work (Lewis, 2000). It is usually focused on students—for example, "Students will become confident and creative thinkers and innovators." Lesson study teams often focus on the same research theme through multiple cycles of lesson study over the course of several years (Yoshida, 1999). Ideally, the goal will serve as a focus for the whole professional development program, not just lesson study. The research theme helps to ensure that lesson study addresses important issues that will have an impact on student learning.

Figure 1.2   Core Elements of Lesson Study

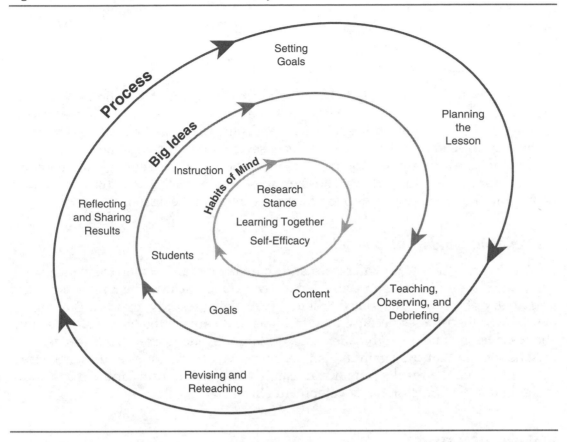

Planning the Lesson

Using the research theme to guide their work, the lesson study team collaboratively develops a classroom lesson, which is called a **research lesson**. The lesson study team identifies specific lesson goals that often come from examining assessment data or identifying a common problem. The teachers spend time investigating teaching materials and draw on their own experiences, ideas they have read about, and strategies they have seen other teachers use (Lewis, 2000). The plan for the research lesson is very detailed, with descriptions of anticipated responses from students. It is a guide for teaching the lesson, but it also serves as a communication tool for the lesson study team by clarifying the goals and ideas being tested.

Teaching, Observing, and Debriefing

When the plan is complete, one person teaches the lesson to his or her students. The other team members serve as data collectors, and sometimes they are joined by invited guests, including **knowledgeable others**—educators with expertise in content or pedagogy relevant to the research lesson. The observers take notes on what the teacher and the students are doing and saying and collect evidence of student thinking. The purpose of the observation is to gather data about the effectiveness of the lesson, not to evaluate the teacher. After a break, the teachers and guests conduct a **debriefing** to discuss the lesson and their observations. The members of the lesson study team—and other observers if they are present—share the evidence of student learning that they have collected.

Revising and Reteaching

Based on the evidence collected and discussed during the observation and debriefing, the lesson study team makes changes to the lesson. The teachers will use the data to craft revisions that will address problems and student misunderstandings identified in the first presentation. The team may meet several times to revise the lesson, which is taught to a new group of students. The same processes for observing and debriefing are used for the second teaching. The team sometimes uses the data collected and the notes from the discussion to develop the final version of the lesson.

Reflecting and Sharing Results

The lesson study team will record and share the research lesson they developed. The teachers publish a **report** about their work and include their reflections and a summary of group discussions (Yoshida, 1999). Lesson study reports are an important part of the process because they facilitate and capture the teachers' reflections about the lesson and about broader issues of teaching and learning. The teachers use the knowledge that they gain to plan and improve other lessons and their instructional practice. The results from one research lesson will inform future lesson study cycles and other professional development efforts.

Habits of Mind

The habits of mind are the qualities that teachers build and use in order to grow professionally through lesson study. These qualities may be unfamiliar to many teachers and therefore inspire a significant shift in the way they think about their work.

Research Stance

Lesson study involves posing questions and problems, researching possible solutions, trying out ideas, collecting data, and analyzing findings. Teachers engage in inquiry, reflection, and critical examination of their practice. They look at the classroom as a place in which to investigate teaching and learning.

Learning Together

It is important for all team members to establish and sustain a safe environment for collaboration. Communication within the team is clear and respectful. Team members are open to new ideas and approaches.

Self-Efficacy

Teachers are motivated and persistent in improving their craft. They take responsibility and believe that they can make a difference in student learning.

Big Ideas

The big ideas are the topics that teachers explore as they engage in lesson study. Focusing on important issues in teaching and learning helps to ensure that the teachers' work will have broad impact. The big ideas guide the teachers toward building knowledge that will endure beyond the research lesson.

Instruction

Linking the key concepts underlying the content and students' current understanding, team members consider instructional approaches that will help students reach the goals. Some of the issues that the team considers include how to begin the lesson, what questions to pose, and how to summarize the key concepts. The team members collect and examine existing lessons, research best practices, and identify effective tools.

Students

Teachers consider students' prior knowledge and think about how children learn. They also identify anticipated responses and misconceptions, discussing and planning how a teacher might address students' reactions and build on their ideas and actions.

Goals

Teachers establish long-term goals for their students by considering what they want their students to become and where they are now. In addition, teachers establish short-term goals for their students, which typically focus on content and process.

Content

Teachers explore the topic of the unit and the research lesson. They consider the key concepts underlying the topic as well as connections to other concepts. Teachers sometimes identify gaps in their own knowledge as they develop the lesson.

Engaging in the process of lesson study without considering the other core elements is a problem that teams can overcome by continually reflecting on their lesson study practice. If teachers do not ground their work in important ideas and adopt the necessary habits of mind, lesson study is not likely to bring about significant improvements in teaching and learning.

ALL THIS WORK FOR ONE LESSON?

The extended time devoted to planning the research lesson is a concern for many teachers and administrators when they first hear about lesson study. Putting so much time and effort into a lesson that occupies a few hours of one school day does not seem like a good investment. Others mistakenly believe that lesson study teams are charged with developing exemplary lessons that other teachers can take up and use.

It is quite natural to assume that the purpose of an activity that is named "*lesson* study" would be to develop lessons. Although the research lesson is an important aspect of the process, it is not the only—or even the primary—product. The lesson serves as an organizer that the teachers use as they engage in the real work of lesson study: studying teaching materials, discussing content and instruction, reflecting on their practice, investigating student learning, and applying all that they learn to their practice. The purpose of lesson study is to improve instruction by generating professional knowledge, *not* by developing a bank of exemplary lessons. Lesson study teams do share their research lessons with each other, but they do so in order to communicate what they have learned.

Although lesson study shares a number of features with other forms of professional development, there are details that set it apart. Figure 1.3 is intended to identify key aspects of lesson study that make it unique. All of these approaches to professional learning are valuable; however, they have different strengths and serve different purposes.

Figure 1.3   Comparing Professional Development Approaches

Action Research	**Lesson Study**
Examining teachers' own teaching and their students' learning by engaging in a research project in their classroom	Emphasis on collaboration Common focus
Study Groups	**Lesson Study**
Engaging in regular, structured, and collaborative interactions regarding topics identified by the group, with opportunities to examine new information, reflect on their practice, or assess and analyze outcome data	Direct link to planning and classroom practice Focus on a specific topic or problem related to goals for student learning
Curriculum Development	**Lesson Study**
Creating new instructional materials and strategies or tailoring existing ones to meet the learning needs of students	Research lessons are learning tools rather than products Teachers often use existing curriculum and learning activities
Peer Coaching and Mentoring	**Lesson Study**
Working one-on-one with an equally or more experienced teacher to improve teaching and learning through a variety of activities, including classroom observation and feedback, problem solving and troubleshooting, and co-planning	Focus on the lesson rather than the teacher All team members contribute equally
Examining Student Work	**Lesson Study**
Carefully examining students' work and products to understand their thinking and learning strategies and identify their learning needs and appropriate teaching strategies and materials	Live observation of students Common understanding of the context of student work

SOURCE: Loucks-Horsley, S., Hewson, P. S., Love, N., & Stiles, K. E. (1998). *Designing professional development for teachers of science and mathematics.* Thousand Oaks, CA: Corwin Press.

BUILDING A RESEARCH BASE FOR LESSON STUDY

Lesson study is gaining momentum in the United States as a practice that can inspire profound changes in teaching and school organization, leading to improvements in student learning and achievement. Much of what is known about the impact of lesson study comes from Japan, where it is an established practice. According to Japanese teachers, the results of lesson study include improved instruction, improved understanding of subject matter, tighter connection between their daily work and long-term goals for students, and improved ability to "see children" (Lewis, 2000; Lewis & Tsuchida, 1997).

In the United States, knowledge about the impact of lesson study is slowly beginning to accumulate. What is known so far is quite limited because although lesson study—and in particular, interest in lesson study—has grown very quickly, it is still a new practice. The educational community is in the midst of finding out what lesson study looks like in a U.S. setting and investigating how teachers engage in lesson study. Rather than looking only at impact, Catherine Lewis and her colleagues call attention to the need for research that describes lesson study as it is practiced in Japan and the United States, as well as investigations of how lesson study results in improved instruction (Lewis, Perry, & Murata, 2006).

To build a strong rationale for lesson study, it is necessary to draw on multiple sources of evidence. The following sections are organized around themes from research on effective professional development. Each theme is linked to the features of lesson study and the related outcomes. Evidence comes from descriptive studies about lesson study practice as well as emerging research and evaluation conducted on U.S. lesson study projects.

Collaborative, Comprehensive, and Ongoing

Professional development has a stronger impact when it involves groups of teachers organized around common subject areas or grade levels rather than individual teachers (Garet, Porter, Desimone, Birman, & Yoon, 2001). Short-term experiences that change topics are less effective that professional development that is continual and maintains a constant focus over time (Clarke, 1994; Office of Educational Research and Improvement, 1999).

Reducing Isolation

Increased collaboration among teachers is often a direct and immediate outcome of lesson study (Byrum, Jarrell, & Munoz, 2002). Lesson study teams often find outcomes related to collaboration the most valuable—decreased isolation, increased trust, and collective effort toward common goals (Wilms, 2003). Rather than simply increasing the amount of collaboration, lesson study also increases the teachers' capacity to learn together. The teachers develop common understandings of content knowledge and the means to improve instruction. The process of planning a lesson together and discussing evidence of student learning helps teachers develop a common language and a shared vision of effective teaching (Liptak, 2005).

Exploring Different Perspectives

One potential problem in collaborative work is that teachers will feel pressure to minimize disagreements or to avoid talking about areas of potential contention. Lesson study provides teachers with a forum to discuss disagreements and perhaps to test different approaches and gather evidence about the impact on student learning (Lewis 2002a). Lesson study also has the potential to help teachers try out new ideas. It can help to gently nudge teachers out of their comfort zone while also providing essential emotional support.

> *Research lessons ensure that teachers with differing beliefs will continue to see and give feedback on one another's practice—rather than talking only with like-minded colleagues. We suspect that such shared discussion of real classroom lessons helps teachers keep in mind education's many goals, recognize the benefits of approaches different from their own, and avoid extreme pendulum swings as innovations are put into practice.*
>
> ~Lewis & Tsuchida (1997, p. 325)

Continual Improvement

Schools are not designed to be places where teachers can engage in continual learning and improvement (Elmore, 2002). The lesson study process has the potential to transform classrooms into places where teachers can investigate student learning and use what they discover to guide their instructional decisions on a continual basis. Instead of thinking of professional development as something that has a beginning and an end, teachers will begin to see their work as a means of conducting research and learning more about their students and how to meet their needs.

When lesson study is conducted schoolwide, its potential impact grows because it is a vehicle for teachers to share what they learn. Lesson study can transform teachers' informal knowledge into professional knowledge that is public, sharable, accurate, and verifiable (Hiebert, Gallimore, & Stigler, 2002).

Focused on Subject Matter

Professional development focused on curriculum, content knowledge, and on how students learn specific content is more likely to impact teacher practice and student learning (Cohen & Hill, 1998; Kennedy, 1998). This category can include pedagogical content knowledge—learning focused on how to teach specific subject matter—as well as the understanding of the content that teachers need to effectively guide student learning.

Increasing Knowledge of Subject Matter

As they develop their research lessons, teachers delve deeply into the subject matter and increase their content knowledge (Turner, 2004). Lesson study is a means for teachers to identify gaps in their own understanding, and it provides motivation for them to learn more (Fernandez, Cannon, & Chokshi, 2003). With the help of knowledgeable others, teachers develop new insights about content and how to explore it with students. Their improved understandings of how concepts are related to each other enable teachers to help students make connections. Teachers may also gain a broader scope in their understanding of content by examining how specific topics are addressed in other grade levels. Catherine Lewis and her colleagues have been investigating lesson study's impact on teachers' knowledge, and they have found that engaging in lesson study was a means for teachers to develop new understandings about mathematics (Perry, Lewis, & Akiba, 2002).

Teacher Driven and Classroom Based

Teachers need to design their own professional development experiences to address questions and issues that they identify as important (Clarke, 1994; Wilson & Berne, 1999). Professional development is effective when it is explicitly connected to teachers' work with their students (Corcoran, 1995; Darling-Hammond & McLaughlin, 1995). Professional conversations about teaching and learning must be centered in the classroom and in artifacts of practice (Ball & Cohen, 1999).

Focusing on Concrete Tasks and Experiences

Lesson study provides both a well-defined task—planning the lesson—and a common episode of teaching that teachers can analyze and discuss (Hiebert, 2000; Yoshida, 1999). Another benefit of the focus on lesson planning is that it is a familiar activity in which to ground reflective practice (Fernandez & Yoshida, 2000). Lesson study makes the process of reflection more concrete by providing goals and questions that teachers can use to examine and think about their experiences.

Improving Instructional Knowledge

Lesson study provides a means for teachers to gain instructional knowledge and direct evidence of the effectiveness of specific strategies (Stewart & Brendefur, 2005). The Northern Michigan Lesson Study Initiative involved four lesson study groups from a variety of grade levels. The teachers reported that lesson study helped them to improve their instruction and planning. Two of the specific areas of instruction that they identified were more effective questioning strategies and a more effective approach to gauging student understanding (Turner, 2004). In another lesson study project, evaluators used classroom observation data to document improvements in interactions between teachers and students (Petrescu, 2005). The knowledge that teachers gain is not isolated to the research lesson but can be applied to other lessons, other subject areas, and instruction in general. Paterson School No. 2 in New Jersey is one of the first lesson study sites in the United States. Paterson teachers report that they have noted changes in the nature of students' learning activities—they have more opportunities to share and discuss their thinking (Jackson, 2005).

Active and Hands On

Effective professional development provides opportunities for active learning—teachers become inquirers and problems solvers (Garet et al., 2001; Wilson & Berne, 1999). Professional development involves teachers in identifying problems and questions, thinking about and discussing their work, gathering data, and using what they learn to inform their practice (Borasi & Fonzi, 2002; Thompson & Zeuli, 1999).

Teachers develop understanding of their own knowledge as well as acquiring new knowledge of content and students (Wilson & Berne, 1999). Opportunities should be designed to enable teachers to share their knowledge and develop communities of practice (Darling-Hammond & McLaughlin, 1995).

Generating and Sharing Knowledge

In the push for research-based strategies and practices, teachers are rarely portrayed as sources of knowledge about teaching. Lesson study can counteract this tendency because it enables teachers to enter into this role. Through their lesson study work, teachers have a means of articulating and organizing their knowledge (Saul, 2001).

Lesson study provides a process that teachers can use to learn from their practice, verifying the effectiveness of their methods and identifying less-effective routines. Rather than relying on researchers to verify what works, lesson study is a means for teachers to develop and employ professional judgment, honing their abilities to gather, analyze, and interpret evidence.

Developing a Researcher Stance

Lesson study helps teachers gain a better understanding of how their decisions and actions contribute to student learning. They create research questions about instruction and student learning and develop a lesson plan that enables them to collect evidence about their questions. As teachers take on an inquiry stance, they learn how to investigate and gain knowledge from their daily practice and from observing students. Other characteristics that teachers develop include being eager to try new strategies, engaging regularly in reflection, and focusing on the details of instructional practice (Byrum et al., 2002). Teachers also report feeling more like professionals as a result of their lesson study work (Wilms, 2003).

Focused on Student Outcomes

Positive changes in student outcomes are the ultimate measure of professional development's success. Gaps between goals for student learning and actual student performance should drive teacher learning (Hawley & Valli, 1999).

Attending to Student Learning

Lesson study focuses professional development on student learning (Takahashi & Yoshida, 2004). The process begins with identifying goals for students. During the planning phase, the team spends time researching and thinking about how students learn. The teachers anticipate how the students will respond to the lesson, altering their plan to address students' likely reactions. When they observe and discuss the lesson, the teachers maintain their focus on students, gathering evidence that they will use to refine the lesson plan.

Rather than focusing only on what to teach and how to teach, the lesson planning process inspires teachers to adopt a student perspective on instruction and to antici-pate how students will respond to questions and tasks (Byrum et al., 2002; Stewart & Brendefur, 2005). Teachers explore student thinking and how to facilitate it (Fernandez et al., 2003). Engaging in lesson study also helps teachers gain a better understanding of students and their learning needs (Lewis, Perry, & Murata, 2003; Petrescu, 2005).

Improving Lesson Planning

Lesson study helps teachers develop more effective approaches to planning their work (Stewart & Brendefur, 2005). Teachers gain a better understanding of long-term goals and standards (Lewis et al., 2003). Teachers report that they become more focused on goals in their daily planning and that their instruction becomes more purposeful (Byrum et al., 2002; Petrescu, 2005).

Like all efforts to bring about meaningful change and significant learning, lesson study requires a long-term view. It may not have an immediate and measurable impact on teachers and students, especially if teachers' first steps are to learn how to engage in lesson study. Stigler and Hiebert (1999) speculated that one of the obstacles that lesson study would face in the United States was the lack of this long-term perspective. There is a danger that the educational community may abandon lesson study before its impact can be established.

Catherine Lewis also suggests the need for a careful and steady pace in conducting research on lesson study (Lewis et al., 2006). Rather than rushing into randomized controlled trials, U.S. researchers need a much deeper understanding of the processes through which teachers' lesson study practice leads to improvements in teaching and learning.

Form 1.1 is a short overview of lesson study. It includes a description of the phases of the lesson study cycle. It also highlights the fit between lesson study and research-based characteristics of high-quality professional development. The purpose of this tool is to provide a overview that can be shared with people who are unfamiliar with lesson study. There are more ideas about how to share information about lesson study in Chapter 2.

FROM THE FIELD

The sixth-grade lesson study team from North Marion Middle School in Aurora, Oregon—Bill Brown, Carolyn Donnelly, Heidi Friesen, Christie Jackson, and Angela Turner—have experienced many of the research findings for themselves. They identify several areas in which lesson study has had an impact on their professional knowledge and growth.

Collaboration

Being able to talk together as a whole group is such a big part of lesson study. It just widens your whole perspective because you are getting ideas from other people and you're not just going down this narrow little road of your own.

~Carolyn Donnelly

Focus on Students

One of the changes I've made as a result of lesson study is anticipating how students are going to respond to my questions and to my style of teaching.

~Bill Brown

Improved Planning

It's really helpful just to take the time to think about things that might be a problem in my lessons. It's much better to be able to do that than to always be dealing with things right on the spot.

~Angela Turner

KEY IDEAS

- Lesson study addresses teaching as a cultural activity—one that is improved through deep thought, inquiry, and a collective focus on teaching rather than individual teachers.
- There is not a single model of Japanese lesson study. In Japan, lesson study takes many different forms and is used for a variety of purposes.
- The process of lesson study is only one part of its substance. Equally important are the habits of mind that teachers develop and the big ideas they explore.
- The purpose of lesson study is to improve instruction by generating professional knowledge, *not* by developing a bank of exemplary lessons.
- Lesson study provides learning experiences for teachers that are congruent with effective professional development. Lesson study is collaborative, comprehensive, and ongoing; focused on subject matter; teacher driven and classroom based; active and hands on; and focused on student outcomes.

Form 1.1   Overview of Lesson Study

Lesson study is a professional development practice in which teachers collaborate to develop a lesson plan, teach and observe the lesson to collect data on student learning, and use their observations to refine their lesson. It is a process that teachers engage in to learn more about effective practices that result in improved learning outcomes for students.

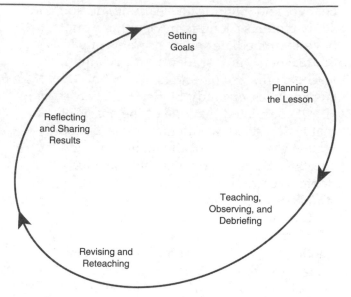

Phases of the Lesson Study Cycle

- Setting Goals
- Planning the Lesson
- Teaching, Observing, and Debriefing
- Revising and Reteaching
- Reflecting and Sharing Results

Lesson Study: High-Quality Professional Development

Collaborative, Comprehensive, and Ongoing

Lesson study involves groups of teachers organized around common subject areas or grade levels. It is designed to be an ongoing effort that is most effective as one element of a schoolwide program for continual improvement.

Focused on Subject Matter

As they develop their lesson plan, lesson study teams draw on resources about a specific topic and how students learn. The teachers then collect evidence and apply it in subsequent planning and day-to-day teaching.

Teacher Driven and Classroom Based

Lesson study teams are responsible for identifying the focus of their work, finding and using information, conducting research, sharing results, and identifying areas for further learning. The teachers conduct lesson study in their own classrooms and with their own students.

Active and Hands On

Lesson study provides support for teachers to develop their own knowledge, placing their learning within their work rather than outside of it. Lesson study provides a process that teachers can use to learn from their practice, honing their abilities to gather, analyze, and interpret evidence.

Focused on Student Outcomes

Lesson study begins with teachers identifying student goals to guide their work. Teachers continue their focus on students by anticipating and observing student responses to instruction.

From Our Team to Yours

The Detroit Lesson Study Group

In Detroit, Michigan, lesson study got its start in the summer of 2002. Thanks to the work of the Detroit Lesson Study Group—the original team of five teachers who got it off the ground—the district's program is not only viable but also growing and gaining momentum. Brandon Graham, Byron Timms, Vicki Vorus, Elana Webster, and Jason White teach middle school mathematics; all five were teaching summer school and participated in the lesson study pilot.

It was the district administrators who first brought lesson study to Detroit Public Schools. They were interested in starting lesson study in the district because it seemed like a good fit for their needs. Aleatha Kimbrough, the executive director of student support programs was one of the people who helped introduce it.

Aleatha Kimbrough: "At Detroit Public Schools, we saw lesson study as a powerful strategy that integrates the best of what we know about quality professional development. It incorporates knowledge and skill building through practice and provides the kind of strong collegial support we want for our teachers. Lesson study supports teachers going deep into the study of teaching and learning in the interest of deepening student thinking."

The members of the Detroit Lesson Study Group are now serving as facilitators for new teams in the district as Detroit's lesson study effort expands. Having served both as team members and as facilitators gives the teachers insight into what it takes for teachers to get the most out of lesson study.

Brandon: "I think all of us have done lesson study long enough to experience and to notice different levels of success. The one key ingredient for a group that is going to reach the optimal level of success is people who want to improve. We believe that there's always a better method to teach something, and we're always trying to explore new and better ways to impact student learning."

Vicki: "I think the majority of people don't mind the commitment if it helps them to become more effective teachers. I think there are more teachers who are committed to teaching and who want to be the best teachers they can be. So I think that lesson study is for the teachers who love teaching."

Byron: "Lesson study is not for everybody. I'd like to think that it is, and I don't want to discourage anyone from trying it. Because I would hope that, particularly as teachers, we would be open to gaining new insight and getting better. I think for the most part, the people who participate in lesson study bring something to it and get something out of it. It absolutely has changed my whole professional life."

Aleatha Kimbrough: "At the end of the first lesson study cycle, we asked the lesson study teams for feedback. One of the lesson study participants said lesson study was the first time in her long teaching career that she had the opportunity to visit another teacher's classroom. It was the first time she was able to interact with other teachers about how to structure teaching for student success. Through lesson study, she became totally reenergized about her teaching."

Laying the Groundwork for Lesson Study

"How do we make this work in our school?" When educators get excited about lesson study, this is one of the first questions they ask. The transition from hearing about lesson study to forming a team requires some initial planning and organization. The conditions that are necessary to support lesson study are not common in most U.S. schools. But working together, teachers and administrators can create an environment in which lesson study can thrive.

> *Lesson study is not something you are taught. Through the process of examining classroom lessons, a teacher gains valuable insights as to how students learn best. Through conversations with others who have the same daily challenges you do, the world of educating children becomes a small team effort, and your group is there to help you in every way it can. The actual observations give you "eyes" to really see what your students are thinking, because you don't sit in the back of the classroom, but among the students as they ponder the new concepts.*
>
> ~Marilyn Carpenter, teacher

BEGINNING WITH THE NECESSARY INGREDIENTS

Creating readiness is the first step in getting lesson study off the ground. When schools do not take time to ensure that the necessary ingredients are in place, lesson study is more likely to falter. This does not mean that a group of volunteer teachers will not be able to do lesson study on their own. But without the following elements, it is less likely to be successful and sustainable. Many of these ingredients are not unique to lesson study—they are the common characteristics of any effective school-based professional development.

Willing and Engaged Teachers

Lesson study teams are not as likely to succeed if the members have been required or coerced to participate. Teachers must be willing to talk about their beliefs and their practices, to collaborate with their colleagues, to learn from each other and their students, and to make changes to their teaching and try new ideas. Teachers need not be true believers from the start, but making lesson study a required, rather than a voluntary, effort is less likely to lead to an effective and sustainable program.

Time for Collaboration

Lesson study requires time set aside for teachers to plan, observe, and discuss research lessons. The best strategy for creating this time—before or after school, during the school day, during inservice days or weekends—will depend on the preferences of the teachers and the policies and practices of the school or district. There is one exception: If the lesson is taught during regular school hours, the team members must be released from their classroom duties during the teaching of the lesson. There is no substitute for live observation—the observers must be able to see the lesson from every angle and to investigate the learning of all students in the classroom.

Administrator Support

Without at least one administrator who understands and values lesson study, it will be difficult (if not impossible) to sustain it. Administrators who are involved in the process will help ensure that teachers have the resources and support they need and will provide encouragement to teams as they face the many challenges of lesson study. Ideally, administrators will support lesson study as a means of increasing their own knowledge about teaching and students and finding new ways to support effective practices throughout the school or the district.

An Action Plan

To put the necessary elements in place—teachers, time, and support from administrators—the lesson study team will need to develop an action plan. The later sections of this chapter will help guide the team through the decisions that need to be made and the issues that need to be resolved. Developing and sharing a well-thought-out plan can help to convince others who are skeptical that lesson study can be a viable investment of professional development time and dollars.

ADDITIONAL SUPPORTS

The four elements listed above (willing and engaged teachers, time for collaboration, administrator support, and an action plan) are essential, but there are other features that will also support lesson study work. These features may not be *necessary*, but they will enable teachers to participate more effectively and contribute to the likelihood that lesson study will be sustainable. Lesson study may also serve as a way for a school to develop and improve the following sources of support.

High-Quality Curriculum

The purpose of lesson study is not to create curriculum or even necessarily to design a lesson from scratch. Instead, team members should focus their efforts on studying and building on existing materials. When teachers do not have a high-quality curriculum to work with, they often must spend more time identifying or creating the learning activities. This, in turn, slows down the lesson study cycle.

Collegial Relationships

When teachers are already accustomed to working together, lesson study is more likely to take off quickly. Positive relationships and group norms will already be established and teachers will be less isolated than they typically are in U.S. schools. Hopefully, teachers will have a sense of collective responsibility for student learning and the belief that their work together can improve outcomes for students. Where such qualities are not already in place, more time will be needed as the teachers begin lesson study.

Collaborative School Climate

Creating an environment that nurtures teacher learning as well as student learning helps to support lesson study. Learning can be an uncomfortable and even a painful process for teachers as they deal with the disequilibrium of changing familiar practices. Emotional safety, caring, and respect enable teachers to question each other, explain their ideas, take intellectual risks, and give and receive feedback. Teachers will not be able to engage effectively in lesson study without a climate that is conducive to these activities.

Outside Support

Lesson study is a complex process that is a challenge for most teachers. Although it is not always possible, many teams begin working with a **facilitator**, who helps ensure that the teachers are going beyond the surface features of lesson study. Teams who do not have access to a facilitator can still draw on the expertise of more experienced practitioners. The advice of others who are knowledgeable about lesson study can be very helpful in avoiding common pitfalls, identifying solutions to problems, and refining lesson study practice.

Schoolwide Participation

Lesson study will be most powerful when all teachers in a school are engaged, because there is a common focus for teacher learning as well as cross-team sharing. It also prevents misunderstandings among the staff about the purpose or substance of the lesson study work. Nevertheless, taking lesson study schoolwide is something to work toward gradually, rather than mandating teachers' participation from the start.

CREATING A LESSON STUDY ACTION PLAN

The sections that follow provide strategies and suggestions for putting the necessary ingredients for lesson study in place. Developing an action plan can be very helpful in preparing a school or district to support the teachers' work. In some situations, the action plan can be used to help make the case for lesson study. For example, sharing the plan with district administrators or school board members might help a team to gain support for common planning time and substitutes. The action plan may also serve as a basis for grant proposals or applications to other funding sources.

Form 2.1 is a template for a lesson study action plan. (Please note that the recording areas have been compressed to save space.) It is organized around the following categories:

- **Expected outcomes.** Explain the reasons for engaging in lesson study and what the team members hope to get out of it. Think about how to demonstrate the value of lesson study to the school, the district, and especially the students.
- **Team members.** Identify the lesson study team members. If the team or teams have not been formed, describe the plan for recruiting teachers.
- **Time needed.** Provide an overview of the time that will be needed and the strategies that will be used to create that time. If this has not been decided, describe several of the most feasible options.
- **Administrator support.** (Optional) Describe the strategies and information that will be used to communicate with administrators. This section may not be appropriate when administrators are initiating lesson study.
- **Sources of external support.** Identify the people who are available to assist the team in their work.
- **Documentation.** Describe the records that the lesson study team will maintain of their work and how they will share their activities with others.
- **Compensation.** If applicable, explain how teachers will be compensated for their time and their work.

The sections that follow are organized around the sections of the action plan. They include guiding questions that the team members, administrators, facilitators, or others can use to develop the plan. In Chapter 3, additional sections will be added to the plan on roles/responsibilities and the schedule for the lesson study cycle.

INVITING TEACHERS TO PARTICIPATE

Lesson study is not likely to be successful if it is mandatory. The most effective way to bring lesson study to a school or district is to start small with a group of volunteers. Although this approach does not have the advantage of making lesson study a schoolwide effort, it is more likely to continue and grow over time if teachers come to it out of their own interest.

Lesson study teams are self-directed and require teachers who are willing to learn together. Team members will engage in what are likely to be unfamiliar activities, such as making instructional decisions together, justifying statements and actions to each other, and teaching in front of their peers. This does not mean that every team member must be an enthusiastic lesson study advocate from the very beginning. It makes sense that at least some teachers will come to the process

Form 2.1   Lesson Study Action Plan

Expected Outcomes	
Team Members	
Time Needed	
Administrator Support	
Sources of External Support	
Documentation	
Compensation	

with a wait-and-see attitude. But commitment to the team and openness to new experiences are essential.

FROM THE FIELD

We were invited to attend an open house at the Greenwich Japanese School in Connecticut, and that event was really what got us involved with lesson study. We saw lesson study as a perfect vehicle to empower teachers to improve instruction and help kids learn better. When we came back from the open house, we knew that we needed to be very strategic about introducing lesson study. We did a lot of planning and brainstorming, and we started by pitching it to the district and then we went to a couple of principals that we thought would be interested in it.

Finally, we approached some teachers and started introducing lesson study very slowly. We dropped a few articles here and there. It was almost like a whisper: "Oh, you might want to look at this. . . ." We got some people interested, and we built it up slowly until we had a handful of people who were ready to go forward with it. Eventually, we worked up to eight groups in four elementary and middle schools across all content areas.

One of the teachers came very reluctantly to lesson study. We didn't pressure her to participate, and she eventually came on board. Even though she was reluctant, she said that lesson study was what she needed to see what was working in her classroom. She saw really strong evidence that planning the lesson with her colleagues helped her to improve as a teacher.

~Andre Audette, Regents Fellow,
Rhode Island Department of Elementary
and Secondary Education (former standards
coordinator for the Pawtucket School District)

Inviting teachers to participate in lesson study can be a delicate matter. No matter who is initiating lesson study—individual teachers, administrators, or professional development providers—the challenge will be to convey a sense of enthusiasm without overdefining the nature and scope of the future work.

Personalizing the invitation may help to make it more appealing. Approaching potential team members individually will provide a sense of personal connection. Writing a letter—which could be an open letter to the whole school or district—is another effective approach.

The invitations can be conveyed or followed up with an exploratory meeting. This is an opportunity for teachers to find out more about lesson study before making a commitment to join the team. Print resources and video can be used to provide an overview of the lesson study process, but seeing lesson study in action is the most powerful way for teachers to gain knowledge and enthusiasm. One way to do this is to attend an **open house** or to visit another school where a research lesson is being taught. Hearing from other teachers about their experiences with lesson study can also be beneficial.

Building time for lesson study into the school day will help teachers to see it as a viable approach to professional development. When this is not possible, compensating teachers for their additional time and work is an alternative strategy. Many teachers say that they were initially uncertain about lesson study because they did not know how to fit it into the existing demands on their time.

Although it can be very helpful, the members of a lesson study team will not necessarily work at the same school. Especially in rural settings, teams may extend across schools and even districts. A disadvantage of this situation is that time for team members to work together cannot be built into the school day. Yet teams whose members come from different settings may benefit from the diversity of perspectives and experiences they are able to share with each other.

Ideally, a group of volunteers who begin doing lesson study will generate interest among the other teachers as they see the results and hear about the benefits from their colleagues. It will be helpful to consider how to bring new people into lesson study as interest grows. For example, experienced lesson study team members may go on to help facilitate new teams.

Some teachers may be interested in lesson study and yet still be reluctant to join a team. It may be helpful to find ways to keep them peripherally involved so that they can participate when they are ready. Teachers are often reluctant about the idea of teaching in front of their peers. It may be helpful to allow some teachers to participate initially in the planning and observing of the lesson without requiring them to teach a research lesson. Hesitant teachers often become more comfortable when they see the respectful and collaborative nature of the debriefing.

The following questions are designed to help identify strategies for inviting teachers to participate in lesson study. This information can be included in the lesson study action plan.

Guiding Questions

- What strategies will we use to invite teachers to participate in lesson study?
- What information will we share to pique their interest? How will we share it?
- Who will we invite?
- Are there likely to be teachers who are reluctant?
- What concerns might they have? How can we address those concerns?

FINDING TIME

To conduct lesson study, teachers require time to meet together. Making opportunities for teacher collaboration a regular part of the school schedule is the best way to provide support. Providing time is often the first obstacle that people encounter as they consider how to begin lesson study in their school. It is an enduring problem that affects most forms of professional development. The belief that teachers' work consists only of time spent with students often makes common time for teachers a low priority.

Lesson study requires two types of collaborative time: (1) time for meetings in which the team members develop and revise the lesson plan and (2) time to observe and discuss the teaching of the lesson. Team meetings can be held during school or outside of regular school hours—each option has advantages and disadvantages. Some teachers do not like to meet after school because they are too tired at the end of the day. When they meet during school, teachers are sometimes more easily distracted. The best option will always be the one that most closely matches the wants and needs of the teachers in the group.

The teaching and observation of the research lesson will usually be held during regular school hours. Therefore, substitutes will be required for the lesson study team and any other teachers who will be observing the lesson. It is also preferable to hold the debriefing soon after the lesson is taught, but if that will not be possible, the session can be held later in the day or after school. A full-day release can allow the team to begin revising the lesson immediately.

To avoid the need for substitutes, the teaching of the research lesson can be held outside of school hours. It can take place at the beginning or end of the day if the school is using a late start/early release schedule, or it can be held on a professional development or inservice day. Both of these options will involve bringing in or keeping one group of students for an extra class period.

There are a number of excellent resources that specifically address the problem of finding time for school-based professional development. Schools have used the strategies in Figure 2.1 to create more time for teachers to work together (Darling-Hammond, 1997; Little, 1999; Loucks-Horsley et al., 1998; Murphy, 1997; Pardini, 1999). Although there is no single strategy that will work for every situation, this list will provide some initial ideas.

Compensation

An alternative to making changes in the school schedule or finding others to cover classes is to compensate teachers for their extra work. This can be accomplished by paying teachers on an hourly basis for their lesson study time or by providing a stipend. The contractual obligations in the district are likely to dictate these issues.

Another form of compensation is providing teachers with continuing education or graduate credits, or enabling them to use lesson study to fulfill requirements for continuing certification. Some schools or districts have excused teachers from annual evaluations of their teaching in return for their lesson study work.

Electronic Tools

When schools have difficulty creating time for teachers to meet together, they sometimes try to conduct lesson study via electronic means. This may be the only way for teachers in small, rural schools to collaborate with their peers. E-mail is useful for saving time and keeping communication active between face-to-face meetings. When team members work at different schools, planning meetings can be held via video conferencing. Lesson study teams have also used online forums such as Blackboard.com to share the work of planning the lesson. As helpful as these tools can be to the planning process, the observation and debriefing must be conducted in person.

Funding

Some schools have pursued grant funding to support their lesson study efforts, using the money to compensate teachers or to hire substitutes. Unfortunately, outside

FROM THE FIELD

We did a statewide pilot project in Ohio in which teams were composed of teachers from multiple districts. Because of the long distances separating team members, the teachers planned their lesson using Blackboard.com, an online electronic forum, videotaped their lesson, and physically came together in a central location to watch the video lesson and debrief. Conducting the observation via video posed numerous challenges. Observers saw only what the videographer chose to focus on, and it was hard to capture the continuity and variety of conversations among students. It was also difficult to view student work as it was performed. The benefit of multiple perspectives collected from different vantage points within the classroom was lost. Though the debriefing conversation was somewhat useful, it was less robust than other debriefings I have participated in.

Following the debriefing, teams revised and refined their lessons online. Because of the drawback of their video observation experience, team members decided to physically travel to the site of the reteaching for the observation and debriefing. The live and in-person nature of the observation and debriefing was substantially more dynamic and offered a wider and richer array of data and evidence than the video observation. And teachers had a much greater sense of satisfaction. Overall, given the choice between video and real-time lesson study, I recommend real-time. But there are some situations where real-time is just not practical and video offers a next-best choice.

~Gary Appel

Figure 2.1   Finding Time for Lesson Study

Adjusting the School Schedule

Early Release/Late Start

Four days a week, the school schedule is extended by several minutes. One day a week, students come to school one hour later or go home one hour earlier. A variation on this schedule is to have teachers come to school 30 minutes early, with students arriving 30 minutes late; a similar strategy can also be used at the end of the day. (An early release/late start schedule does not have to be used on a weekly basis but can be spread out over the course of several weeks.)

Professional Development Days

The daily school schedule is extended by several minutes in order to release students for a full day once a month or every six weeks.

Prep Time

Teachers in each grade level or each department have a common prep time that can be used weekly (or as needed) to work together.

Covering Classes

Specialist Days

Each day of the week, students from one grade level spend most of the day with specialists, in the computer lab, and in the library. (Elementary/middle school)

Service Learning

For one half-day each week, students spend their time conducting service learning or community projects. (High school)

Paraprofessionals/Administrators/Parents/Volunteers

Teachers' classes are taken over for one hour each week.

Teaming

Teacher teams pair up and take each other's classes for one hour each week. For example, each second-grade teacher takes one class of first graders so that the first-grade teachers can meet together. (Elementary level)

Substitute Teachers

Substitutes are hired to rotate through the classes one day every other week.

Reallocating Existing Time

Staff Meetings

Weekly staff meetings are cut back to once or twice a month and replaced with grade-level or department meetings.

Adjusting Planning Time

Teachers' daily planning time is used for collaborative work one day a week. The number of minutes that teachers are expected to stay after school can be cut back by 10 minutes on four days during the week in order to create an extra 40 minutes for meeting together on one afternoon.

Professional Development/Inservice Days

Teachers are excused from staff development days to compensate for weekly meetings outside of school hours.

funding may enable a school to avoid making the organizational changes that are necessary to sustain lesson study over time. A grant may be a good way to get lesson study started, but it also is important to have a plan for how to continue lesson study after the funding has ended.

The following questions are designed to help identify strategies for finding time for teachers to participate in lesson study. This information can be included in the lesson study action plan.

Guiding Questions

- How many meetings are needed to give us enough time to conduct research and plan the lesson?
- What are our options for creating time to meet?
- What are the preferences of the team members?
- When will the teaching/observation be held? How will we cover classes or bring in students?
- Who has the authority to help us find or create time for lesson study?

FROM THE FIELD

When Sharon Baum, the principal of North Marion Middle School, came across lesson study in the summer of 2001, she was already looking for ways to give her teachers more time to collaborate and plan together. "I wanted to take advantage of the fact that our team of sixth-grade teachers had the perfect setup, because they taught all subjects and they had self-contained classrooms," she says. By coordinating the time that students spent with specialists, Sharon developed a schedule that gave the teachers time to work together during the school day.

After reading about lesson study, Sharon realized that it was a good fit with what she believed her teachers needed. When she introduced the idea of doing lesson study at North Marion, the teachers were intrigued but also caught off guard. They gradually overcame their uncertainty as they learned more about lesson study. In the end, it was Sharon's enthusiasm that won them over and encouraged them to give lesson study a try. "At first, I wasn't sure because it was so different from what we thought we were going to do," says Bill Brown. "I wasn't sure that we were really going to have time to do it. But Sharon was so excited about it, that we just went with it."

GAINING SUPPORT FROM ADMINISTRATORS

The building principal is perhaps the key person who can make a difference in the success or failure of lesson study. The bottom line is that lesson study will not happen if the administration does not—at the minimum—give approval. Teachers are often the people who are enthusiastic about lesson study, but they rarely have the power to make the necessary changes in the policies and procedures of the school or district.

The strategies for gaining support from administrators are similar to the methods used to develop interest among teachers. Presenting information about lesson study at a meeting is often the first step, but providing an opportunity to experience lesson study firsthand is ideal. Preparing a well-developed action plan for lesson study will also help bring an administrator on board.

Sometimes administrators will give their approval without giving their full support. One way to generate more enthusiasm is to invite administrators to participate in observations and debriefings. Providing copies of reports and evaluations may also help administrators gain an understanding of teachers' lesson study work and the benefits to instruction and learning. Sharing the information from Chapter 1 also may be helpful in communicating the power of lesson study.

In the United States, it is common for administrators to initiate lesson study in their schools and districts. In such cases, it may not be necessary to spend time educating administrators before beginning lesson study. Yet, as the program grows or as leaders change, providing an overview and the rationale for the teachers' work is likely to be an ongoing concern.

The lesson study team will benefit from being proactive in communicating with others about their work and seeking their support. In addition to administrators, there are other important stakeholders to consider, including school board members, union leaders, and parents. All of these groups have potential roles in supporting and sustaining lesson study. For example, the American Federation of Teachers has sponsored lesson study in several sites, and the United Teachers of Los Angeles initiated lesson study in their district (Gill, 2005; Wilms, 2003).

More important, these stakeholder groups also have the ability to derail lesson study if they do not see its value. At a middle school where the principal organized the schedule to provide a lesson study team with a common daily planning period, some of the other teachers in the school filed a complaint with the union. They charged that the team members were receiving an extra prep period. The union ruled in favor of the complaint and required that the common planning time be eliminated from the schedule. Misunderstandings such as this can potentially be avoided by including as many as possible in all efforts to gain support for lesson study.

The following questions are designed to help identify strategies for communicating with administrators about lesson study and gaining their support. This information can be included in the lesson study action plan.

Guiding Questions

- Who are the administrators who need to approve our plans?
- Who are the administrators who are likely to support lesson study?
- What can they do to help?
- Are there other stakeholder groups that should be included in our outreach efforts?
- How will we gain their support?
- How will we keep them informed of our activities and our progress?

FINDING EXTERNAL SUPPORT

Substantial improvements in teaching and learning are not likely to result from simply engaging in the lesson study process. As Sonal Chokshi and Clea Fernandez (2004) have written, "Lesson study is easy to learn but difficult to master" (p. 524). Guidance and advice from experienced practitioners can help ensure that the teachers' work is grounded in the core elements of lesson study: not just the process, but the big ideas and habits of mind. In addition, the purpose of lesson study is for teachers to think about their work in new ways and to examine it from different perspectives. It is difficult to do this without the knowledge and views of other educators.

External support is not a requirement for lesson study. Nevertheless, most novice teams will reap great benefit from drawing on the support of those with more expertise. The nature of the support may change over time, but it is often an ongoing need. Less-experienced teams may need more help as they get started with lesson study. As teams gain more experience, they will be able to provide assistance to others.

One avenue of support is providing access to resources, including research and other forms of information that can inform the research lesson. Many teachers lack direct access to these types of materials. Another form of support is providing expertise in content or pedagogy to inform both the planning of the research lesson and the assessment of its effectiveness during the observation and debriefing.

Before the lesson study cycle begins, it may be helpful to identify potential sources of support. Figure 2.2 is a brief overview of the assistance that teams often require and the people who may be able to provide support.

Figure 2.2   Sources of External Support

Lesson Study Phase	Type of Support	Providers of Support
Planning Revising	Access to resources	Curriculum specialists Professional development providers Librarians or resource specialists
Planning Teaching, observing, and debriefing	Content expertise Instructional expertise	Higher-education faculty Professional development providers Instructional specialists or coaches
All phases	Lesson study advice	Lesson study facilitators Lesson study teams Professional development providers Researchers Consultants

The Web site for the Lesson Study Research Group at Teachers College/ Columbia University in New York is a useful resource that lesson study teams can use to find people to help them with their work. The site features lists of lesson study practitioners, including lesson study projects, researchers, and consultants. The group also manages a Listserv where individuals can post questions and requests for assistance. (See Resource C: Additional Resources for information on the group's Web site.)

The following questions are designed to help identify sources of external support for lesson study. This information can be included in the lesson study action plan.

Guiding Questions

- What types of resources do we need? Who can help us gain access to resources?
- What content do we want to research? Who can provide content expertise, or how will we find experts?
- What questions do we have about lesson study? How can we get in touch with existing lesson study teams?
- What additional support do we need? Who can provide that support?

DEVELOPING A
COLLABORATIVE SCHOOL CULTURE

The process of creating and sustaining a lesson study team is a complex and challenging endeavor. It requires time, trust, and commitment from all participants. Even if a school has only one lesson study team, the climate of the whole school will have an impact on the work of the team. Lesson study is more likely to thrive in schools that function as professional learning communities.

A school culture that is grounded in a sense of community will support lesson study by creating a dynamic and congenial workplace and establishing relationships that encourage continuous inquiry and improvement (Collay, Dunlap, Enloe, & Gagnon, 1998; Lieberman & Miller, 1999). Research on school improvement suggests that the presence of a professional learning community in a school has a positive impact on student achievement and is an essential component of effective teaching and learning (Ancess, 2000; Bryk & Schneider, 2002; Langer, 2000; Newmann & Wehlage, 1995).

There are a number of characteristics associated with professional learning and collaboration (Bierema, 1999; Dufour & Eaker, 1998; Hord, 1997; McLaughlin, 2001; Supovitz & Christman, 2003; Zederayko & Ward, 1999):

- **Common Goals.** Teachers take on collective responsibility for student learning, sharing a common purpose and criteria for measuring the success of their efforts. The overarching focus is on student learning, but teachers articulate and negotiate the specific goals.
- **Mutual Trust and Respect.** Teachers have a sense of emotional safety that enables them to share their thinking and their practice. They are willing to open up their classrooms to each other, observing instruction and providing each other with feedback.
- **Collective Inquiry.** Teachers are accustomed to observing and discussing each other's teaching methods and philosophies. All staff engage in learning new ways to talk about teaching. Teachers work together to develop materials, activities, and strategies and to choose and create professional development opportunities.
- **Reflective Dialogue.** Teachers talk to each other about their practice and their students. Topics may include content knowledge, assumptions and rationale behind instructional decisions, or the process of adopting new strategies.
- **Supportive and Shared Leadership.** Teachers have the freedom and authority to make decisions and to explore alternatives and innovations in instruction. The organizational norms and structures support and encourage collaboration and inquiry.
- **Continuous Learning Opportunities.** The professional learning community is not a one-time effort but a way of working together that is embedded into the school culture. All staff put in the time and effort required to maintain collaborative relationships and focus on inquiry and improvement. Teacher learning is given a high priority, and teachers' efforts are supported and celebrated by the whole school.

It may be helpful to look at these characteristics and think about what they might look like in a specific school or district. Are there elements of a learning community that are already in place in this school? What characteristics are not in place? The school staff should consider the following questions (Dufour, 1999; Watkins & Marsick, 1993):

- What knowledge and skills do we need to function as a professional learning community?
- How big of a transition will be involved? Are there norms and structures already in place, or will a major shift in school culture be required?
- Are there current policies and practices that may interfere with our efforts? How can we deal with possible barriers?
- What avenues are in place for teachers to share what we learn?
- How frequently do teachers talk about our work and exchange information and ideas?

CHALLENGES OF LAYING THE GROUNDWORK

Dilemma: Our team does not have common planning time.

Designated time for teachers to work together is still rare in many schools. Staff meetings and departmental meetings are often devoted to administrative issues rather than teaching. Many districts place a high priority on bringing in experts rather than giving teachers control over their own professional learning. Lesson study may seem impossible when time for the team members to work together is not built into the school day.

Another Perspective

A lack of common planning time is a significant obstacle to overcome, but it should not prevent teachers from considering the possibility of lesson study. The first step is to find out who might be able to help the team find some time to work together. If no progress can be made, teachers might want to consider working together on their own time. This should be considered only when all other options have failed, but it may demonstrate the power and feasibility of lesson study and help to make the case to administrators.

Questions to Consider

- Are there alternative ways to compensate teachers for their time?
- What do we need to convince administrators to invest in lesson study?

Dilemma: We do not have enough teachers to form a team.

Teachers may be understandably reluctant to participate in lesson study. Some may be uncomfortable with the idea of opening their classrooms to others. Teachers may feel they are already overwhelmed with other duties, or lesson study simply may not appeal to them. Some schools have addressed reluctance by making lesson study mandatory.

Another Perspective

Ideally, lesson study teams are made up of three to six teachers. One group of three is a perfectly viable start for a new lesson study initiative in a school or district. Even individual teachers can get a team started if they can find just one other colleague to join. A two-person team will face some obstacles, including more responsibility for the members. Yet starting with a small team will probably be a better strategy for getting lesson study off the ground than coercing teachers to participate.

It may be necessary to extend the search for team members to other schools in the district, or even to other districts. Again, teams with members from multiple sites will face some additional challenges, but many districtwide lesson study efforts have started out this way.

Questions to Consider

- Are there teachers from other schools in the district who may be interested?
- Are there teachers from other grade levels?
- How can we address the concerns of teachers who are interested but also reluctant?

> **Dilemma:** Our team needs training in lesson study.

First-time lesson study teams often hesitate before beginning their work because they feel unprepared for the demands of lesson study. Many teachers are afraid of doing lesson study "wrong" or believe that they do not have the requisite content knowledge or research skills. People who are skeptical about the viability of lesson study in the United States often share these concerns.

Another Perspective

Lesson study is a departure from the professional development that most teachers are familiar with. To be done well, it requires knowledge and skills that some teachers have not had the opportunity to develop. Yet these facts should not discourage a team from getting started. Lesson study is not something that teachers can be fully trained to do before they begin doing it.

In Japan, teachers learn how to engage in lesson study by attending open houses and participating in observations and debriefings. If possible, lesson study teams in the United States should also begin their work this way. Because lesson study is just beginning, there may not be many opportunities for U.S. teachers to do this, and many will have to learn as they go. Reflecting on the core elements of lesson study and monitoring the teams' progress will help teachers build their lesson study "skills."

Questions to Consider

- What opportunities are there for us to see lesson study in action?
- Are there other lesson study teams that we can call on for advice?
- Are there knowledgeable others who may be able to help us?

MOVING ON TO THE NEXT PHASE

Once the teachers are on board and the time for collaboration is available, the lesson study team is one step closer to planning their first research lesson. It may take an extended period of time to bring together the people and resources to support lesson study. The next phase will be to establish positive relationships among team members and to craft a research theme or long-term goal for lesson study.

The team may want to start a collection of documents and other artifacts. Creating a running record of lesson study artifacts and activities will save time and prevent frustration when preparing a lesson study **report.** Also, it is never too early to begin thinking about how to evaluate the team's work. Keeping track of professional growth and other outcomes will help to improve lesson study practice and expand the number of people involved.

KEY IDEAS

- Lesson study requires interested teachers, time for collaboration, support from administrators, and a well-thought-out action plan.
- Starting out small with a group of enthusiastic teachers will help lesson study to grow and gain momentum.
- Finding time for lesson study may seem like the biggest obstacle, yet there are actually many opportunities and options to choose from if schools are willing to adjust the allocation of time and money for professional development.
- Lesson study is supported and sustained by a collaborative school culture.

From Our Team to Yours

Getting the Word Out

The members of the Detroit Lesson Study Group have found that frequent communication with administrators is essential for many reasons. The teachers take responsibility for ensuring that administrators know about the impact of their work. Inviting administrators to attend observations and debriefings has also helped administrators understand and support their work.

Vicki: "I think it's important for administrators to buy into what we're doing. Sometimes we have to have substitutes in our classrooms, and obviously subs are not usually as strong as you with your students. And so I think our principals do need to buy into the lesson study process and to see professional development as something that is important."

Byron: "We have tried to be proactive about communicating with administrators about lesson study. If principals don't know anything about lesson study, they are going to be reluctant to support it. We have to make sure that we tell them about what we are doing in lesson study and how it is going to help us become better teachers."

Elana: "It's very helpful when administrators can participate and observe a research lesson. One of our goals is for our students to have a positive experience with math. During one lesson, the principal got right in there with the students. So we had the children's interest as well as the principal's—even he had a positive experience."

3

Starting the Lesson Study Cycle

Once the invitations to join the lesson study team have been issued and the members have signed on, the teachers can begin their work. The lesson study cycle will soon be under way, but before the team begins planning the research lesson, a few issues must be addressed. The first steps toward beginning lesson study are both logistical—creating a schedule and agreeing on responsibilities— and relational—laying the ground rules for effective collaboration. Another preliminary task is crafting a research theme or long-term goal for lesson study. Taking time to establish good working relationships and mapping out the work with a long-term goal will help to ensure the effectiveness of the rest of the lesson study cycle.

In regular team or department meetings I can't think of a time where I've been in a group that actually agonized over the minute details of a lesson together. Normally, we just don't have time to do that. But lesson study gave us that time, and I think we've gotten to be really comfortable with each other—the good, the bad, and all of that. I would say we are much closer than any other team I've been on.

~Christie Jackson, teacher

ROLES AND RESPONSIBILITIES

Lesson study teams are intended to be self-directed and democratic. The members will make all decisions about their work together, and they will contribute equally— from the first-year teacher to the experienced veteran. Therefore, it is important for the team members to begin their work with a clear understanding and agreement about their responsibilities. Becoming a member of the lesson study team will involve much more than a willingness to attend meetings.

Lesson Study Team

The responsibilities of the lesson study team members include a commitment to participate in all lesson study activities. This includes conducting research on content and best practices and studying curriculum materials; planning and writing the research lesson; participating in the teaching, observation, and debriefing; and contributing to the report or other final product. Lesson study team members are also expected to take notes, communicate between meetings, and share their knowledge. Some teams may also want to trade off responsibility for leading meetings among the team members.

Facilitator

There are additional responsibilities for the lesson study facilitator—the person who will guide the lesson study process. The facilitator can be a team member or someone outside the team. When a school is just starting out with lesson study, it is often helpful to work with a facilitator who is *not* a member of the team. The facilitator can be a professional development provider from outside the school district or a local teacher, administrator, or specialist.

Many groups begin working with an outside facilitator who has experience conducting lesson study and then move on as an independent team. Working with an experienced facilitator has many advantages. For example, the facilitator pushes the teachers to go deeper and to change the way they do things. The facilitator also helps the lesson study team gain access to resources outside the school—both information and people.

The many demands on teachers' time make it difficult for them to take on these responsibilities. Time constraints rather than the capabilities of teachers are what drive the need for a facilitator. The role should not be misinterpreted—the facilitator's job is not to teach the team members or to direct their work.

Outside facilitators are not readily available for all lesson study teams, and therefore the teachers may decide to drop the facilitator role. It will be far better to identify a team member who can take on the facilitator responsibilities. Even a teacher who is new to lesson study can take on the role with success.

The primary responsibility of the facilitator is to monitor and guide the lesson study process. This includes gaining an understanding of the core elements of lesson study, looking outside the team for feedback and suggestions, and helping the team maintain the integrity of the process—ensuring that any necessary adaptations are sound. Facilitators sometimes provide subject-matter expertise, but this is not required for the role. Nevertheless, the facilitator should be able to help the teachers make connections to bigger ideas and identify the implications for teaching that go beyond the one lesson. Calling on knowledgeable others and carefully selecting **invited guests** for the observation and debriefing can help to accomplish this.

Keep in mind that an outside facilitator's ultimate goal will be to help the team become independent. Once the team has more experience and a thorough understanding of lesson study, the facilitator will not be needed. As one experienced facilitator sagely put it, "The magic of good facilitation is teaching the team how to drive their own professional development."

Sometimes, the facilitator also takes responsibility for coordinating the team's work. This includes dealing with logistics—scheduling meetings, arranging for facilities, and communicating with administrators. If a team member is serving as the facilitator, another team member should take on these responsibilities, or the members can share the coordination duties.

Knowledgeable Others

In lesson study, teachers "own and operate" the process. They become the drivers of their professional learning. Nevertheless, the team will often call on knowledgeable others who they believe will add value to their work. Knowledgeable others are sometimes called **outside advisors** or **outside experts**. They can come from a school, district office, community college, university, or a regional service agency. They can also come from the community at large.

Knowledgeable others often bring content expertise to the table. Other times they bring valuable instructional knowledge or provide a fresh perspective to the team. The most effective knowledgeable others will have experience with lesson study and an understanding of the role they play. They often push the teachers to think more deeply about content and pedagogy, but their job is not to instruct the teachers or to manage their work.

Another valuable role that knowledgeable others fulfill is in connecting the work of individual lesson study teams (Watanabe & Wang-Iverson, 2005). When they work with multiple teams, knowledgeable others can share the professional knowledge that the teams generate, extending the impact of lesson study across schools, districts, and even states.

Form 3.1 is a list of the lesson study responsibilities that can be included in the lesson study action plan (see Chapter 2). It is not necessary to designate who will take responsibility for each task at the outset, but it is helpful to come to agreement on as many duties as possible. A notable exception is deciding who will teach the lesson: It is usually best to leave this role open until the lesson plan is almost complete. See Chapter 5 for more information and advice about this issue.

CREATING THE SCHEDULE

Developing the schedule for a lesson study cycle is a complex task. The first cycle is especially challenging because it is difficult to anticipate what will happen and how much time each phase will take. There is also a balance to maintain between providing enough time and getting bogged down. The following suggestions may make the scheduling process easier. They are not meant to be a prescription for how all lesson study teams should conduct their work.

Getting Started

Before the team begins working on their research lesson, they should devote at least one meeting to developing group processes and setting a research theme or long-term goal. These activities will usually take two to three hours, and can take more time for first-time teams. Depending on how much meeting time is available, this may take one dedicated meeting of three or more hours or two or more shorter meetings.

Form 3.1   Lesson Study Action Plan: Team Responsibilities

Task	Person Responsible
Facilitating the Team	
Coordinating Meetings and Events	
Finding meeting space	
Scheduling planning meetings	
Scheduling first teaching and debriefing	
Scheduling second teaching and debriefing	
Arranging for food and drinks	
During Planning and Revising Meetings	
Leading the meeting	
Taking minutes	
Typing up the research lesson	
Communicating With Others	
Keeping administrators up to date	
Keeping other teachers up to date	
Contacting knowledgeable others	
Inviting guests to events	
Maintaining Records	
Gathering notes and other documents	
Making and distributing copies	
Maintaining logs and other artifacts for the report	

First Teaching, Observation, and Debriefing	
Conducting the pre-observation	
Teaching the lesson	
Moderating the debriefing	
Keeping time	
Taking notes	
Second Teaching, Observation, and Debriefing	
Conducting the pre-observation	
Teaching the lesson	
Moderating the debriefing	
Keeping time	
Taking notes	

All team members will be responsible for the following:

Attending meetings and events

Taking notes

Conducting research on content and best practices

Studying curriculum materials

Contributing to the planning and the revision of the research lesson

Participating in the teaching, observation, and debriefing

Contributing to the report or other final product

Scheduling the Planning Meetings

To ensure plenty of time for the planning phase, it may be better to err on the side of designating too much time. Chapter 4 provides an overview of the in-depth work that is involved in creating the research lesson, and it may help provide a sense of how much time will be needed. Alternatively, first-time teams may want to conduct a somewhat shorter planning phase to get a feel for the process and then devote more time to planning in their second cycle and beyond. Figure 3.1 suggests some scheduling options.

Remember that the purpose of the research lesson is to provide a common experience that teachers can use to learn from their practice. Some lesson study teams intentionally spend more time on revising the lesson than they do on the first planning phase. This enables the teachers to invest more of their time and energy in using the concrete examples and evidence that were gathered during the observation and debriefing.

Figure 3.1 Scheduling Options—Planning

When	Number of Sessions
Class period – 45–60 minutes	6–8
After school – 60 minutes	6–8
Late start or early release – 90 minutes	4–6
Half-day release time	3–4
Full-day release time	2–3

Akihiko Takahashi, an assistant professor of mathematics education at DePaul University who is also a lesson study expert, suggests the schedule in Figure 3.2 for developing a research lesson. This schedule will not work for all teams, but is a useful starting point to consider. It may take new lesson study teams more time to develop their first research lesson. What the schedule demonstrates is that the planning can be a very streamlined process. Teams can develop a well-planned research lesson even if they do not have extended time available.

Scheduling the Teaching and Debriefing

Scheduling the teaching of the research lesson in the context of many districts' curriculum pacing constraints can seem like a daunting task. Many teachers tend to have little latitude in adjusting the timing of instruction around particular units and concepts. Carefully allowing sufficient planning time in advance of the point where the concept or strategy that is the focus of the lesson study is normally taught usually works. Sometimes, in spite of everyone's best effort, the schedule gets off-track. When this happens, it may be necessary to look beyond the team to find a classroom not yet past that place in the flow of the curriculum. The research lesson is usually presented to a team member's students because the teachers are then able to develop it with a specific group of students in mind.

Figure 3.2   Sample Planning Schedule

Five weeks before: teaching the lesson	**Goal Setting.** Identify your research theme or goal.
	Identifying the Topic. Decide on a topic to investigate. A topic should be thought of as a unit of lessons rather than a single lesson.
Four weeks before:	**Conducting Research.** Investigate a variety of materials to develop a research lesson.
	Mapping the Unit. Develop a simple unit plan before planning the research lesson.
Three weeks before:	**Developing the Research Lesson.** Begin writing the research lesson.
Two weeks before:	**Completing the First Draft.** Complete the first draft of the research lesson. It might be useful for a group to include ideas from members' classrooms. One or two group members teach lessons to their own classes based on the ideas from the first draft in order to complete the final draft.
One week before:	**Completing the Final Draft.** Complete the final draft of research lesson.

SOURCE: Takahashi, A. (2005, June). *Facilitating the process of lesson study.* Paper presented at the Detroit Lesson Study Conference, Detroit, MI.

Devoting a full day to the observation and debriefing ensures that the team will have ample time to do their work. It allows for a substantial pre-observation session to introduce the lesson, time for the observers to go over their notes and gather their thoughts before the debriefing, and time for the lesson study team to reflect on the debriefing as a closing activity. Many teams begin revising the research lesson immediately after the debriefing. Chapter 5 provides a few examples for organizing the agenda and schedule for the observation and debriefing.

Scheduling the Revising and Reteaching

Revising and reteaching the lesson has sometimes been given less emphasis than the previous phases of the lesson study process because it can pose problems for scheduling. A hurdle that many teams run into is the need to teach the same lesson at

---

FROM THE FIELD

By the time we were ready to conduct the teaching and observation, everybody on the team had already taught the concept. Nobody was at a point in the unit where they could do the lesson. My students were already out of the light unit and into density. Our team felt stuck. But then I figured out that my colleague at another school, who had done lesson study before, was just diving into the unit with his students. I called, explained the situation, and asked if our team could borrow his class so one of us could teach the lesson while the others observed. He agreed and oriented us to the specific dynamics and background of his students. It worked tremendously well. It was neat for him to watch his class respond to a lesson. He was able to view his students as an observer, something he is never able to do, and contribute to the debriefing based on his knowledge of his class. Another team member retaught the lesson later in another borrowed classroom. With a little creativity, we were able to make it all work.

~Karen Nelson, teacher

the same time in all of their classes. If the teachers are on the same schedule, they may have to move on to other topics by the time the revisions are made and the lesson is ready for the second teaching. If the team members are on different schedules, the lesson may not fit where they are in the curriculum.

The revising and reteaching may pose a challenge for scheduling, but much learning takes place during this phase. Every effort should be made to find the time. The amount of time that the team will need to revise the lesson will vary—approximately two to six hours is often sufficient. The time for revision can be broken up into different meetings, or the team can spend an entire day working together.

If there is a sufficient block of time between the two teaching episodes, providing this time should not be problematic. Yet it is likely that there will be occasions when the turnaround time is tight. If possible, the team should have additional out-of-class time to meet together and to work on the lesson. If the schedule is very tight, the team can observe and debrief the first lesson in the morning, revise the lesson in the afternoon, and reteach the following day.

Again, the team may have elected to spend more time on revising the lesson than the first planning phase. Yet the revision process should not drag on to the extent that the team loses momentum and motivation to continue.

Listed here are some alternative ways to organize the revising and reteaching phase if it is not possible to fit it into the current cycle.

- The team revises the lesson together, but the team members reteach it on their own and then report back.
- The team uses the data from the teaching and debriefing to plan a different but related lesson that occurs later in the unit.
- The team uses the revisions they make to the research lesson to inform the next lesson study cycle.
- The team revises the lesson immediately after the first teaching and debriefing but reteaches the lesson the following year.

Reflecting and Sharing

After the second teaching, the team will need time to reflect on and capture their learning and to develop the lesson study report. Not all lesson study teams will develop a report, yet the team will need to develop a means of sharing what they have learned. The schedule for this phase of the lesson study cycle will depend on how elaborate the team decides to make their report and how much work can be completed individually and between sessions. Typically, two to four hours will be sufficient.

Form 3.2 is a template that lesson study teams can use to develop a schedule for the cycle. This schedule will be included in the lesson study action plan.

DEVELOPING INTO A TEAM

Lesson study provides a means for teachers to work together, but the opportunity alone will not automatically result in effective collaboration. In spite of the proven benefits of collaboration, providing frequent opportunities for teachers to work together is still not the norm in U.S. schools. Many teachers have not had a chance to build their skills for collaborative inquiry and learning, and they may be reluctant to open up their classrooms and share their teaching with colleagues.

Form 3.2   Lesson Study Action Plan: Schedule

Getting Started (Group Norms, Research Theme)		
Date	*Time*	*Location*

Planning Sessions		
Date	*Time*	*Location*

Teaching, Observation, and Debriefing		
Date	*Time*	*Location*
Pre-observation		
Teaching		
Reflection		
Debriefing		
Post-debriefing		

(Continued)

Form 3.2 (Continued)

Revising Sessions		
Date	*Time*	*Location*

Reteaching, Observation, and Debriefing		
Date	*Time*	*Location*
Pre-observation		
Teaching		
Reflection		
Debriefing		
Post-debriefing		

Reflecting and Sharing		
Date	*Time*	*Location*

To learn from the lesson study process, teachers must be willing to collectively examine their practice, seek out areas for improvement, and acknowledge challenges. Taking a self-critical perspective can be very difficult, especially in front of others. The supportive relationships among the team members build a foundation for dialogue, analysis, and critique.

Teachers who begin the lesson study process with hesitation often say that they were quickly reassured and became more comfortable. The collective ownership of the research lesson is key. Rather than singling out one teacher's practice for scrutiny, the team is examining their collective ideas and decisions.

Before establishing goals or planning a lesson, the lesson study team must devote some time to getting to know each other and to establishing group norms for their work together. Many professional development experiences begin with an ice-breaker. When teachers will be working together on short-term projects, an informal, "getting-to-know-you" process is appropriate and sufficient. For the long-term effort that lesson study requires, a deeper process is essential. Even when the team members know each other well, they will ultimately benefit from laying the groundwork for their collaboration.

Creating a supportive and productive environment means establishing trust, safety, rapport, and respect. The lesson study team should identify the qualities they need to develop and the ground rules they need to establish to work effectively together. These group norms will provide a set of shared expectations for how the team members will interact and how they will support each other's learning.

Group norms are also important because they enable teachers to build the habits of mind that are a key component in the substance of lesson study. A productive team environment will enable teachers to learn together, to adopt a research stance toward their practice, and to build a sense of professional authority.

Identifying Group Norms

Establishing group norms will be the lesson study team's first collective effort and should be the focus of the first group meeting. There are many different ways to identify the expectations, and each team will select the appropriate method and adapt it to fit their needs.

Generating the list can begin as an individual brainstorming task, in which each person creates his or her own list and then shares it with the group. Using Post-it notes to record each item will make it easy to group similar ideas together. Or the team can forego the individual brainstorming and generate the list together.

The following are some guiding questions that may help the team identify the group norms.

- What are our expectations for how we will work together?
- What conditions will contribute to our learning?
- What conditions will get in the way?
- What conditions are necessary to create and maintain a sense of belonging and support?
- How will we resolve our differences and disagreements?

Another strategy is to generate a set of expectations based on completing the following sentence fragments. For example, "I expect that my colleagues will share their opinions, even if we disagree."

- I expect . . .
- I assume . . .
- Effective groups need . . .

No matter how the team creates their expectations, it will be helpful for each person to provide a description or an example of the characteristics they wish to be included. This will help ensure that everyone has a common understanding of the final list.

It may be helpful to begin with a list of the characteristics of effective teams as a starting point for the discussion. An existing list can also be helpful to check against the one the team generated. There may be characteristics that do not come up in the initial discussion but that the group agrees should be included. What follows is a sample list of group norms (Bray, Lee, Smith, & Yorks, 2000; Collay et al., 1998; Dufour & Eaker, 1998; Preskill & Torres, 1999).

Communication Is Open and Honest; There Is a Climate of Trust

Team members must feel that they are able to share their ideas and opinions without inspiring defensiveness or reprisals. It will be difficult for members to learn from each other if they cannot be honest. Although the ability to share their views openly and honestly is important, members will be unlikely to do so if they fear their contributions will be ignored or belittled. The balance between honesty and trust may not be easy to establish and maintain at first, but it is crucial to the team's work.

Members Are Encouraged to Both Challenge and Support One Another

Team members do this by asking questions, building on each other's ideas, and respectfully disagreeing. They are expected to ask for clarification, explain their reasoning, and provide evidence to back up their assertions.

Methods for Resolving Conflict Are Established and Agreed On

No team should begin its work with the assumption that it will be easy to work together. Members must agree to listen and focus on the problem rather than on the people involved, give the process adequate time, and try to see the issue from another person's perspective.

Mistakes Are Viewed as Opportunities

It is difficult to try new things or to take risks if there is fear of the consequences. It may be helpful to keep in mind that the purpose of lesson study is not to create the perfect lesson but to learn. Mistakes are fruitful sources of learning—so in many ways, the more the better.

All Members Are Held Accountable for Their Actions

Part of engaging in lesson study is making a commitment to the other team members. All must agree to fulfill their specific responsibilities, to share the work as equally as possible, and to support each other and maintain productive and respectful interactions.

Maintaining Group Norms

When it is complete, the list of group norms will serve as a charter for the lesson study team. All members should have a copy of the list that they can refer to on a continual basis. It may also be helpful to create a poster that can be put up on the wall during meetings. Some groups sign an agreement to symbolize their commitment.

Remember that establishing the group norms is only the first step. Each team will also need a strategy for continuing to monitor their behavior, rather than waiting until a problem arises. This can be accomplished with a periodic self-assessment or a check-in at the end of each meeting. The "Reflecting and Assessing Progress" sections in each chapter provide questions about group norms. It may also be helpful to take time to reflect on a specific norm.

Becoming a Community of Practice

As team members build their relationships and become accustomed to working together, they will be able to reflect on and deepen their sense of community. Teachers who begin lesson study with collaborative relationships already established may also want to use this as an opportunity to improve.

To develop more meaningful collaboration, lesson study teams may benefit from considering the characteristics of collective communities of practice. Westheimer (1998) has attempted to identify the differences between the surface features of collaboration that make it sound so appealing and the qualities of groups that develop a collective sense of their work, their knowledge, and their learning.

> **FROM THE FIELD**
>
> At the San Mateo–Foster City School District in California, teachers and leaders have developed a systematic approach to maintaining positive group relationships. The lesson study teams have learned that it is important to take time and establish norms, as well as to actively monitor them throughout each lesson study cycle.
>
> Each team devotes time during the first meeting of the year to review the group norms from the previous year and make adjustments if they are needed. At each subsequent meeting, the teachers will select one of the group norms to monitor. At the end of the meeting, they reflect on the norm, discuss their success in demonstrating it, and identify ways to improve future meetings.
>
> At the end of the year, the teams reflect on the group norms as a whole and their success in maintaining them. Using this self-evaluation process, the teams continually improve their collegial relationships and their lesson study practice.

Collective Responsibility

Many groups start out with the idea that their purpose is to support each other and their individual work in their classrooms. Over time, the team may develop a sense of their work as a collective enterprise. Creating the research lesson together is only the first step. Drawing on each other's strengths, sharing resources, and distributing responsibilities are approaches that teachers can use every day as they work together to foster student learning. A sense of interdependence develops, which the team values and models for others.

Philosophical Conversations

As they develop a research lesson, teachers discuss activities they have developed, strategies they use, the students in their classrooms, and experiences they have had. Exchanges on this level can be valuable, but the lesson study process is more than just a means of sharing ideas. Teachers may work toward developing an atmosphere in which they can regularly explore principles and philosophies of education: to think about and share their deeply held beliefs about teaching, how students learn, and the nature of the disciplines they teach.

Addressing Problems Together

When teachers run into problems, they sometimes approach their colleagues for support and professional advice. As they build a stronger sense of community, teachers approach problems as challenges that they will face together rather than individual occasions when they might go to each other for guidance. Collaborative problem solving is the norm rather than the exception.

Valuing Dissent

Many people approach collaboration as an environment in which everyone must agree. Therefore teachers are often quick to avoid the possibility of conflict when they work together. The tendency to suppress dissenting opinions will lessen as teachers gain an understanding that it is through sharing their differences that they build professional knowledge.

Community as an End

Most lesson study teams will quickly gain an understanding of the positive outcomes that collaboration helps them to achieve. Over time, the teachers may develop a sense of the intrinsic value of collaboration. It becomes the way that they prefer to work rather than just a means of achieving specific objectives. Teachers will participate not out of a sense of professional obligation but because being a member of the community is part of their identity.

TYPES OF LESSON STUDY GOALS

Goals are an essential part of the lesson study process. There are several different types of goals involved in lesson study.

The research theme is a broad, long-term goal that is focused on students, not teachers or instruction. It provides a common theme for multiple cycles of lesson study, and it may also serve as a collective focus for individual teams within a school.

The **unit goal** or goals are the overall goals for the unit within which the research lesson is located. Unit goals help connect the research theme to the lesson-specific goals. There are two different types of unit goals. A **content goal** identifies the specific concepts or understandings that students will develop. A **process goal** identifies the skills or habits of mind that students will develop. Identifying both content

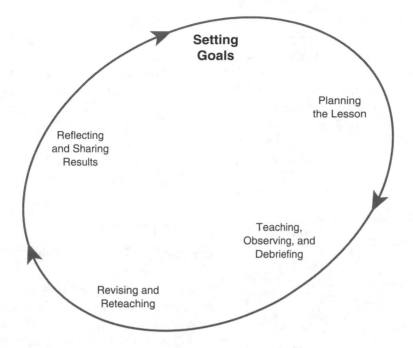

and process goals may not be appropriate for every lesson study cycle. For example, a content goal is required for most mathematics and science lessons, but it may not be essential for a language arts lesson.

The **lesson goal** or goals narrow down the previous goals even further. They are the specific student learning outcomes for the lesson. Figure 3.3 provides an example of the three types of goals from a science lesson.

Many teachers are not accustomed to making goals such a prominent part of their planning. Clear goals make it possible to plan focused and coherent research lessons with measurable outcomes. The goals help the lesson study team develop a stronger understanding of student learning and how to support it.

Figure 3.3   Sample Goals—Science

Research Theme	Developing scientific habits of mind such as use of the senses, use of evidence to warrant assertions, and use of controlled investigations.
Unit Goals	Students will investigate, describe, and analyze ways in which matter changes.
	Students will develop an awareness of the need for evidence in making decisions scientifically.
Lesson Goals	Students will make careful observations of both positive and negative results.
	Students will use deductive reasoning based on evidence to narrow choices.

Linking immediate and long-term goals allows teams to think not only about individual lessons but also how each one builds on the next to help reach more challenging outcomes that take time to develop.

High-quality lessons are focused on important learning goals and reflect the teacher's understanding of how each lesson relates to the goals (Weiss, Pasley, Smith, Banilower, & Heck, 2003). Clear learning goals also contribute to higher student achievement (Lipsey & Wilson, 1993).

This chapter focuses on one type of lesson study goal: the research theme. Chapter 4 describes the unit goals and lesson goals in more detail.

FROM THE FIELD

Frankly, I had significant reservations as the lesson study process began. We were six teachers who had never worked together. We came from different districts using different curriculum materials, and we taught widely varying classes in high schools and junior high schools. I thought it unlikely that we would be able to create and work effectively toward a common goal. I also questioned whether we would have enough of a common frame of reference to offer useful feedback to each other.

We began with a rather fitful attempt at goal setting. At first this activity felt hopeless, but in retrospect it was in fact the perfect way for us to begin. As we talked of our dreams for our students and the gaps that prevented their fulfillment, we were getting to know each other. This discussion allowed each of us to share our visions and frustrations, and it became apparent that, despite our differences, we had a great deal in common. What seemed like something of an aimless, philosophical discussion actually created the beginnings of the common ground from which we could work together. We also created a pretty good goal—one that each of us found worthwhile and that we were willing to extend ourselves to achieve:

"Our goal is to encourage students to create their own conceptual framework of mathematics. We believe that if we can increase the frequency and quality of student questions, then we will improve their conceptual understanding. We see a quality lesson as creating a need and providing an opportunity for students to ask critical questions."

~Rich Dixon, teacher

CRAFTING A RESEARCH THEME

Before a lesson study team begins conducting their research and planning the research lesson, they will establish a research theme to guide their work. The term "research theme" comes from lesson study practice in Japan. It is also sometimes called a "**research focus**." In some Japanese schools, the teachers identify a research theme and all professional development, including lesson study, is focused around this theme (Fernandez & Yoshida, 2004). Many themes continue across multiple years.

The goals and their connection to each other help maintain the coherence of the lesson study cycle. Even for a single team within a school, it is still a good idea to take time to identify a research theme. It will help tie the more specific goals to long-term goals for students. The team will also be able to demonstrate how their work is connected to the goals of the school as a whole. The research theme can help maintain convergence across multiple cycles of lesson study and additional professional development experiences.

Teachers say that one of the benefits of the research theme is that it helps them to keep an eye on the big picture, which they often lose sight of in the rush through the school day. It encourages them to step back and reflect occasionally on the "why," rather than just the "what" and the "how" of their teaching. Responsibility for common goals also contributes to collegiality among teachers (Little, 1990).

Strategies for Identifying the Research Theme

Lesson study teams can use one of the following methods to craft their research theme. Some teams may want to combine more than one strategy.

Identify Ideal Student Qualities

In Japanese schools, the teachers often identify the research theme by comparing the qualities they want their students to develop in the future with the qualities their students currently possess (Fernandez & Chokshi, 2002; Fernandez & Yoshida, 2000; Lewis, 2002b). Teachers brainstorm a list of the characteristics that an ideal student will be able to demonstrate. After this first list is complete, the team identifies the characteristics that best describe where students are. The third step is to examine the gap between the two lists and consider: What can schools do, and what can teachers do, to close the gap? One way to develop a broader perspective is to involve parents and students in this activity.

Barbrina Ertle, Sonal Chokshi, and Clea Fernandez of the Lesson Study Research Group at Teachers College have developed a Goal Selection Worksheet that will help guide a team through this process. The worksheet is available on the Internet at www.tc.columbia.edu/centers/lessonstudy/resources.html. Figure 3.4 provides some sample responses that might result from this process.

Figure 3.4   Students: Ideal Versus Actual

Example 1		
Ideal Student Qualities	*Actual Student Qualities*	*Research Theme*
Independent thinkers Mastery of basic skills Ability to work with others Self-motivated learners Positive self-concept	Dependent on the teacher Enthusiastic Scattered Lack responsibility Friendly Immature	To develop students' confidence and to encourage them to take responsibility for their own and others' learning.
Example 2		
Ideal Student Qualities	*Actual Student Qualities*	*Research Theme*
Problem solvers Proficient with technology Good communication skills Lifelong learners who understand *how* to learn	Have difficulty applying what they know Oral communication less than satisfactory Intimidated by unfamiliar situations Lack metacognitive skills	To engage students in learning how to learn and apply what they know to new situations.

More than one goal may be identified through this process, so planning for ways to prioritize the different areas may be helpful. Perhaps the easiest way to prioritize is for teachers to choose the area that is most compelling to them or the quality that they are most passionate about.

One pitfall to watch out for with this strategy is the tendency to create a laundry list, which will make the research theme less meaningful. The list from Example 1 in Figure 3.4 could have been turned into the following goal: "For students to master basic skills and become independent thinkers while also developing the abilities to be self-motivated and confident learners."

Build on Existing Goals

Many schools and district have school improvement plans and goals already in place. These can serve as a research theme for lesson study as well. In fact, even when teachers use a different strategy for selecting the research theme, it should be aligned to any existing goals that guide the school. Figure 3.5 provides examples of research themes that are derived from school improvement goals.

Figure 3.5   School Improvement Goals

Example 1	
School Improvement Goal	*Research Theme*
Provide support to students and staff to foster writing literacy.	For students to understand the qualities of effective writing and how to develop those qualities in their own work.
Example 2	
School Improvement Goal	*Research Theme*
Cultivate a positive learning environment.	For students to feel safe and supported as they encounter challenging learning situations.
Example 3	
School Improvement Goal	*Research Theme*
Increase opportunities for all students to build relationships with student peers and with adults.	For students to develop good relationships with their peers and with the adults in their lives.
Example 4	
School Improvement Goal	*Research Theme*
Promote improvement of students' informational reading skills across the curriculum.	For students to value reading for a variety of purposes.

Use the School Mission Statement

This approach may help maintain a long-term and broad perspective. Checking the actual practices and learning environment against the stated ideal can illuminate areas for improvement. A brainstorming process similar to the one used to identify ideal and actual student qualities can be used.

Mission statements are often very broad and lengthy—they can fall into the laundry list category. The lesson study team should select one aspect of the mission to focus their work. This can be a quality that they feel is the most important or interesting. Alternatively, a team might select the aspect of the mission statement that needs the most improvement. Figure 3.6 provides examples of research themes that are based on school mission statements.

Figure 3.6   School Mission Statements

Example 1	
Mission Statement	*Research Theme*
Our mission is to develop an environment and curriculum that foster the growth of students in becoming creative thinkers, innovators, and responsible members of society and to instill in all students a strong sense of self-worth, a commitment to reach the highest levels of excellence in academic achievement and physical and emotional growth, and a genuine concern for others.	To help students become confident and creative thinkers and innovators.
Example 2	
Mission Statement	*Research Theme*
Our school supports inspired learning, leading to responsible action through dedicated teaching, caring relationships, a challenging curriculum, and community service. We value each person's effort, imagination, and positive contributions to the community.	To help students value each other and develop caring relationships.
Example 3	
Mission Statement	*Research Theme*
Our mission is to develop within each student: 　Respectful, responsible, and ethical attitudes and behaviors 　An awareness and appreciation of the diverse cultures in our learning community and our world 　An ability to think critically and solve problems 　An ability to communicate effectively 　An ability to appreciate and demonstrate creativity 　A lifelong desire to pursue knowledge	To foster students' problem solving and responsibility for learning.

Combine All Three Strategies

Some lesson study teams may want to use all three sources of information to create their research theme. Doing so will help increase the coherence of the school's or district's professional development. If this is not done, lesson study may become "one more thing" rather than a means of supporting existing priorities.

Do not be afraid to spend time developing the research theme and getting the wording right. The team may also want to ask for feedback on their long-term goal. At Paterson School No. 2 in New Jersey, the lesson study team worked closely with teachers from a Japanese school in Greenwich, Connecticut. The Japanese teachers helped the Paterson team to hone their original goal into a more meaningful one (Fernandez et al., 2003). These questions may help the team to evaluate their research theme and to ensure that it is appropriate and workable.

- Can the research theme be addressed in different subject areas?
- Are you interested in the goal? Do you find it compelling?
- Is the research theme important?

When the research theme has been agreed on and the wording is finalized, the team members will record their thinking and the rationale that was used to identify the goal. This will make it easier for the team to explain the goal to other people. It may even serve as a reminder as time passes and the details of the development process begin to fade. In addition, keep any documents or lists that were generated to include in the lesson study report. Form 3.3 is designed to capture the research theme.

A Note on Affective Goals

In lesson study, the research theme often focuses on affective qualities—things like well-being, relationships, and positive emotions—rather than academic achievement or specific content. The tradition of focusing on affective goals has grown out of the emphasis on teaching the whole child in Japanese education. Japanese teachers think of their work as a responsibility to promote the social, ethical, emotional, aesthetic, physical, and intellectual development of their students (Lewis, 1995). Affective goals are important for the same reasons that lesson study teams spend time on identifying the group norms that will support their work together. The climate of the school and the classroom has an impact on student learning.

An affective research theme is not required, but there are many benefits. Affective goals may lend themselves more easily to multiple subject areas. When lesson study is conducted on a schoolwide basis, or even if there are multiple teams in the same school or district, the research theme is very rarely content specific. This allows the teams to share a collective aim. An exception might be an elementary school where all teachers teach all subjects, or a school where teachers in all subject areas agree to share an emphasis on a particular content area. For example, if the research theme is focused on literacy, a team of science teachers might design a lesson that fosters reading skills in their subject area.

A focus on the social or emotional aspects of learning may inspire teachers to think about learning and students in new ways. In a climate of intense accountability, teachers often believe that paying attention to affective goals for learning must be put aside in favor of the demands of improving achievement on test scores and moving as quickly as possible through the curriculum. It is easy to forget that relationships and the classroom climate are the foundations of teaching and learning. Student perceptions of the classroom environment—their feelings of acceptance, care, and participation—are directly related to their motivation to learn and to academic achievement (Black, 1997; Fraser, Giddings, & McRobbie, 1995; McCombs & Whisler, 1997; Pierce, 1994; Voelkl, 1994).

Form 3.3   Research Theme Statement

Our Research Theme:

We created this goal by:

We believe this is an important goal because:

CHALLENGES OF GETTING STARTED

> **Dilemma:** We may be too different to work together well.

When people think about collaborative work or professional communities, they assume that teams are supposed to be congenial, with common ideals, teaching philosophies, and experiences. Community is often equated with conformity and expectations that members will suppress their differences.

Another Perspective

The members of a lesson study team bring their individual experiences, ideas, and opinions to their work together. Differences help to create more opportunities to learn and to look at situations and problems from a variety of angles. This does not mean that extended debates or disagreements that deteriorate into arguments will be productive. When the team establishes group norms, they have an opportunity to decide collectively on how to engage in dialogue rather than debate, how to question each other in a supportive manner, and how to deal with disagreements when they occur.

Questions to Consider

- How might our differences contribute to our learning?
- How can we ensure that disagreements are productive rather than disruptive?

> **Dilemma:** We want to get started on planning the lesson right away.

The planning phase may seem like the point where the *real* work of lesson study begins. When a team will be spending so much time on just one lesson, taking even more time before planning begins may be the breaking point. Slowing down and laying the initial foundation may also feel like a roadblock that will interrupt a team's growing momentum.

Another Perspective

Collaboration does not happen automatically, and working together productively requires skills that teachers often do not have time to practice in their daily work. A lesson study team that takes time to establish good relationships among the members will find that their work together goes more smoothly and they will be able to learn more from their experiences. Instead of trying to invent a method for dealing with disagreement in the midst of a problem when tension may be high, the team will be able to rely on the guidelines they established from the beginning of their work together.

Questions to Consider

- What are the risks if we do *not* have collective agreement about our work together?
- What are some potential problems that we should plan for?

> **Dilemma:** Why so many goals? The research theme
> does not seem very important to the lesson study process.

Developing the research theme may seem like an extra layer of work in a process that is already quite labor-intensive. Realizing that they will soon be identifying goals that are more directly related to the research lesson, team members may be reluctant to spend time on identifying the long-term goal.

Another Perspective

The research theme may not seem like a necessity to the overall lesson study process. There are teams that have chosen to skip over this step. When this happens, there are trade-offs for the time that is saved. The team will lose the opportunity to connect multiple research lessons through a common focus. The lack of an explicit connection may lead to learning that is only applied to individual lessons. Teachers may be less likely to strengthen and accumulate knowledge of student learning and effective instruction. The lack of connection may also increase the threat that lesson study will be a one-time experience that teachers try for a year before moving on.

Questions to Consider

- How will the research theme contribute to the planning process?
- How will a common schoolwide research theme affect our learning?

REFLECTING AND ASSESSING PROGRESS

The team has just begun its work, but it may be a fruitful time to reflect on the progress so far. It is helpful to pause at the end of each phase in the lesson study cycle. Devoting time to reflection will help the team members to ensure that their learning is intentional and cumulative and that their lesson study practice improves over time.

After the research theme has been created, take a few moments at the end of the meeting to think about the following questions. Sharing responses via e-mail is another option if time is limited.

- What concerns do you have about working as a team?
- Were these addressed by the process of establishing group norms?
- What surprised you about the process of developing the research theme?
- What benefits do you anticipate from the research theme?
- Do you have any new insights about your school? Your students? Your colleagues? Yourself?
- What have you learned so far?

MOVING ON TO THE NEXT PHASE

Before the planning phase begins, there are a few logistical details to address. First, all members of the team will need a copy of the Lesson Study Action Plan: Team Responsibilities (Form 3.1), the Lesson Study Action Plan: Schedule (Form 3.2), the group charter or list of group norms, and the Research Theme Statement (Form 3.3). The purpose of these forms is to help teams organize and record their work, but they are optional. Facilitators and teams should select the tools that seem helpful and adapt or ignore those that they find less meaningful.

It also will be helpful to prepare tools and materials for the planning meetings. The facilitator or a team member might prepare a template agenda for future meetings. The team can tailor the agenda for each meeting while also ensuring that the team stays on track and that there is adequate time for reflection. Other tools include an enlarged copy of the group norms and the research theme that can be posted on the wall.

At this point in the lesson study cycle, the team will also want to collect the artifacts they have created so far and add them to the documentation. The items to be included are

- Group charter or set of group norms
- Artifacts from the development of the research theme
- Research Theme Statement
- Team Responsibilities and Schedule for the lesson study action plan

KEY IDEAS

- The lesson study team members share responsibility for guiding and monitoring their work.
- Relationships among team members and a common understanding of how to work together enhance teamwork and collegial learning.
- Teachers craft a long-term goal for student to guide their lesson study work.

From Our Team to Yours

Group Size

When the members of the Detroit Lesson Study Group reflect on the things that have contributed to their success, group size is revealed as a crucial issue. After trying to work with larger groups—up to 12 members—the teachers have decided to limit teams to a maximum of six people. One of the obstacles for bigger teams is scheduling: It can be challenging to find a time when even six people are all available. The group also has found that it is difficult to make sure that everyone can contribute when the lesson study team is too large.

Brandon: "One thing I've noticed with the larger groups—people get discouraged because they don't have a defined role. If you don't have a defined role, you really get a little displaced and you're not really involved. That's why I think a group with five or six people works best—definitely a maximum of six members. Everybody has a defined role and everybody has a direct impact on the quality of the lesson."

Elana: "When we first started with lesson study, we each defined a role for ourselves on the team. Everyone used their strengths, met their responsibilities, and did what they were supposed to do. That really helps make the whole team effective."

Jason: "I agree. It's almost like less is more. When there are five people, you have an impact. You need to have a mixture of people—females, males, different races, different ages, different areas. The more diverse the team is, the more flavor it's going to have. Everybody has a value or something to contribute."

4

Planning the Research Lesson

T he planning phase of the lesson study cycle takes time and focused effort. It is an opportunity for teachers to adopt the stance of "teacher as researcher"— creating a lesson as an inquiry into the complexities of content, instruction, goals, and student learning.

The lesson study team will move outside the familiar confines of educational practice to think more deeply than ever before about how lessons interact and

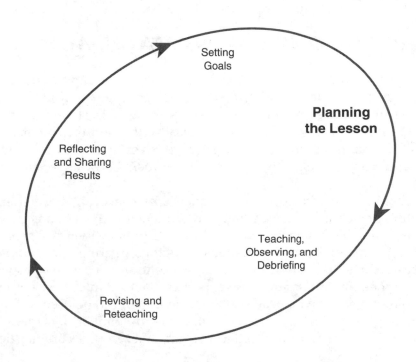

Setting
Goals

**Planning
the Lesson**

Reflecting
and Sharing
Results

Teaching,
Observing, and
Debriefing

Revising and
Reteaching

support each other. The research lesson will help them explore their ideas and questions about how students learn challenging concepts. The teachers will develop their knowledge about crafting learning experiences that anticipate and plan for student responses.

> *The most rewarding thing about lesson study is the opportunity to discuss ideas with your colleagues. . . . With lesson study you have the chance to talk about all of those ideas floating around in your head to improve a lesson. We were able to look at research and curricula with other teachers in developing this lesson which has led to a rethinking of the unit.*
>
> ~Karen Nelson, teacher

PROCESS FOR PLANNING THE LESSON

Many aspects of planning a research lesson run counter to the experiences of educators in the United States. From the collaborative nature of the process, to the extended time devoted to planning, to the detailed nature of the plan itself, lesson study challenges long-held notions about how teachers accomplish their work.

After the lesson study group has agreed on a research theme or long-term goal (see Chapter 3), the planning process can begin. During the planning phase, the group will identify a topic, study how that topic fits into a larger unit, and identify unit and lesson goals. The team will conduct research and investigate teaching materials, consider a variety of instructional approaches, and anticipate student responses. Based on their work together, the team will create a detailed lesson plan.

The process outlined in Figure 4.1 can be used to structure this phase of the lesson study cycle. It will not meet the needs of every team—more specifically, many teams find that their planning is less linear than this example. The sequence presented here is a place to begin and is one that teams can refine.

INVESTIGATING TEACHING MATERIALS

The practice of thinking deeply about a particular topic and how students learn is at the heart of teachers' journey to improve content and pedagogical content knowledge. The lesson study team will investigate a variety of teaching materials to help them plan the research lesson. They will typically draw on these materials during every step of the planning phase. The purpose of investigating teaching materials is to broaden the team's perspective, contribute to their knowledge, and to bring in fresh ideas.

The teachers investigate scope and sequence of concepts, instructional materials, research on teaching and learning, and student misconceptions or challenges (Takahashi, Yoshida, & Watanabe, 2005). This process is known as ***kyozaikenkyu*** in Japanese. The team members share responsibility for gathering information and conducting research. The teachers may want to concentrate on different aspects of this task, based on their areas of interest and expertise. For example, a teacher who enjoys using technology may take the lead on exploring how it can be used in the lesson.

Approaching materials in this way may be unfamiliar for many teachers. Unfortunately, most curricula and other instructional resources are not designed to

Figure 4.1   Process for Planning the Lesson

Guiding Questions	Description
Step 1: Identify the Topic	
What areas are challenging for our students? What are common challenges from research on student learning? What areas are difficult to teach? Are there weak or missing topics in our curriculum? What topic will contribute to our knowledge about the research theme? Will the topic we identify work within the lesson study schedule?	The lesson study team pinpoints a topic for the research lesson by looking at: Student achievement data Challenging concepts and common misconceptions Teacher learning needs Curriculum gaps
Step 2: Map the Unit	
Which lesson will have the most impact on the unit? Why focus on this particular lesson? How does a focus on a single research lesson affect the other lessons in the unit? What will students learn in the activities leading up to the research lesson? Where will they be going next?	The lesson study team examines the unit for the topic they identified in Step 1. The teachers will select the research lesson and consider the connections with the other lessons in the unit.
Step 3: Identify Lesson Goals	
What are the content and process goals for this unit? What do the standards say about these goals? What makes these goals worthwhile? How can the research theme and unit goals be brought to life with the research lesson?	The lesson study team identifies the unit goals that apply to the research lesson. The lesson goals are derived from the unit goals and the research theme.
Step 4: Create the Lesson Plan	
What is our research question or hypothesis? How does our design support the goals of the research lesson? Have we anticipated student responses based on our experience and the research? What kinds of prior knowledge of the topic should students have? How will the teacher respond to student reactions and misconceptions? What kinds of evidence would be sufficient for demonstrating student understanding? Do we have a plan for evaluating the lesson?	The team develops the research lesson. The lesson plan is extremely detailed and represents the team's research and their collective questions and ideas about how best to foster student learning.

serve as sources of professional knowledge for teachers (Ball & Cohen, 1996; Davis & Krajcik, 2005). This aspect of lesson study may be challenging as a result. Yet the research that the team members conduct is essential to develop the detailed plan for the research lesson.

Types of Materials

There are many kinds of resources available to help lesson study teams plan their research lesson. How many different materials the team will use depends on how much time is available for the planning phase. It is helpful to draw on as many different sources as possible.

Curricula, Textbooks, and Activities

The team will find answers to scope and sequence questions and will investigate how different resources organize the topic related to the research lesson. The team will also compare how different materials approach teaching the topics of the research lesson. Looking at materials from different grade levels can also inform the team's understanding of students' prior knowledge and future challenges.

National and State Standards

The team will use standards and benchmarks to help them formulate the unit goals and lesson goals. Standards can inform both the content of the lesson and the types of learning experiences that will help students achieve expected skills.

Curriculum Frameworks and Teacher Guides

District or state frameworks will illustrate the scope and sequence of topics through the grade levels. The benefits are similar to those from investigating curricula for different grade levels.

Books and Journals

Research and classroom-based experiences can address questions about instruction, student learning, and assessment. For example, teachers will investigate research on how students build understanding and fluency, common misconceptions, developmentally appropriate strategies, and how to provide multiple access points and suitable levels of challenge for diverse learners.

Research Lessons

Lessons developed by other lesson study teams may be available to inform the team's planning. Looking at other research lessons also can help the team to get a feel for the format of the research lesson and the level of detail required.

Video

Another aspect of conducting research is developing a vision for what effective instruction looks like in the classroom. It is often productive to watch a segment twice to gain a more complete understanding of the content of the video.

The following questions may be helpful to guide the process of investigating print materials and viewing videos. They can also be used to organize the team members' discussions about their research.

Guiding Questions—Print Resources

- Why is this concept or skill taught at this point in the curriculum?
- What are some alternative ways of representing the concepts and the relationships among them?
- What are the strengths and weaknesses in the design of different activities?
- What decisions went into the design of the lessons and activities?
- What questions are used to frame the concept in different activities?
- Is the approach something we have tried before?
- What is the value of trying something new?

Guiding Questions—Videos

- What do you think are the goals of instruction demonstrated in this video?
- What is it about the featured task(s) that supports these goals?
- What do you notice about the teacher's role in this classroom?
- What do you notice about the students' roles in this classroom?

STEP 1: IDENTIFY THE TOPIC

The first step in identifying the topic will be to agree on the content area. For lesson study teams whose members specialize in a common subject, the content for the lesson will be clear. Other teams—including groups of elementary teachers, other teachers who teach more than one subject, and interdisciplinary lesson study teams—will need to agree on the content area of the research lesson.

When the content area is set, the team will identify a more specific topic for the lesson. In many schools, this will be dictated by the curriculum or by a pacing chart. The team will look at the lesson study schedule and compare it to the curriculum, selecting the topic based on what will be taught at the time that the observation and debriefing are likely to take place.

If the team is not constrained by other demands, there are several sources of information that can inform the identification of a topic for the research lesson. The team can select one source or combine several: student achievement data, research on student learning challenges, teacher learning needs around content and pedagogical content knowledge, and new topics or gaps in the curriculum. No matter what topic is identified, the teachers will keep their research theme in mind as they explore the possibilities.

Assessment Data

Through the disaggregation and analysis of student achievement data from state or district assessments, patterns may emerge that indicate weaknesses in student understanding or skills. By using data to select the topic, the teachers ensure that their work will focus on the areas of greatest need, such as reading expository text in English/language arts, problem solving in math, or making sense of phenomena in physical science. The team members can also conduct a classroom assessment to obtain a more specific understanding of student learning needs.

Research on Student Learning

There is extensive literature available on student misconceptions in science and mathematics, and learning challenges can be found in all subject areas (American Association for the Advancement of Science, 2001; Driver, Squires, Rushworth, & Wood-Robinson, 2003; National Council of Teachers of Mathematics, 2000; National Reading Panel, 2000). Learning challenges may also include specific skills that cut across subject areas, like reading comprehension, problem solving, and writing. The National Research Council has developed a publication on student learning in three specific subject areas: mathematics, science, and history (Donovan & Bransford, 2005).

Teacher Learning Needs

Teachers may want to select a topic that they want to learn more about themselves. Teacher content and pedagogical content knowledge are frequently linked to student learning (Hiebert et al., 2002; Hill, Rowan, & Ball, 2005). Team members can reflect on the areas they feel less prepared to teach or on the topics they find difficult to teach.

FROM THE FIELD

During our first planning meeting together, our team began to think about a topic within the Light Unit taught in fifth grade. We began to consider refraction as a possible research lesson topic, but as we talked, it became evident that there must be a more elemental understanding of light that refraction is built on. Constanza, who was a knowledgeable other for our team, posed a simple, yet powerful question to us: "What is important about refraction?"

At that moment, we realized that reflection and reflected light were where we needed to focus the research lesson. The materials provided by the curriculum and district about this topic were limited. Based on data from district assessments, we knew that students had very uneven levels of prior knowledge about reflected light and that misconceptions about light were persistent. In addition, our team wanted to plan a more inquiry-based lesson, develop a deeper understanding of the behavior of light among students, and strengthen our own pedagogical content knowledge about light.

~Fifth-Grade Lesson Study Team

Curriculum

Lesson study teams may want to focus on gaps in the curriculum—significant topics that are missing or weak. Also, the adoption of new curricula usually requires teachers to examine how concepts are taught and in what sequence.

Figure 4.2 provides a series of questions that may be helpful in examining these sources of information. Choosing a topic for lesson study is often an iterative process. Teams may work through several possibilities before they finalize the topic. Form 4.1 may be helpful for thinking through the possible topics for the research lesson. Teams can use this tool to generate concepts that are challenging to teach or difficult for students to understand.

During the process of identifying a topic (see Figure 4.3), it is helpful to have access to a knowledgeable other who has strong content knowledge and an awareness of the research base on the content area. It is also helpful to have input from individuals who understand the curriculum, student misconceptions, and how to teach difficult topics.

Form 4.1   Planning Tool: Identifying the Topic

Research Theme

Areas for Improvement: Assessment Data

Areas for Improvement: Research on Student Learning

Areas for Improvement: Teacher Learning Needs

Areas for Improvement: Curriculum

Figure 4.2   Guiding Questions—Identifying the Topic

Assessment Data	What topics represent strengths and weaknesses in student achievement? Are there areas that specific groups of students are struggling with?
Research on Student Learning	What topics are perennially difficult for students to understand? What does the research say about student misconceptions and learning challenges?
Teacher Learning Needs	Are any of these evident in the student work or in the questions students ask? What topics are especially challenging to teach? Are any of these topics significant in terms of future student learning? What topics do you feel the least comfortable or least prepared to teach?
Curriculum	Does the new curriculum introduce topics not taught before? Are the scope and sequence of topics different than the way we are currently addressing them? What topics are missing from our curriculum? Are there lessons that are weak or that need to be developed further?

Figure 4.3   Step 1: Identify the Topic

Guiding Questions	Description

• What areas are challenging for our students?
 • What are common challenges from research on student learning?
 • What areas are difficult to teach?
 • Are there weak or missing topics in our curriculum?
 • What topic will contribute to our knowledge about the research theme?
 • Will the topic we identify work within the lesson study schedule?
	The lesson study team pinpoints a topic for the research lesson by looking at:
	   Student achievement data
	   Challenging concepts and common misconceptions
	   Teacher learning needs
	   Curriculum gaps

Example
We chose the concept of equality for our first-grade lesson. There were several factors that helped us to select that concept. Last year when we aligned our current math curriculum with our state standards, we found this gap. We decided to address one of these gaps in our research lesson— the concept of equality/inequality. We also realized that this concept is one that spans the math continuum. It is an essential concept because it is a major part of algebraic sense and is a prerequisite to understanding and performing higher math.

STEP 2: MAP THE UNIT

In many ways, lesson study should be called unit study. Not only did we create a great lesson to use within a unit that needs help, but we also talked a lot about ways to improve the unit in the future. I don't feel that our lesson study group is done with our work on the light and sound unit . . . we are inspired to do more work on other areas of the unit.

~Jessica Unger, teacher

After the topic for the research lesson is identified, the lesson study team examines the unit in which the lesson will take place. "The word 'lesson' sometimes creates a misunderstanding of the lesson study process. Teachers do work to plan a research lesson, but it must be connected to other lessons in the unit in order to maximize the learning results" (Takahashi & Yoshida, 2004).

An understanding of the unit and how concepts develop within the unit inform the planning of the research lesson in several ways. Through the process of mapping or unit planning, the team gains a better understanding of how the research lesson fits with other lessons, and how skills and understanding of concepts are developed. It may be helpful to identify unit goals during this process—see Figure 4.7 for more details.

Depending on how broad the topic is, the team may begin with mapping out the unit to identify the research lesson. Looking at the sequence can help the teachers pinpoint the lesson that covers a key topic within the sequence. They may choose an introductory lesson or a lesson at the end of the unit that will bring all of the important concepts together.

For a narrower topic, the team may already have a specific lesson in mind. The process of mapping the unit will help them to situate the research lesson within the broader context. What will students learn in the activities leading up to the research lesson? Where will they be going next? The teachers may also want to broaden their scope and look at how the topic is addressed in other grade levels.

It may be helpful to look at how the unit is organized in several different sources and to draw on state and national standards as well. A unit outline in which the big ideas and activities are described for each lesson is another useful tool. If this type of document does not already exist, the teachers will need to create a brief outline. A sample unit map for a fourth-grade science research lesson on "Chemical Tests" is included in Figure 4.4.

STEP 3: IDENTIFY GOALS

The lesson study team uses goals to shape the details and design of the research lesson. Articulating these goals can be challenging for many groups and for schools new to the lesson study process. The team will consider unit goals—the overall goals for the unit within which the research lesson is located. The team will also create lesson goals that are the specific student learning outcomes.

Unit Goals

Unit goals are often broad and help connect the research theme with the goals for the research lesson. There are two different types of unit goals. A content goal identifies the specific concepts or understandings that students will develop. A process goal identifies the skills or habits of mind that students will develop. Identifying both content and process goals may not be appropriate for every lesson study cycle. For example, a content goal is required for most mathematics and science lessons, but it may not be essential for a language arts lesson.

The lesson study team may identify unit goals in the process of mapping the unit. The content goals may already be in place, based on the textbook or a

FROM THE FIELD

The lesson study team at Traverse City Area Schools in Traverse City, Michigan, developed a fourth-grade research lesson for a science unit on "Chemical Tests" (see Figure 4.4). To select a lesson, the teachers walked through the unit and began to focus on a group of lessons that were most problematic for students. These lessons required students to use their prior knowledge about testing and identifying solids to unravel the identity of a mixture using chemical indicators. The teachers discussed their previous experiences in teaching these lessons. One member of the team confessed, "As a first-year teacher, I skipped this lesson because I was afraid to teach it." A more experienced teacher said, "This is the lesson where kids use what they observe to identify chemicals. But students tend to ignore evidence in the form of nonreactions."

Why Lesson 14?

In many units there are lessons or a cluster of lessons that pose a greater challenge for teachers to teach, for students to learn, or both. The lesson study team, as they mapped the unit and discussed unit goals, began to hone in on Lesson 14 of this unit: Modeling for Student Observations and Deductive Thinking. This lesson got to the heart of the process that scientists use to eliminate choices: using deductive thinking. The teachers agreed that students have difficulty using evidence to make deductions.

This lesson was originally called "Testing Mixtures of Unknown Solids." In many ways it is a culminating lesson for all of the student work that came before. Students use data they have collected and knowledge about chemical test results to identify unknown solids. Experienced teachers on the cross-district team, as well as district assessments, indicated that students tend to focus on positive test results when trying to identify an unknown solid, rather than making deductions based on both positive and negative results. Students also tend to jump to conclusions about the identity of an unknown. These learning challenges become most pronounced in Lesson 14.

Figure 4.4   Sample Unit Map—Chemical Tests

Lesson 1: Thinking About Chemicals
This lesson serves as a pre-unit assessment of students' prior knowledge about chemicals.

Lesson 2: Investigating Unknown Solids—Getting Ready
Students observe and describe properties of classroom objects. Students also become familiar with the tools and the five unknown chemicals that they will be investigating.

Lesson 3: Exploring the Five Unknown Solids
Students begin observing the five unknowns using both their eyes and magnifying lenses. They begin recording and organizing their data: how it looks, feels, smells, and sounds.

Lessons 4 and 5: Testing Unknown Solids With Water
Students test their unknowns with water and record results. In Lesson 5, students observe both solutions and suspensions and filter water mixtures.

Lesson 6: Discovering Crystals
Students discover the effect of evaporation on the filtration dishes from Lesson 5. Students begin to understand that some solids are best separated from water by evaporation, some by filtration.

Lessons 7–9: Testing Unknown Solids With Vinegar, Iodine, and Red Cabbage Juice
Students predict and test their unknowns with vinegar, iodine, and red cabbage juice. Students record the chemical reactions that occur. Here students are introduced to the concept of a control.

Lesson 10: Testing Unknown Solids With Heat
Students use heat to test their unknown chemicals.

Lesson 11: Reviewing the Evidence
In this lesson, students review and analyze all of the data from the two physical tests (water) and four chemical tests (vinegar, iodine, red cabbage juice, and heat).

Lessons 12 and 13: Identifying the Unknown Solids
In this lesson, students identify each unknown, comparing their test data with known data from scientists. Students identify a mystery bag chemical.

Lessons 14a and 14b: Modeling for Student Observations and Deductive Thinking
These are the lesson study lessons.

Lesson 14c: Finishing Testing Mixtures of Two Unknown Solids

Lessons 15–16: Testing Household Liquids With Red Cabbage Juice

Lesson 16: Using the Known Solids to Identify Unknown Liquids

Figure 4.5   Step 2: Map the Unit

Guiding Questions	Description
• Which lesson will have the most impact on the unit? • Why focus on this particular lesson? • How does a focus on a single research lesson affect the other lessons in the unit? • What will students learn in the activities leading up to the research lesson? • Where will they be going next?	The lesson study team examines the unit for the topic they identified in Step 1. The teachers will select the research lesson and consider the connections with the other lessons in the unit.
Example	
Our team decided to develop a lesson related to the broad topic of reading comprehension. We wanted to focus on a lesson that would have an impact on other subject areas and help students improve their performance on state assessments. We decided to focus on reading and comprehending nonfiction text. The research lesson was part of a yearlong unit on reading comprehension strategies. We looked closely at the other lessons in the unit and identified some of the previous strategies that students would be learning prior to the research lesson. Because this was the first lesson in the unit that addressed nonfiction text, it was clear that one of the concepts we would need to address was the difference between narrative stories and nonfiction.	

curriculum guide. Figure 4.6 includes examples of both content and process goals from different subject areas.

Lesson Goals

From unit goals, it is easy to begin honing in on those that represent particular challenges for students to understand or do and often for the teacher to teach. The topic within a unit that is problematic for students—like understanding the interaction of light and our ability to see objects, or understanding how to derive an equation from a pattern—provides the focus for the research lesson.

The goals of the lesson should function not only as a beacon when teams lose their way in developing the lesson but also as touchstones for determining whether the lesson was effective. The goals will guide the observation and the debriefing of the research lesson. One way to think about the lesson is as a **research hypothesis** about how to achieve the specific student learning goals. Figure 4.7 includes examples of lesson goals from several different subject areas.

In *Understanding by Design* (1998), Grant Wiggins and Jay McTighe present a model for planning instruction that is based on the idea of backwards design. The process for planning a research lesson follows a similar sequence. Instead of starting with an activity or a text, the lesson study team begins with the end results and makes instructional decisions based on the goals of the lesson. *Understanding by Design* is a resource that can help lesson study teams to identify goals and to plan the research lesson.

When the goals for the lesson have been identified and articulated (see Figure 4.8), the team will revisit the research theme. The connection between the long-term goal and the lesson goals should be explicit. If the connection is not obvious, the goals should be revised.

Figure 4.6   Sample Lesson Goals

	Research Theme	Unit Goals		Lesson Goals
		Content Goals	Process Goals	
Science	Developing scientific habits of mind such as use of the senses, use of evidence to warrant assertions, and use of controlled investigations.	Classify common objects and substances according to observable attributes and properties.	Generate questions about the world based on observation.	Student will use deductive reasoning based on observable evidence to narrow choices. Students will make careful observations of both positive and negative results.
Language Arts	For students to value reading for a variety of purposes.	Identify and compare the text features of nonfiction and fiction genres.	Use appropriate strategies to support one another's learning through partner work.	Students will note nonfiction features that signal importance. Students will compare narrative and nonfiction text.
Mathematics	To foster students' problem-solving ability and responsibility for learning.	Understand area of plane figures by composing and decomposing them into familiar shapes.	Apply and adapt a variety of appropriate strategies to solve problems.	Students will recognize that the area of a triangle can be found by transforming the shape of a triangle into familiar shapes. Students who are struggling will find at least one way to transform the triangle and understand that two congruent triangles can be composed to form a parallelogram.

STEP 4: CREATE THE LESSON PLAN

The lesson study team works together to develop the plan for the research lesson. The plan represents their collective ideas and questions about teaching the topic. A sense of collective ownership is essential.

To preserve this sense of collective ownership, it is best to put off deciding who will teach the lesson until the plan is almost complete. If the teacher is identified too early in the planning process, the other members tend to become less invested in the research lesson or to defer all decisions to the person who will be teaching.

The lesson plan does not need to be created from scratch (Lewis, 2002b). In fact, it is more efficient to begin with an existing lesson. The team can use an activity from

Figure 4.7   Step 3: Identify Goals

Guiding Questions	Description
• What are the content and process goals for this unit? • What do the standards say about these goals? • What makes these goals worthwhile? • How can the research theme and unit goals be brought to life with the research lesson?	The lesson study team identifies the unit goals that apply to the research lesson. They use the research they conducted—including curricula, activities, and standards—to craft a goal or goals for the research lesson. The lesson goals are derived from the unit goals and the research theme.

Example

To develop the goals for our lesson, we applied our research theme:

- Develop in all students the ability to make, analyze, and evaluate conjectures, arguments, and generalizations.

To national standards and the unit goals:

- Students will explore the concept of volume and formulate strategies for finding the volume of small paper boxes and larger spaces such as their classroom.

We identified the following lesson goals:

- Develop, describe, and justify a strategy for determining the number of cubes that fit in a box.

Students will:

- Build and/or visualize a three-dimensional object from a two-dimensional representation.
- Describe a "package" as an arrangement of congruent layers; these layers are rectangular arrays of cubes.
- Explore the relationship between the number of cubes that will fit inside a rectangular box and the box's dimensions.

their curriculum or another source, adapting it to reflect their ideas and the needs of their students.

Components of a Research Lesson

There is no required lesson template used in lesson study, yet there are common elements that most research lessons will include. One of the differences that teams will note between familiar lesson plans and research lessons is the level of detail evident in the research lesson. Just as the teachers have carefully crafted the research theme and the goals, they will also take time to plan the instructional sequence, learning activities, key questions for students, and anticipated student responses.

Research lessons often include background information, such as the rationale for selecting the lesson. This is a means of documenting the thought and effort that go into developing a well-planned lesson. The background information is especially important when outside observers will be invited to participate in the observation and debriefing.

Form 4.2 is a **research lesson template**. It is intended to provide an overview of the common content and format for presenting lesson plans. In the following sections, the common elements are described in more detail and illustrated with examples from a fourth-grade science lesson. This research lesson is the plan that resulted from the unit map in Figure 4.4.

Opening Section

The opening section of the research lesson includes the following:

- Heading (subject area, grade level, etc.)
- Title of the lesson
- Goals (including the research theme)
- Standards addressed in the lesson
- Unit map

Some teams also include standards from other grade levels to provide context for the lesson. This helps to demonstrate that the lesson is appropriately challenging and addresses important content. The unit map enables outside observers and other readers to follow and understand the instructional sequence.

Many research lessons also include a "Background Information" section that describes the rationale for selecting the lesson and the instructional decisions made by the team. The teachers should include any information that they feel is relevant to understanding their research lesson. The team will draw on and summarize the research they conducted and their investigation of teaching materials. The teachers can also use this section to describe their students and their school. Consider these questions:

- Why did we choose this topic for lesson study?
- Why is it important to have this lesson at this particular time in students' learning?
- Why did we choose the main activities?
- What are the key instructional strategies that are needed for this lesson?

Figure 4.9 is an example of the opening section of a research lesson. (The unit map for this lesson was included in Figure 4.4.)

Lesson Process

The opening section is followed by the **Lesson Process** section, which describes the flow of the lesson in detail. Most research lessons are presented in a four-column format.

The first column outlines the **Learning Activities and Teacher Questions**—what students will be doing and how the teacher will set up and facilitate the tasks. Someone from outside the team should be able to envision what will be happening throughout the lesson.

It is often helpful to estimate how much time each phase of the lesson will take. The team uses this column to describe important points for the teacher to remember

Form 4.2   Research Lesson Template

[Grade Level] [Subject Area] Research Lesson

School:

Date:

Instructor:

Lesson Study Team:

Title:

Goals:

Standards Addressed in the Lesson:

Sequence of the Unit (Unit Map):

Background Information:

Why did we choose this topic for lesson study?

Why is it important to have this lesson at this particular time in students' learning?

Why did we choose the main activities?

What are the key instructional strategies that are needed for this lesson?

Lesson Process

Learning Activities and Teacher Questions	Expected Student Reactions	Teacher Support	Points of Evaluation

Evaluation:

SOURCE: Makoto Yoshida, Sonal Chokshi, & Clea Fernandez. © 2001, Lesson Study Research Group. www.tc.columbia.edu/lessonstudy/tools.html. Adapted from guidelines developed by Global Education Resources LLC, Paterson Public School 2 (Paterson, NJ), and Research for Better Schools.

Figure 4.8   Sample Opening Section

Science Research Lesson—Fourth Grade

School: Traverse City Area Elementary Schools (Bertha Voss, Cherry Knoll, Norris, Oak Park, and Westwood)

Date: November 16, 2004

Teacher:

Lesson Study Team:

1. **Title of the Lesson**: *Modeling for Student Observations and Deductive Thinking*

2. **Lesson Study Goals**

(See Figure 4.6)

3. **State Science Curriculum Framework**

   Constructing New Scientific Knowledge
   a. Generate questions about the world based on observation.
   b. Develop solutions to problems through reasoning, observation, and investigation.
   c. Construct charts and graphs and prepare summaries of observations.

   Reflecting on Scientific Knowledge
   a. Develop an awareness of the need for evidence in making decisions scientifically.

   Physical Science: Matter and Energy
   a. Classify common objects and substances according to observable attributes/properties.

   Physical Science: Changes in Matter
   a. Describe common physical changes in matter (i.e., dissolving).
   b. Prepare mixtures and separate them into their component parts.

4. **Unit Map**

(See Figure 4.4)

About This Lesson

Why did you choose the main activities?

We chose the main activities in the lesson because we wanted students to apply what they know about mixtures and about the tests they could perform to figure out the two chemicals. The lab sheet was designed to help students focus on both positive and negative results and to make deductions about what the solids could and could not be.

---

in setting up the learning activities, such as allowing time for student discussion. The team may describe how the teacher and students will use the blackboard or other visual aids in the lesson. The questions that the teacher will pose to students are also included in this section. The team works together to carefully craft the wording of the key questions. The questions are designed to help students work toward the goal of the lesson.

The second column describes **Expected Student Reactions** to the learning activities and teacher questions. Many teachers are not accustomed to considering how students will respond as a means of planning instruction. As a result, this aspect of lesson study often inspires a significant shift in the way teachers think about their work.

One strategy that many teams use to generate possible responses is to engage in the activities or problems of the research lesson as learners. The teachers may try out several different activities before they decide on the one they believe will be most effective. These strategies will help teams to identify potential difficulties that students may encounter with the content or learning activities.

The team will try to identify prior knowledge and potential misconceptions that the students will bring to the lesson. In doing so, it is helpful to draw on both research and past experience. Some teams choose to interview students or gather other data to gain a better understanding of students' struggles.

Figure 4.9 shows an example from the first two columns of the science research lesson.

Figure 4.9   Lesson Process—Part 1

Learning Activities and Teacher Questions	Expected Student Reactions
Launch (5–10 min.) I have two chemicals and they got mixed together. How can we figure out what's in there? I need your help.	Students may say: *We could do the heat test . . .* *Baking soda and vinegar.* *You're mixing two things.*
Talk in pairs. I will check in with you in a few minutes, and then we will share ideas in small groups.	
What tests could we perform to figure out these chemicals?	*We could look at our charts.* *We could see how it feels.* *They may suggest tests like vinegar, iodine, etc.*
Explore (25–50 min.) Teacher models heat test and models how to fill in the lab sheet. (5–10 min.)	
Why do you do the test and what evidence are you looking for?	*It's melting.* *It's boiling.* *It smells like it's burning.*

The third column—**Teacher Support**—describes how the teacher will respond to the anticipated reactions from students. The team provides questions that the teacher can pose to extend student thinking or to help students reevaluate their misconceptions. It can provide a contingency plan to enact if students are struggling.

The team also uses this section to provide questions that the teacher can pose to students as they are working. They might list things to look for to identify the strategies that students are using or the ideas they are discussing. This will help the teacher to facilitate the closing of the lesson by identifying the students to call on or by anticipating how to bring new ideas into the discussion.

Figure 4.10   Lesson Process—Part 2

Learning Activities and Teacher Questions	Expected Student Reactions	Teacher Support	Points of Evaluation
Launch (5–10 min.) I have two chemicals and they got mixed together. How can we figure out what's in there? I need your help.	Students may say: *We could do the heat test . . .* *Baking soda and vinegar.* *You're mixing two things.*	What am I doing? What are you thinking that makes you think I'm mixing? How do you know it's two?	Are there common responses to the question?
Talk in pairs. I will check in with you in a few minutes, and then we will share ideas in small groups.			Informal assessment of prior knowledge; gather evidence of student misconceptions
What tests could we perform to figure out these chemicals?	*We could look at our charts.* *We could see how it feels.* *They may suggest tests like vinegar, iodine, etc.*		
Explore (25–50 min.) Teacher models heat test and models how to fill in the lab sheet. (5–10 min.)		What evidence would the heat test give us to prove it's a chemical?	Do students bring up both physical and chemical tests?
Why do you do the test and what evidence are you looking for?	*It's melting.* *It's boiling.* *It smells like it's burning.*	What could we learn from the heat test? Because it didn't react, what does that tell us?	

The final column describes **Points of Evaluation**—questions to help assess student progress throughout the lesson. These are points that the teacher will use to guide instruction and that the observers will use to document student learning.

Figure 4.10 provides an excerpt from the science lesson that brings all four columns together.

Evaluation Section

The lesson process section is followed by **Evaluation**, the final section of the lesson plan. This part of the research lesson includes questions that the team will use to analyze its effectiveness and to address the team's questions about teaching and learning that have guided their research lesson.

This is a good opportunity for the teachers to revisit the research theme, unit goals, and lesson goals. In the process of planning the lesson, it is easy to leave the goals behind. Yet the learning activities, teacher questions, and all the details of

Figure 4.11   Evaluation

---

a. Do students attend to both positive and negative results as they make deductions and narrow their choices as to the chemicals in the mixture?

b. Do students work collaboratively to problem solve?

c. Do students use vocabulary and descriptive words appropriately and consistently?

d. Do students utilize previously learned knowledge and skills to identify unknown chemicals?

---

instruction should contribute, in some way, to helping students achieve the goals that guide the research lesson.

Figure 4.11 is the Evaluation section for the science research lesson.

Planning all of the details of instruction and organizing the research lesson is a challenging endeavor. Figure 4.12 provides a set of planning questions organized around the sections of the research lesson template. These questions may help teams in planning and recording their ideas. To assist teams with more specific challenges, there is a FAQ about planning the research lesson in Resource B. The questions addressed include the following:

- How do we know the right amount of time to spend on planning the lesson?
- Is it necessary to use the research lesson template?
- What if the whole unit needs work? Should we still spend time on one lesson?
- We are having trouble coming to consensus about some parts of the lesson. What should we do?
- What if the research lesson is not very challenging?
- Why is the research lesson so scripted?

Drafting the Lesson Plan

Sometimes a subset of team members will take responsibility for drafting the research lesson based on the team's discussions and decisions (see Figure 4.13). The writing team includes the people who have stepped forward to teach the lesson. For teams who are new to lesson study, it is more effective for the entire team to draft the lesson together. One person may be in charge of taking notes or typing up the plan, but the teachers will make the underlying decision together. This will reinforce the teachers' collective ownership of the plan, and it will help them to think differently about lessons and how they are developed.

If the lesson study team is using an existing lesson, they will adapt it to the research lesson format and add the additional information. For the process of creating the lesson plan, it is helpful to have an LCD projector and laptop to project an image of the template as the team is working on the lesson. When these tools are not available, chart paper and markers will suffice.

Sample research lessons can be found in the Resources section at the end of the book. Sample Lesson 1 is included in Resource A. It is the plan for the fourth-grade science lesson that resulted from the unit map in Figure 4.4 and that is featured in the previous examples of the sections of a research lesson. This lesson also is featured in Chapter 6: Revising and Reteaching the Lesson. Sample Lesson 2 is a third-grade language arts lesson that is also included in Resource A.

Figure 4.12 Guiding Questions—Lesson Process Section

Learning Activities and Teacher Questions	How do lessons in various textbooks address the selected content and process goals?
	Are these lessons deficient in any way? If yes, in what way?
	Discuss possible instructional activities that will support students in reaching the content and process goals.
	What key question(s) will students explore?
	How will the activities need to be adapted?
	How can we promote productive discussions among students?
	What scaffolding can we provide to meet the needs of all learners?
Expected Student Reactions	What prior knowledge do students have of the content goal?
	What is confusing for students about these concepts? What is at the root of this confusion?
	What prior experiences do students have of the process goal?
	What difficulties do students have with these process goals? Why do they have these difficulties?
	How can we build on students' prior knowledge and experiences?
	What will students think and do in response to the instructional activities?
	How might students respond to the questions? What strategies might students use? What answers might they give?
	When is it okay—or even desirable—for students to be confused?
Teacher Support	How can student misconceptions and confusion be addressed?
	What questions will further student understanding?
	What supports are necessary to provide access for all learners?
	How will the teacher help students who are struggling or frustrated?
	How can we rephrase the questions if students do not respond?
	How can we make the task more or less complex without undermining the goal?
Points of Evaluation	What kinds of data will help us assess students' progress toward the goals?
	What work will students produce? What will this work tell us about student thinking?
	How will we check for understanding?

REFLECTING AND ASSESSING PROGRESS

It is possible for teachers to move through the mechanics of planning a research lesson and yet gain little new knowledge. It takes time to learn how to do lesson study well. For this reason, it is important for teams to reflect on the planning process. Team members should think about and discuss not only what they learned about students, content, and instruction of the specific research lesson but also what is transferable to other lessons.

Figure 4.13   Step 4: Create the Lesson Plan

Guiding Questions	Description
• What is our research question or hypothesis? • How does our lesson design support the goals of the research lesson? • Have we anticipated student responses based on our experience and the research? • What kinds of prior knowledge of the topic should students have? • How will the teacher respond to student reactions and misconceptions? • What kinds of evidence would be sufficient for demonstrating student understanding? • Do we have a plan for evaluating the lesson?	Using the template, the team collaborates on developing a lesson that will result in students meeting the goals and in teachers gaining knowledge about the research theme. The lesson plan is extremely detailed and represents the team's research and their collective questions and ideas about how best to foster student learning.

Example
We started planning the lesson by looking closely at the textbook, trying out several different activities, and drawing on the research we did on the topic of the lesson. We decided to use the lesson from the textbook, changing the order of the tasks and adding a context for the key question that we think will draw on students' interests. We planned out what the teacher will say and tried to think about different ways that students may respond. We identified some potential difficulties that students may have and decided how to address them. We also identified some places in the lesson that will help us determine if students are understanding the concept and making progress toward the goals of the lesson.

The following questions may be helpful in guiding the team's reflections. The questions are organized around the core elements of lesson study (see Figure 4.14). The team members may want to devote time during a planning meeting to share their responses. If time together is hard to come by, it may be more efficient to reflect independently and conduct the discussion via e-mail.

Lesson Study Process

- Was the planning process effective?
- What would you do differently next time and why?
- Did the long-term goals and lesson study goals help focus your learning?
- Were we able to generate anticipated student responses?

Big Ideas

- Summarize your learning in each of the following areas:
  - ○ Goals
  - ○ Content
  - ○ Student learning
  - ○ Instruction
- Beyond the research lesson, what are the implications of what we have learned?

Figure 4.14 Core Elements of Lesson Study

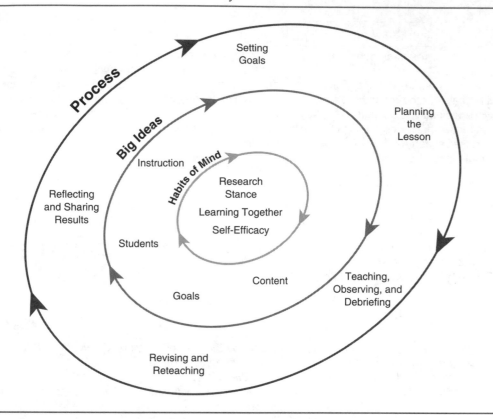

Habits of Mind

- Were we open to new ideas and to challenges that stretched our thinking?
- Did we actively seek out research on content-specific student learning?
- Were we able to move beyond the familiar curricula and lessons to bring in fresh ideas?
- Are there any areas for improvement in our group norms? How can we address them?
- What were my contributions to the planning process?

Two tools are included to help the team capture and reflect on their learning so far. The logs for team members and facilitators are designed to be completed at the end of each planning meeting (see Forms 4.3 and 4.4). When there are gaps between planning meetings, the logs can be especially helpful for teams to keep track of their work. The logs will also help the team to document the planning process for the lesson study report.

MOVING ON TO THE NEXT PHASE

The lesson study team is likely to create several drafts of the research lesson before they feel prepared for the observation and debriefing. It is important to take the time necessary to develop a well-planned research lesson, but it is also helpful to remember that the goal is not to develop the perfect lesson. Teachers should strive to develop a

Form 4.3   Team Member Log—Planning Meeting

School/Team _____	Date _____
Recorder _____	

What were the objectives of the meeting?

Briefly describe what happened during the meeting.

Describe any discussions around the following topics:

Content
Instruction
Student Learning
Goals (short- and long-term)

What are my/our next steps?

What will be on the agenda for our next meeting?

Other notes:

Form 4.4   Facilitator Log—Planning Meeting

School/Team _____   Date _____
Facilitator _____

What were the objectives of the meeting?

Briefly describe what happened during the meeting.

What actions did you take to guide the teachers toward effective lesson study practice?

Were there any problems during the meeting? If so, how did you deal with them?

How did all of the team members participate?

Have you noticed evidence of an increase in teacher collaboration or change in the ways that the teachers work together? Please describe.

Things to keep in mind for next time:

Other notes:

lesson that reflects their knowledge, research, and best thinking. When the lesson is presented to students, the team will collect data about the effectiveness of the lesson.

When the research lesson is finalized, the preparations for the teaching and debriefing can begin. Chapter 5 provides suggestions for getting ready and planning for the observation and debriefing.

Before moving on, the team should make sure that they have gathered and saved the documents that will inform the lesson study report. Artifacts from the planning phase might include the following items:

- Agendas, notes, and minutes from the planning meetings
- Teacher and facilitator logs
- Records of the background research that the team conducted
- Documents related to the process of mapping the unit and developing the goals
- Drafts of the research lesson
- The final version of the research lesson

KEY IDEAS

- Research lessons should focus on significant content that is challenging to teach and challenging for students to learn.
- Teachers' research into pedagogy and student learning influences the design and content of the research lesson.
- The lesson study team will map the unit before they begin planning the lesson to get a broader perspective on its context.
- The research lesson is focused on student learning goals that are connected to the research theme.
- The team will develop a detailed plan that includes the instructional sequence, learning activities, key questions for students, and anticipated student responses.

From Our Team to Yours

It's *Our* Lesson

During the Detroit Lesson Study Group's initial lesson study cycle, Brandon was the first person to teach a research lesson. The other team members say that his approach helped them to get a better understanding of the lesson study process: He emphasized their collective ownership of the lesson.

Jason: "Brandon did something repeatedly that helped us a lot: He kept using the word 'our.' '*Our* lesson. . . . ' When one of us would ask him, 'Are you ready for it?' he would say, 'Yeah, *we're* ready for it.' It was never 'I.' After it was over, I'm sure he could hold his shoulders back and head up high with confidence, but he never said, 'I did it!' We were almost like a sports team—even the people sitting on the bench can say, 'We won the championship.' We celebrate together in the good times and we share the bad times too."

Brandon: "I was really trying to understand the process. I went back to the idea that it was a lesson developed by the group and it was the job of the person who teaches it to convey the group's message to the students."

Byron: "When he stopped and said, 'No, **our** lesson,' it helped bring all of us back to the fact that *we* planned the lesson. It brought me back to the point: 'Yeah, I had a hand in it. We all contributed to it.' And we all had that mind-set after that. It almost became our mantra."

5

Teaching, Observing, and Debriefing

N ow that the hard work of goal setting and collectively drafting a research lesson is complete, it's time to test the team's ideas and understandings with students. The teaching, observing, and debriefing phase of the lesson study cycle creates the occasion for teachers to bring their learning together and to see how

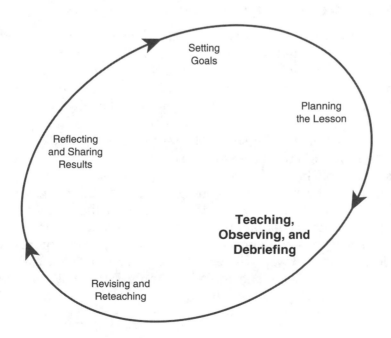

their ideas play out with students in the classroom. Remember, the research lesson is a draft—really a work in progress.

After the lesson is taught, the team and invited observers meet to debrief and share ideas based on their observations. The debriefing is a structured discussion that provides the chance to make sense of data collected about student learning and to prepare for revising and improving the lesson.

The observation was really eye-opening. The first thing I noticed was how difficult it was for me to focus on the students and not on the teacher. That really says a lot about our culture as teachers and our focus on the teacher being at the center. That was powerful, but when I really started focusing on the students, really watching them and their interactions, I realized so clearly how much we are unaware of what's happening with the students when we are teaching.

~Kristy Krahl, elementary coordinator

ROLES AND RESPONSIBILITIES

Lesson study requires a variety of players who serve different functions. From the teacher to the **moderator** to the invited guests, the observation and debriefing usually involve people from outside the team. In addition to the team member who teaches the lesson, players include a variety of people who serve as observers:

- Members of the lesson study team
- Invited guests
- Knowledgeable others
- A moderator for the debriefing (a member of the team or someone who facilitated the team's earlier work)
- The **final commentator** (a knowledgeable other who will wrap up the debriefing)

Teaching the Research Lesson

Because many teachers have not observed or been observed by other teachers since their student teaching days, the idea of stepping up and teaching the lesson in front of colleagues and guests can be intimidating. For novice teams, determining who will teach the team's lesson is best done late in the process of planning the lesson. Prematurely choosing the teacher who will be observed can undermine team members' investment. It becomes all too easy for the team to relinquish shared ownership and to perceive the lesson as the teacher's lesson. Building collaborative ownership of the process and the lesson is essential to the success of the team.

In Spokane Public Schools in Washington State, some of the district's lesson study teams drew straws at the end of the planning process to determine who would teach the research lesson. Keep in mind that the selection of the teacher should happen enough in advance of the observation to allow the lesson design to reflect the particular needs of the teacher's students. As team members become more accustomed to the process, decisions about who will teach the lesson can be made earlier in the cycle.

Often a volunteer will emerge quite naturally. Maybe it's a teacher who is taking some leadership responsibility on the team or acting as the team's facilitator.

Sometimes the reluctance is strong and additional encouragement is needed. Highlighting the focus of lesson study on the lesson and not the teacher and reinforcing that notion at every phase of the cycle can be helpful. Some teachers may be more willing to volunteer in pairs and team-teach the lesson.

Another approach that may help to make teachers more comfortable is to forego any invited guests and limit the observation to team members. Although this may reduce the diversity and depth of the debriefing, it can diminish the teacher's anxiety and allow the team to become comfortable with the process. An alternative is a guest teacher. It is most powerful to have a team member teach the lesson to the students, but in the absence of a volunteer, it is acceptable for a guest teacher to convey the lesson to a team member's students or to his or her own students. If the team has an outside facilitator, the group may ask the facilitator to teach the lesson. These options, though not ideal, can be viewed as a transition step for the most hesitant teams.

Observing the Research Lesson

Why have observers in the classroom? Observers can offer new and multiple sets of eyes that can capture evidence of student thinking and understanding. Except for the teacher who is presenting the lesson, all the adults in the classroom serve as observers. They take detailed notes and gather evidence to share at the debriefing. They use the lesson plan as a guide, paying close attention to the points of evaluation. Observers do *not* evaluate the teacher, act as trainers or professional developers, or serve as additional teachers in the classroom.

> ### FROM THE FIELD
>
> *When I first heard about lesson study and thought about being observed, my initial reaction was that I just didn't want to do it. I was really nervous about being observed. Once I understood it was not about fixing "Vicki," that it was about the learning that was taking place and about student thinking, I was more open to the idea. I saw the value of having more pairs of eyes in my classroom.*
>
> *My eighth-grade students were really excited. I had explained the reason for the observers coming into the room and they had a sense of pride about people wanting to see what they were learning. Once I started teaching, I really forgot that all those people were in the room. I was so pleased the children responded in their normal way—they stayed focused on the content and the task in spite of having so many observers moving around the classroom.*
>
> *Even though I felt relieved when the observation was over, I still had my guard up when the debriefing started—what were they going to say about me? The moderator did a good job of keeping everyone focused on the lesson—it was all about what the students were learning: Were the objectives of the lesson met? Was it the best possible way to present that lesson? How could it be tweaked to provide the most effective introduction to exponential growth?*
>
> *When I first heard about lesson study, the theory and how it worked, it sounded ideal but I wondered if it was just another great idea that wouldn't translate into my world in Detroit Public Schools. But it did. We had to think and learn differently about planning lessons. The lesson represented the team's collective work. The team's voice became the lesson and the lesson became the team's voice.*
>
> ~Vicki Vorus, teacher

People who engage in lesson study are willing to take a risk. Whether you are part of the team that writes the lesson or one of the observers or the person being observed, you put yourself and your ideas under scrutiny.

~Colleen Longville, principal
(former teacher and lesson study team member)

Initially, it may not be feasible to have outside observers in the classroom. It is quite natural for the team to be hesitant about inviting other people. After the team gains experience, striving to expand the pool of observers beyond the lesson study team members is critical and helps stretch the team's thinking.

The team needs to allow time to orient the outside observers and help them understand how lesson study focuses on understanding students' thinking rather than critiquing or evaluating the teacher. Building trust among lesson study team members is fundamental to the success of a group. Helping everyone to approach lesson study with a spirit of respect and gentle inquiry will support the trust-building process and enhance the team's work.

Invited Guests

Principals, district office staff, other teachers, and even parents can be invited guests. In addition to valuable contributions to the team's learning, opening the teaching of the research lesson to others can provide many benefits. The observation can foster schoolwide learning, building knowledge around the research questions and establishing better cross-grade articulation.

The team may also strategically select invited guests to build support for their efforts. The principal or district administrators may be invited to help garner resources for lesson study. Colleagues who are interested in learning more about lesson study can be welcomed. A parent serving on a school improvement committee or district curriculum task force may gain insight into new strategies for professional development.

Ensuring that the principal will not evaluate the teacher is essential. Building the principal's understanding of lesson study is also important. Understanding the process helps the principal to demonstrate support for the team and the teacher who decides to teach the lesson. The greater the value the principal places on lesson study, the easier it is for a team member to take a risk and volunteer.

Knowledgeable Others

Knowledgeable others sometimes work with the team throughout the lesson study cycle, but it is common for them to be present only during the observation and debriefing. Knowledgeable others can be district specialists with content expertise, professors from local colleges and universities, subject area consultants from the local intermediate agency, or teacher leaders from nearby schools or districts. To create a trusting relationship in a very short period of time, knowledgeable others

---

FROM THE FIELD

As a knowledgeable other with expertise in physics, I was able to use my knowledge to contribute to the lesson study team in several ways. In the observation, my broader and deeper knowledge of the subject allowed me to quickly assess what the students were learning or not learning. Maybe more important, I observed when the students were developing misconceptions. In my science experience, misconceptions often occurred in experiments where procedures or equipment introduced errors that masked or altered the physical phenomenon being studied. In the debriefing, I shared observations based on my knowledge and background. This helped the team in revising the lesson, as they worked to prioritize the learning goals, refine the activities to meet those goals, and to bring in real-world examples that could be used to help make meaningful connections for the students.

The challenge for a knowledgeable other is this: You need to be grounded in the lesson study process, the level of the students, and the curriculum. I had some background on the students and the district's curriculum, but found I was more effective in my second lesson study observation and debriefing as I came to better understand the lesson study process.

~Matt Cauchy, engineer (and former Teach for America teacher)

need to consider how they use their actions and their words to demonstrate respect and appreciation for the teacher. Careful attention to mutual trust is the key to supporting teachers as they open up their classrooms, often for the first time.

In addition to sharing their own observations, knowledgeable others contemplate how they can inspire teachers to reflect on and learn from their observations. For example, it may be helpful to identify ways to phrase guiding questions or how to express suggestions as a range of possibilities using sentence stems such as "I wonder . . ." or "In what ways could the team . . ." or "How might. . . ."

Seasoned knowledgeable others approach each lesson as a learning opportunity. The observations and conversations can provide new insight into teaching strategies, how students learn specific content, and the lesson study process itself—to name just a few possibilities. Knowledgeable others who can take on the learner role and articulate what they hope to get out of their experiences are more likely to establish rapport and trust with lesson study teams.

The most effective knowledgeable others model how to observe carefully and record detailed notes about student interactions and student work. In the debriefing, they push the team's thinking with thoughtful questions and observations.

Form 5.1 is a tool that lesson study teams can use to help knowledgeable others understand their responsibilities. It is an excerpt from the previous section.

Choosing a Final Commentator

Another important role for the team to designate is that of the final commentator. Most often the final commentator is selected from the pool of knowledgeable others. In the absence of knowledgeable others, a team member or the moderator can fill this role. Choosing a thoughtful and articulate final commentator can set the tone for the team's work moving forward from the debriefing.

The final commentator is responsible for the following:

- Contributing any new insights or questions not previously shared in the debriefing
- Summarizing the key ideas and questions that emerged from the debriefing
- Highlighting the areas and issues the team might want to pay attention to as they revise the lesson
- Expressing appreciation to the teacher for opening his or her classroom to the group
- Extending thanks to the team for all of their work

PREPARING FOR THE OBSERVATION AND DEBRIEFING

Before the observation can take place, there are a number of tasks the team will need to attend to in preparation. First is getting the students and the classroom ready for the observation. The team will also need to plan the agenda for the observation and debriefing and arrange for meeting space. If guests have been invited, the teachers will need to plan the pre-observation meeting.

Form 5.1   Your Role as a Knowledgeable Other

Knowledgeable others play a crucial and delicate part in the lesson study process. Lesson study focuses on understanding students' thinking rather than critiquing or evaluating the teacher. Building trust among lesson study team members is fundamental to the success of a group. Knowledgeable others will approach lesson study with a spirit of respect and gentle inquiry that supports the trust-building process and enhances the team's work.

To create a trusting relationship in a very short period of time, knowledgeable others need to consider how they use their actions and their words to demonstrate respect and appreciation for the teacher. Careful attention to mutual trust is the key to supporting teachers as they open up their classrooms, often for the first time.

To avoid falling into the role of instructor, knowledgeable others contemplate how they can inspire teachers to reflect on and learn from their observations. For example, it may be helpful to identify ways to phrase guiding questions or how to express suggestions as a range of possibilities using sentence stems such as "I wonder . . ." or "In what ways could the team . . ." or "How might. . . ."

Seasoned knowledgeable others approach each lesson as a learning opportunity. The observations and conversations can provide new insight into teaching strategies, how students learn specific content, and the lesson study process itself—to name just a few possibilities. Knowledgeable others who can take on the learner role and articulate what they hope to get out of their experiences are more likely to establish rapport and trust with lesson study teams.

The most effective knowledgeable others model how to observe carefully and record detailed notes about student interactions and student work. In the debriefing, they push the team's thinking with thoughtful questions and observations.

As a knowledgeable other with expertise in physics, I was able to use my knowledge to contribute to the lesson study team in several ways. In the observation, my broader and deeper knowledge of the subject allowed me to quickly assess what the students were learning or not learning. Maybe more important, I observed when the students were developing misconceptions. In my science experience, misconceptions often occurred in experiments where procedures or equipment introduced errors that masked or altered the physical phenomenon being studied. In the debriefing, I shared observations based on my knowledge and background. This helped inform the team's thinking as they worked to prioritize the learning goals, refine the activities to meet those goals, and to bring in real-world examples that could be used to help make meaningful connections for the students.

The challenge for a knowledgeable other is this: It's helpful to be grounded in the lesson study process, the level of the students, and the curriculum. I had some background on the students and the district's curriculum, but found I was more effective in my second lesson study observation and debriefing as I came to better understand the process.

~Matt Cauchy, engineer
(and former Teach for America teacher)

Preparing Students

Because of the distraction of observers in the classroom, teachers are often concerned about the ability of students to focus on the lesson. Teachers worry about their students acting out, but that very seldom happens. In fact, the opposite is often true. Preparing students and the classroom for the observation in advance is enormously productive. Explaining the purpose of lesson study in general terms, including what will happen in the debriefing following the observation, helps put the observation in context for students. One teacher explained to her students, "All these people who will be in the room observing are helping all of us become better teachers." Lesson study can help students see teachers as learners, modeling an inquiry approach to their work. Thinking of teachers as learners, Regie Routman (1996) writes, "If we want our students to be thinkers, researchers, collaborators, readers, writers, and evaluators, then they need to see us thinking, researching, collaborating, reading, writing, and evaluating. We need, literally, to live the life we're asking them to lead" (p. 166).

> *It's wonderful for students to see the people they respect—their teachers and their administrators—so willing to learn. The message we're sending with lesson study is this: We're learners, too, and we're going to work hard to study and improve what we do. We're modeling for our students that learning is truly a lifelong process.*
>
> ~Colleen Longville, principal
> (former teacher and lesson study team member)

Preparing the Classroom

To facilitate data collection by the observers, prepare a seating chart of the class and provide name tags and name tents for the students. If space allows, add chairs to the perimeter of the classroom for observers to use while the teacher or students are addressing the whole class.

Reducing Interruptions

Many U.S. schools experience constant classroom interruptions with people coming in and out and intercom announcements punctuating instruction time. For the teaching of the lesson, it is imperative that interruptions be kept to a minimum. Alert the office that intercom announcements and people coming into the classroom during the lesson will reduce the value of the observation. Enlist the principal and the staff to help protect the continuity of the lesson. Post a sign on the door that reads, "Lesson Study in Progress: Please do not enter unless an emergency." Although it is often challenging to accomplish, it is useful to work toward policies and practices that reduce the number of classroom interruptions on a daily basis to protect the integrity of instructional time.

FROM THE FIELD

An eighth-grade lesson study observation was in process in a large district with numerous observers, some who had traveled from a university almost an hour away. The lesson was also being professionally filmed. In the middle of the lesson, the school secretary came over the intercom demanding the class attendance list from the young teacher. While the cameras were running, the teacher explained what was going on in his classroom and pleaded for a short reprieve so he could finish the lesson. He was refused and had to stop the lesson to complete the attendance list. One of the observers, a district math specialist, carried it to the office.

Developing a Schedule

The day set aside for teaching, observing, and reflecting on the team's lesson requires considerable organization in advance. The most successful lesson study teams provide a strong structure for the designated day to guarantee the richest possible experience that will take advantage of their investment of time and energy.

Although it is not always possible to arrange, it is often best to release all team members from their classrooms for the entire day. The observation and debriefing will require demanding and intense work from everyone involved. A full-day release also enables the team to begin revising the research lesson right away. Figure 5.1 is a sample schedule for a full-day event.

Figure 5.1 Sample Schedule—Full Day

8:00–9:00	Gathering and pre-observation meeting
9:00–10:00	Teaching and observing
10:00–10:15	Individual reflections
10:15–10:30	Break
10:30–11:30	Debriefing
11:30–12:30	Celebration and lunch with team and invited guests
12:30–3:00	Team revises lesson plan

If a full-day release cannot be arranged, an alternative schedule beginning two hours prior to the end of the teaching day is effective. The pre-observation meeting and the teaching and observation take place prior to the dismissal of students. Time for individual reflection and the debriefing are held after the students leave school. The team's lesson revision is scheduled for subsequent meetings. Figure 5.2 is a sample schedule for an observation and debriefing held at the end of the day.

Figure 5.2 Sample Schedule—Half Day

1:00–2:00	Pre-observation meeting
2:00–3:00	Teaching and observing
3:00–3:15	Individual observer reflective writing
3:15–3:30	Break
3:30–4:30	Debriefing
4:30	Celebration

Sometimes, especially at the secondary level, it is not possible to conduct the teaching and observation at the very end of the school day. Ultimately, teams will adapt their schedules to the time and resource constraints they face. At the same time, the team can work with school and district leaders to create allies, structures, and policies that are more supportive of lesson study. No matter what the schedule, don't forget to celebrate the team's hard work either over lunch or at the end of the day.

THE PRE-OBSERVATION MEETING

A pre-observation meeting should be held any time guests or knowledgeable others are invited to the teaching of the lesson. It is not necessary to conduct a formal pre-observation meeting if the observation is limited to the lesson study team's members. The meeting is designed to build common understanding of the team's goals and to introduce the lesson plan to the invited guests and knowledgeable others. It is also a time to clarify roles and responsibilities and orient all observers to the **observation guidelines**. The meeting will occur immediately prior to the observation. Ensure that an adequate block of time—usually 45 to 60 minutes—prior to the teaching is protected and a quiet space is reserved.

The members of the team who will not be teaching the lesson take primary responsibility for conducting the pre-observation meeting. It is helpful to plan the presentation and to decide in advance who will be speaking about each of the topics. Other preparation tasks include making copies of handouts, creating any necessary visuals, gathering supplies, and posting the team's meeting norms in a visible place in the room.

Typically, the meeting begins with introductions and a review of the day's schedule. The agenda of the pre-observation meeting includes the following items:

- Understanding the content addressed in the lesson
- Sharing the team's goals
- Introducing the lesson plan
- Providing observation guidelines
- Framing the observation

Understanding the content addressed in the lesson (optional). The team engages the observers (either individually or in groups) in a task from the lesson that will help them understand the concepts. As a whole group, they discuss the key content in the lesson and identify the important ideas in the task. The team also discusses how students develop an understanding of the concepts in the lesson, how they might respond to the task, and what misconceptions they might have around the concepts. What guests learn from this process might help in their observations of students as they build understanding of the concepts during the lesson.

Sharing the team's goals. The team provides background on the research theme, the goals of the lesson, and how they relate to student learning. They discuss their research questions and how they arrived at the questions, and they share evidence or data that helped inform their choice of goals and share why they believe the goals are important to the content area.

Introducing the lesson. After establishing the larger picture, the team distributes the lesson plan and student handouts and explains the planning they went through in developing the lesson, including some of the key instructional decisions they made. The team provides an overview of the research lesson and its context within a larger unit of study. Anticipated student responses are shared by the team, and points of evaluation are highlighted. Time is allowed for observers to review the plan and ask clarifying questions. The teacher will also share background about the students, as well as any relevant information on class dynamics and culture.

Providing observation guidelines. Providing a structure for the observers supports the collection of richer data that will feed an evidence-based debriefing. A member of the team shares the observation guidelines, such as the sample guidelines in Form 5.2. The guidelines are adapted from those developed by Global Education Resources LLC, Paterson School No. 2 (Paterson, NJ), and Research for Better Schools.

A fruitful debriefing is the result of in-depth observations of the lesson and student thinking. The guests need to have an understanding of the expectations for their role in the lesson study process. It is essential that observers take detailed notes to record the flow of the lesson and the actions and conversations of the teacher and students. They can use the lesson plan and the seating chart to record their observations, or they can take notes on additional sheets of paper.

Essentially, the observers will be functioning as researchers, examining the effectiveness of the team's lesson. Though the inclination to teach or assist the students is common and often strong, it distorts the research stance, dilutes the value of the observation, and is best resisted. Instead of helping students, observers need to actively pay attention to the many details and nuances of the lesson, the students, and their work. In the long term, this will generate more meaningful evidence to help improve instruction in a more powerful way.

Framing the observation. There are many considerations in determining observer focus. The team should agree in advance what data they would like collected. Defining this well is likely to increase the usefulness of the evidence. Assigning specific tasks to the observers can enhance the value of the debriefing. Most teams find it useful to assign observers to remain with small groups of students to follow their thinking throughout the lesson. Some allow observers to roam at their discretion. It also can be useful to have some observers follow individual students.

The team might also assign observers to collect specific types of data. For example, one observer might record all questions asked by different students during whole-class discussions and another observer might use a class checklist to record how frequently students respond to teacher questions and prompts. When observers are given assignments, their focus should be tied to a lesson goal. In the checklist example, the purpose for the data might be to address a goal related to increasing student participation in class discussions.

The team may want to encourage observers to develop a specific question around which they want to collect evidence. For example, it might be a specific point in the lesson that stands out and arouses curiosity: How will the students react to a question posed by the teacher? Having a good question will help focus the observers and keep them engaged in the lesson.

Form 5.2   Guidelines for Observing Research Lessons

Procedural Guidelines

- Do not engage in side conversations during the lesson.

- Circulate freely when students are working individually or in groups, but move to the side or back of the room during whole-class discussion.

- Make sure you are not blocking students' view.

- Refrain from interacting, teaching, or assisting the students in any way. Very occasional interaction is permissible if done discreetly and with the purpose of understanding student thinking.

- Take notes throughout the whole lesson.

Collecting Data

- Take on a researcher role.

- Use the goals of the lesson and the points of evaluation to guide data collection.

- Take notes on individual student responses, using the students' names.

- Record how students begin their work and approach the tasks.

- Record interactions between students and between students and the teacher.

- Document common misunderstandings the students had and how and when their understanding changed.

- Indicate how individual students constructed their understanding through activities and discussions.

- Document the variety of solutions that individual students use to solve problems, including errors.

SOURCE: Adapted from guidelines developed by Global Resources LLC, Paterson Public Schools and Research for Better Schools.

Transitioning From the Pre-observation Meeting to the Classroom

Before the observers enter, the teacher should return to the classroom, excuse the substitute, and remind the students about the purpose of the observation. When the teacher is comfortable that the students are ready and any needed materials are prepared, the observers can be welcomed into the classroom and briefly introduced to the students.

TEACHING AND OBSERVING THE LESSON

A great deal of work has been invested in planning the team's lesson. It represents the teachers' ideas and questions about teaching and learning. The team has shared their thinking. The guests have been oriented. Observer focus has been determined and observation guidelines shared. Data to be collected have been specified. The final commentator has been designated. The students are prepared. Everything is in place.

The teaching provides the opportunity to test the team's ideas and hypotheses and to bring the plan to life in the classroom. How will it play out with their students? With great attention to detail, observers record what they see and hear with an eye toward understanding and uncovering student thinking. The primary focus is on the students—not the teacher—and on what the team wants students to learn.

Altering the Lesson Plan

Because the lesson plan reflects the collective wisdom of the team and the teacher is representing the team's collaborative work, generally the lesson plan should be followed. If the team has carefully anticipated students' possible reactions to the lesson and identified teacher responses, changing the lesson during the teaching is usually not appropriate. Teachers should not deviate from the plan too easily. However, Dylan Wiliam (2006) points out that "sometimes student learning difficulties will be unpredictable, and an important skill that teachers need to develop is being able to distinguish between situations that can be retrieved within the existing plan and situations that mean the existing plan must be abandoned."

Think of lesson study as a form of job-embedded research to study the effectiveness of the team's design in the real world of the classroom. Occasionally, circumstances warrant a mid-course correction during the teaching of the lesson. For example, if student responses tell the teacher that teaching the lesson as written will generate strong misconceptions that will be difficult to address at a later time, the teacher should make adjustments.

Although it is sometimes necessary, altering the lesson plan during the teaching makes it difficult for the team and knowledgeable others to evaluate the effectiveness of the lesson plan and the team's ideas. If the lesson is changed, Makoto Yoshida (2006) recommends discussing the following during the debriefing:

1. What was different from the original lesson plan?

2. Why did the teacher make the decision?

3. Did the changes that were made help students learn or not?

Keep in mind that lessons should be treated as dynamic and flexible within the framework established by the team. Akihiko Takahashi (2006) writes, "Planning a lesson for lesson study is not drawing a single path to the goal. It is more like drawing a map around the topic that we teach."

Addressing Inappropriate Behavior

Team members should be ready to gently guide observers who may be acting inappropriately—chatting with other observers, assisting students, blocking the students' view of the board—back to the observation guidelines. The most common disturbance is observers talking to one another, often commenting on something interesting or notable taking place. Teachers often find this very distracting and sometimes assume that the observers are evaluating their teaching. It also takes away from the task at hand—observing students.

Interviewing Students (Optional)

Bringing in the student perspective following the teaching of the lesson can add an interesting, useful, and sometimes surprising dimension to the debriefing. Taking a few minutes to ask students the following questions, developmentally adjusted, usually generates rich responses.

> **FROM THE FIELD**
>
> *During the student interviews, the students in my second-grade class surprised the observers with their ideas about running the human tic-tac-toe geography game. This activity concluded the lesson on grid and coordinate systems meant to lead students into an understanding of how maps and globes are designed and read. The students were especially concerned with the equity of participation and how the first student for each tic-tac-toe round was selected. They commented favorably on the use of the map to trace the route they might take to fly home during their periodic visits to their native countries. They asked for more "real" map activities and confirmed the observers' comments about strengthening the lesson by adding additional activities designed to engage students in making connections to their everyday lives and the world around them. We don't often ask students for feedback on this level, and it turned out to be a very interesting addition to the debriefing.*
>
> ~Janie Hubbard, teacher

1. What was the point of this lesson? What did you learn?

2. What worked in this lesson? What did you like about the lesson?

3. What didn't work in this lesson? What didn't you like about the lesson?

4. Your teacher might teach this lesson next year. How could she (or he) make it better?

Students can be interviewed in small groups, or a small sample of students can be selected for the observers to interview.

CONDUCTING THE DEBRIEFING

> *The key to our success has been the supportive and nonjudgmental reflections during the debriefing period after the lesson. The extra adult eyes and ears picked up a lot more information about how students responded to the lesson. The other members of the team would watch a particular group from the start of a task to the end. This provided valuable feedback on how best to modify the lesson.*
>
> ~Kaye Gilbert, Julie Gulden, Owen Peterson,
> Sam Steverson, and Colleen Unger, teachers

If possible, conduct the debriefing in the same classroom where the observation was held. This enables everyone to see the board and any teaching tools used. Before beginning, ensure that a team member is prepared to record debriefing comments and another is acting as timekeeper. If the debriefing is held in another room, the teacher will bring any tools or artifacts from the lesson—such as posters—to the debriefing room.

Individual Reflection

During an observation, much is experienced and enormous quantities of data are usually collected. Immediately following the lesson, it is useful to provide time for the observers to reflect. This will enable everyone to collect any thoughts that they have not yet recorded and to review their notes. They will look back at the goals and the points of evaluation from the lesson plan.

Most important, the observers should consider the evidence they want to share and the questions they want to raise during the debriefing. Having observers write their personal reflections following the observation helps focus and deepen the debriefing conversation and increases the value for the lesson study team. The observers should select the comments that will have the most impact on the learning of everyone involved. Sharing a few comments is more effective than reading off a long list of points.

Flow of the Debriefing

To begin, the moderator—a member of the lesson study team or someone familiar with the team's work—expresses appreciation to the team for their work, thanks the teacher for welcoming everyone into the classroom, outlines the **debriefing protocol**, and reviews the team's meeting norms. The moderator briefly repeats the team's goals and writes or projects the goals on the board, asking observers to refer to the goals in their comments. The moderator encourages everyone to base their comments on data collected during the observation and to avoid offering an exhaustive laundry list of comments. A typical agenda might look like this:

- Teacher comments on the lesson.
- Lesson study team members comment based on the evidence.
- Knowledgeable others and invited guests comment based on the evidence.
- Interviewers share student interview data.
- Open discussion among team, invited guests, and knowledgeable others.
- Final commentator closes the debriefing.

In general, discussion other than clarifying questions should be held off until the "open discussion" phase of the debriefing protocol. This helps avoid a back-and-forth exchange in which a comment is made and the teacher or team defends or goes into too much clarifying detail in response. It is the responsibility of the team to seriously consider the comments of the invited guests and knowledgeable others as they move into the revising and refining of the lesson, but it is distracting and not necessarily productive to respond to each comment during the debriefing.

Teacher comments. The moderator invites the teacher to briefly share impressions of the team's lesson and to describe any challenges that were encountered. The teacher is the one who leads the way, giving everyone permission to genuinely analyze the lesson and to offer perceived difficulties based on the evidence. Many teams are nervous about the debriefing because they fear that harshly critical or judgmental comments will be made. In fact, the opposite is often the case, and issues related to the lesson are sometimes glossed over and superficial comments are made. The teacher's initial observations set the stage for others to take an analytical but supportive approach to the discussion.

Lesson study team members comment. Next, the moderator invites the team members to comment. Remembering that the lesson is collectively owned by the whole team, each person shares one or two comments focused on evidence around student understanding. It is useful to share a strength of the lesson, followed by a challenge or weakness. Team members may also share anything surprising or intriguing that they noticed in relation to their expectation of how the lesson would flow.

> *I had the benefit of watching a team member teach our lesson in her classroom. As an observer, I could immediately see some of the problems the students were having and the misconceptions they were forming. It was tremendously valuable to share and discuss these observations during the debriefing.*
>
> ~Linda Egeler, teacher

> **FROM THE FIELD**
>
> *I believe the worst kind of debriefing is when everyone says the lesson went well, and few useful comments are made. I have seen way too many of this kind of debriefing. To avoid this, all participants should understand the purpose of the lesson study observation—to improve the research lesson and learn more about students and how they think and learn.*
>
> *I appreciate it when the observer has a knowledge of the subject matter . . . and the comments focus more on the mathematics (or science or whatever subject) and how the lesson facilitated (or not) student understanding. I appreciate comments about my teaching, but I think the comments should focus on how particular parts of the teaching (or plan) affected student thinking. Praise is nice, but critique is more helpful. Don't be afraid to critique, but just be careful not to make the teacher and the team feel like they are being attacked. This can be done by focusing on students and the lesson plan.*
>
> ~Bill Jackson, math coach

Knowledgeable others comment. The moderator asks knowledgeable others to share comments based on the data they collected from the classroom conversations, student tasks, and student work. Knowledgeable others should not aggressively prescribe solutions or attempt to fix the lesson. It's helpful to first share lesson strengths, based on the collected evidence, before sharing areas that may require attention. Knowledgeable others are partners in lesson study, with expertise and experience that can add value to the work of the team. Their role is to share data collected, help the team make sense of the data, and assist them in considering where to go with the revision effort.

Interviewers share student interview data (optional). If student interviews were conducted, the moderator asks the interviewers to share responses that could paint a fuller picture of how the lesson went. Student comments that reinforce or challenge the data collected by observers should also be shared.

Open discussion. At this point, the moderator invites a more free-flowing discussion among team members, knowledgeable others, and invited guests. Additional questions can be asked or observations made, comments already offered can be probed at a deeper level, and ideas for strengthening the lesson can be shared. There may be instances where the team prefers not to solicit suggested revisions to the lesson.

If the team does choose to seek more input, knowledgeable others and guests can help the team consider the direction that their revision might take and to make further sense of the evidence collected. It is helpful for the moderator to ask participants to frame suggestions in the form of questions, using sentence stems such as

- I wonder what would happen if . . . ?
- What is another way you might . . . ?
- What might explain . . . ?
- Why did you decide to . . . ?
- In your planning, did you consider . . . ?

The sentence stems can be posted during the debriefing. Using questions helps knowledgeable others and guests to refrain from offering overly prescriptive solutions. It also helps engage the collective wisdom of the group in making sense of the data and improving the lesson.

Sometimes direct suggestions are offered. It can be useful to follow a suggestion with a question that invites the team to imagine or hypothesize how the idea might work in the lesson. Examples include

- How might that look in your lesson?
- To what extent might that work in your lesson and with your students?
- What do you imagine might happen if you were to try something like that?

Final commentator comments. To end the debriefing, the moderator introduces and thanks the final commentator, who will add his or her thoughts and synthesize the discussion. As mentioned earlier in this chapter, the final commentator is responsible for the following:

- Contributing any new insights or questions not previously shared in the debriefing
- Summarizing the key ideas and questions that emerged from the debriefing
- Highlighting the areas and issues the team might want to pay attention to as they revise the lesson
- Expressing appreciation to the teacher for opening her classroom to the group
- Extending thanks to the team for all of their work

> *For me, the debriefing was the best part because I could hear about observations from other places in the classroom that I wasn't able to pay attention to while I was watching my assigned group of students. Hearing from the other teachers about what they saw in their groups was just fascinating. It struck me that I go into my teaching thinking that I know what the students are understanding, but the observation and debriefing helped me realize that I just don't always know.*
>
> ~Dustin Rhoades, teacher

Conducting the Debriefing With a Large Group

Occasionally a large group of invited guests is part of the observation and debriefing. For example, all fifth- and sixth-grade teachers from an adjacent school district may come over on their professional development day to participate in lesson study before forming their own teams, or a group of preservice teachers from the local university may visit to learn about lesson study. When there is a large group of invited guests, especially if they are not very familiar with lesson study, it is sometimes challenging to conduct an effective debriefing. Adapting the debriefing protocol can help retain the integrity of the process while providing an opportunity for visitors to participate.

During the individual reflection (see p. 96) immediately following the observation, everyone can be asked to share a question based on their observations or an actual observation on an index card. The moderator reviews the questions and observations and organizes them into themes. Then, during the debriefing and after the team members and knowledgeable others have had a chance to comment, the moderator shares the themes. The moderator does not address everything, however. Only the most compelling or fruitful questions or observations are shared. With large groups unfamiliar with lesson study, it is often best if the visitors observe, but not comment, during the actual debriefing.

A second approach for a large group that provides everyone with an opportunity to share is to ask the invited guests to tell each other about something they observed. This can also take place after the time for individual reflection, with an opportunity to talk briefly with a person sitting nearby. It is a chance to informally discuss observations, questions, and new understanding that came up during the teaching of the lesson. The informal sharing should take no more than 5 to 10 minutes.

A third, somewhat more formal option, is to break into small groups (three to five people) and share observations. At least one team member or knowledgeable other should be in each small group. During the debriefing, a team member or knowledgeable other from each small group shares the key observations they heard.

For all three options, depending on the time and the inclination of the team and the moderator, visitors can be invited to contribute during the open discussion (see pp. 96–97).

PREPARING FOR THE REVISION

To carry the value of the debriefing forward into the next phase of lesson study— revising and refining the lesson—the team must capture the complexity of the evidence about student understanding discussed during the debriefing. To do this, it is useful to supplement the notes from the recorder and the other team members by having all observers respond to the questions in the post-debriefing reflection log. Form 5.3 is an example of a log for team members, and Form 5.4 is an example of a log for outside observers, including knowledgeable others and invited guests. The team members can collect the logs and bring them to their next team planning meeting for use in the revision.

Form 5.3   Team Member Log—Post-debriefing

Name _____	Date _____

Describe participants' observations of student learning. Include details of what students said, did, and wrote/produced.

Were there any unanticipated student responses? Explain.

To what extent were the goals of the lesson achieved? Please provide supporting evidence.

Which instructional decisions might have contributed to helping students meet these goals? Explain.

What aspects of the goals were not reached? Please provide supporting evidence.

Which aspects of the lesson plan should be reconsidered based on this evidence?

Form 5.4   Outside Observer Log—Post-debriefing

School/Team _____   Date _____

Research Lesson Teacher _____

Knowledgeable Other _____

To what extent were the goals of the lesson achieved? Please provide supporting evidence.

Which instructional decisions might have attributed to helping students meet these goals? Explain.

What aspects of the goals were not reached? Please provide supporting evidence.

Which aspects of the lesson plan should be reconsidered based on this evidence?

CHALLENGES OF THE DEBRIEFING

The debriefing process poses several challenges for the members of the lesson study team, knowledgeable others, and invited guests.

> **Dilemma:** The team members seem to always feel that the lesson went well and the students were engaged, complimenting both the lesson and the teacher.

Many teachers have little experience in observing and analyzing student learning or reflecting deeply about practice with their colleagues. Some are understandably sensitive to being perceived as critical of colleagues' work. In too many schools, teachers are congenial and not accustomed to robust collegial conversations. Teachers working in the isolation of their classrooms may not have had the opportunity to develop a rich vocabulary around student thinking or the refined observation skills needed to gather useful data on the lesson and student understanding.

Another Perspective

It will take time for lesson study teams to acquire and practice the skills required for a productive debriefing. An experienced moderator can help give team members permission to go deeper. Through probing and clarifying comments, a moderator can demonstrate a way of thinking that supports lesson study. Recruiting savvy knowledgeable others who can model a more analytical approach to the debriefing and set a clear tone of respectful inquiry is very helpful.

It may also be helpful for team members and invited guests to watch a video of a Japanese debriefing to get a sense of the type of discussion involved. The account of the debriefing in *Lesson Study: A Japanese Approach to Improving Mathematics Teaching and Learning* (2004)—Clea Fernandez and Makoto Yoshida's book about lesson study in Japan—is also helpful in illuminating the qualities of an effective debriefing.

> **Dilemma:** The comments made by the observers have left the team feeling attacked.

Sometimes, knowledgeable others and observers have not developed the ability to offer critique in a gentle and productive manner. In other cases, the lesson study team may perceive even the most diplomatic suggestion as an attack on their work. This translates into defensiveness on the part of the team and sometimes results in a volleying between the team and the outside observers.

Another Perspective

Providing a strong orientation and clear expectations for knowledgeable others and observers can help avoid this problem. Form 5.1 provides suggestions for knowledgeable others and Form 5.2 provides a sample of guidelines for observers. Framing comments or suggestions in the form of a question can help the team better focus on the content.

Adhering to the debriefing protocol can reduce the feeling of personalization and aid in a constructive discussion. Providing additional guidelines can sometimes be helpful. One approach is to ask each team member, followed by each observer, to make one positive comment about student learning, providing specific examples of how students were working toward the goals of the lesson. The next round of comments then focuses on a question that team members and knowledgeable others pose to the entire group of observers. This strategy can help prevent volleying between the team and invited guests. It can also help focus the discussion on the larger issues, minimizing discussion around less important items.

REFLECTING AND ASSESSING PROGRESS

At this point, it is important for teams to reflect on the process of observing and debriefing. If they have completed the post-debriefing log, the team members have already thought about what they learned about students, content, and instruction around this specific research lesson, as well as what is transferable to other lessons. It may be helpful to share the logs with each other.

It is also important to reflect on the team's work and their progress in developing their lesson study practice. The following questions may be helpful in guiding the team's reflections on the core elements of lesson study—see Figure 5.3. The teachers may want to devote a lesson study meeting to sharing their responses. If time together is hard to come by, it may be more efficient to conduct the discussion via e-mail.

Figure 5.3   Core Elements of Lesson Study

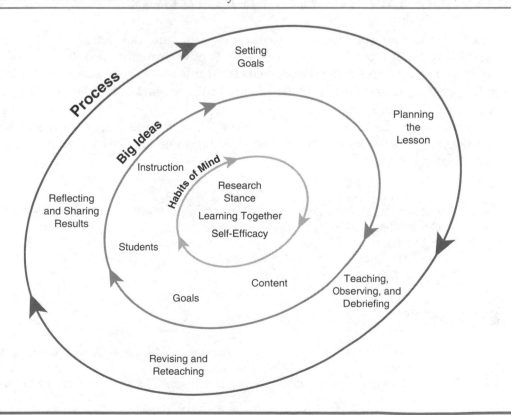

Lesson Study Process

- In what ways was the observing and debriefing phase effective?
- What would you do differently next time and why?
- Were the points of evaluation useful in guiding our observation and debriefing?
- What contributions did the outside observers make?

Big Ideas

- Summarize your learning in each of the following areas:
  - Goals
  - Content
  - Student learning
  - Instruction
- Beyond the research lesson, what are the implications of what we have learned?

Habits of Mind

- Were we able to collect useful data about the research lesson?
- Were we open to ideas and questions from observers?
- Were any of our existing beliefs challenged? What did we learn from this?
- Did we maintain a focus on evidence?
- Are there any areas for improvement in our group norms? How can we address them?
- What were my contributions to the teaching, observing, and debriefing process?

MOVING ON TO THE NEXT PHASE

After celebrating the completion of the first teaching and debriefing of their research lesson and reflecting on their work, the team is now primed to use the evidence they have collected and the proposed revisions. The teachers will continue their work together as they refine and improve the lesson in preparation for reteaching with a different group of students.

The following documents and items from the observation and debriefing should be gathered for the revision process. These artifacts will also be used in preparing the lesson study report.

- Observation notes
- Notes from the debriefing on participants' and team members' observations
- Post-debriefing individual reflection log
- Student work
- Photos of the blackboard
- Videotape of lesson (if available)

KEY IDEAS

- Teachers and observers collect and discuss evidence about student thinking and learning.
- The focus of the observations is on the team's lesson and its effectiveness rather than on the teacher.

- Observers develop an increasingly refined ability to gather and discuss meaningful data about students.
- During the debriefing, observers share the evidence collected about student learning and discuss the implications for the lesson.

From Our Team to Yours

Observing Students

The members of the Detroit Lesson Study Group have discovered that the process of observing the research lessons is a learning experience that extends far beyond the research lesson. They gain insights into their students and how they learn. They have also learned how to observe students, which has changed the way they approach their work on a daily basis.

Brandon: "For our research lessons, we always go in with a game plan. We decide who is going to observe which groups of students. As the teacher is conveying the lesson to the students, we watch them and see how the students respond to the things that we put into the lesson. So you're not just looking at the teacher, you're observing the lesson as it's going through in sequence, and you're watching how each one of these things that are in the lesson affects the students' thinking."

Jason: "I think it's a great opportunity to have a student present at the debriefing. I know the students may be reluctant to say anything negative about their teachers while they are sitting right there. So you need to get the right student who has the right attitude: 'If you give me a bad grade, you give me a bad grade, but I'm going to say what I think.' Because as teachers, we never ask the client. We just give the service, and we never ask the client, 'How do you feel? How do you like it?'"

Vicki: "Before, I wouldn't really look at my students' work until after I had collected it. Now I intervene, because I know how to be an observer. I walk around and look at what they're doing and listen to what they're saying. I'm an observer in my classroom, every day and every hour now that I know how to observe. So when I go to summarize, I can address the things that they were talking about in their groups. And when I do the lesson during the next hour, I change it because I saw the challenges that they had the hour before. So what I've learned from lesson study about being an observer has affected how I teach every day."

6

Revising and Reteaching the Lesson

The revising and reteaching phase of the lesson study cycle is an opportunity for teachers to use the data they gathered during the observation and debriefing of the first teaching to further their learning. The group meets to make improvements to the lesson and prepare for a second implementation.

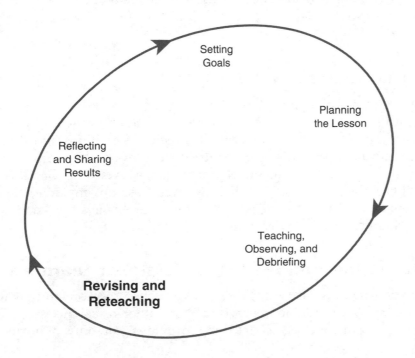

The lesson study team draws on the rich experiences and information collected up to this point. The teachers examine how the data provide evidence of the extent to which students have met the goals of the lesson. They revisit the research hypothesis and points of evaluation for the lesson and analyze the data collected. The lesson is taught again to a different group of students. Observers collect information during the lesson and engage in a second debriefing.

> *We've always approached lesson study as an experiment for teachers. We're going to try this out and see how it works, and we're going have the kids give us the evidence of if it was successful or not. And then we're going to make some changes and try it again. That means that we're going to come away with an understanding of whether or not this type of questioning or this type of learning experience was successful. And to me it's always been the transition from the first lesson to the second lesson that's made the biggest difference. You're missing the finish line if you don't revise the lesson.*

~Andre Audette, Regents Fellow, Rhode Island
Department of Elementary and Secondary Education

WHY REVISE AND RETEACH?

The revising and reteaching phase is an opportunity for teachers to reflect on and improve their lesson study practice. Learning to think deeply about the content, student learning, and effective instruction is not an automatic result of going through the phases of lesson study. Rather, it takes deliberate actions and habits of mind for this to happen.

Making revisions enables teachers to reflect on what they have learned so far and, even more important, to enact their learning. Teachers may be able to file away what they gained from planning and observing the lesson and draw on it in their future work, but revising and reteaching ensures that they immediately begin using what they learned. There are a number of additional reasons that revising and reteaching are a vital part of lesson study.

Uses Actual Classroom Data

During the initial planning phase, the team members rely on their past experiences, their investigations of curriculum materials and best practices, and the advice of knowledgeable others. When teachers use their observations and feedback from observers to inform another iteration of the research lesson, they benefit from having more concrete data to inform the development of the revised lesson. This allows the team to build on the first version of their research lesson by making revisions based on actual data and then to observe whether or not the changes they made will lead to the desired changes in student learning.

Increases Opportunities for Professional Learning

In Japan, a teacher typically engages in two cycles of lesson study with the team and participates as an outside observer in nine other research lessons every year (Fernandez & Yoshida, 2004). Reteaching provides not only a means for team members to enact their learning but also a rich opportunity for teachers beyond the team to engage in lesson study. Outside observers can provide "fresh eyes" and valuable feedback to the team. In return, outside observers benefit from what the team has learned through their research lesson.

Adapts Learning to Various Contexts

When they develop a research lesson, the lesson study team considers how students will respond to each aspect of the plan. What works well for one group of students may fall flat in a different classroom. During the revision process, the team has the opportunity to fine-tune the lesson to meet the needs of the students in a second classroom. As Makoto Yoshida points out, "Re-teaching in a second classroom by a second teacher creates a totally different environment. Since there are no perfect lessons that are successful for every classroom situation, learning how to adjust a lesson is a valuable skill for teachers" (Lewis, 2002b).

Allows Investigation of Different Ideas

Revising and reteaching provide a means for teachers to try out and compare different ideas. In fact, teachers sometimes identify two different strategies that they want to test during the initial planning sessions. When this happens, the lesson study team may use the first and second implementations to compare certain aspects of the lesson. For example, they may use different types of manipulatives or different grouping strategies. This is an effective way to deal with disagreements that occur in the planning of the lesson. Instead of spending time debating their views, the teachers use the lesson study process to gather evidence that can help them achieve consensus.

> **FROM THE FIELD**
>
> Matthew Inman, a high school science teacher in Spokane, Washington, says that he and his colleagues have taken advantage of the reteaching phase when they disagree about things like how to begin a lesson or how to bring closure to it. "There are often significant debates between us, and that's one of the valuable parts of lesson study," he says. "When this happens we usually say, 'Okay, the first time we'll do it this way and the second time we'll do it that way.'"
>
> Matthew sees this as an opportunity to grow as a teacher because it challenges him to test his assumptions. "There are some things that are out of my comfort zone, but I'm working with my fellow teachers, and it's not out of their comfort zone, so I'm challenged to do them." Planning a lesson on cell division, one of the team members suggested that the students should physically act out the process. "Maybe as part of my defense mechanisms, I've told myself that these types of activities are not effective. When I'm challenged to do them or when I get to observe them, I have to acknowledge that they often *are* effective."

PROCESS FOR REVISING THE LESSON

After spending time researching and developing the lesson, teaching the lesson while recording observations, and sharing observations and insights during the debriefing, the team has collected a wealth of information that can be used to revise the lesson.

One of the challenges of revising the lesson is knowing where to begin. The process described in Figure 6.1 is one way to go about revising. It may not work equally well for all teams, but it can serve as a starting point that teams can adapt to their own needs. Regardless of the process they use, the teachers should be deliberate in their reflection on what they have learned, both individually and as a team.

Figure 6.1   Process for Revising the Lesson

Step	Guiding Questions	Description

1: Gather and Review the Data	What evidence do we need to authentically inform the team's learning?	Teams go over the artifacts they have collected throughout their lesson study process. For the revision of the lesson, teams may want to include the following:
		    Student work
		    Photos of the blackboard
		    Videotape of lesson
		    Notes from the debriefing on participants' and team members' observations
		    Post-debriefing individual reflection logs

2: Analyze the Data	What do the data reveal about student understanding and learning? To what extent were the goals of the lesson achieved? What aspects of the lesson contributed to student learning? Which goals are the students still struggling with?	As teams examine the artifacts, they identify evidence of student learning. In addition, teams begin identifying areas where students were still struggling with developing understanding of the goals.
3: Identify Needed Changes	What do the analyses of the data on student learning tell us about the impact of our instructional decisions? How can we change the lesson plan to help students more effectively reach the goals?	Teams connect student learning with the instructional decisions in the lesson. They determine which parts of the lesson support student learning and which parts might be revised to be more effective. Teams might review their research notes from planning for ideas about content, instruction, and student learning to inform the types of changes that could be made.
4: Revise the Lesson Plan	How do we document the changes to the lesson plan?	It is important for teams to retain a copy of the original lesson plan for the reflecting and sharing stage of lesson study. With this in mind, be sure to create a new file in your computer where you will save the revised version of the lesson. It can be beneficial to indicate how the revised lesson is different from the original lesson. Some groups highlight changes with boxes or by using a different font. Teams then make enough copies for members and all observers to use during the reteaching of the lesson.

STEP 1: GATHER AND REVIEW THE DATA

The team has been creating and collecting artifacts throughout the lesson study cycle. The following documents and items may be helpful for the revision process:

- Observation notes
- Notes from the debriefing on participants' and team members' observations
- Post-debriefing individual reflection log
- Student work
- Photos of the blackboard
- Videotape of lesson (if available)

To make the most of their time together, team members will review the data individually before meeting together to start the revision process. Given teachers' busy schedules, this may not be realistic. Often the first part of the revision meeting may be set aside for reviewing the data. Figure 6.2 is a set of sample debriefing notes to illustrate one type of data that the team will use. The lesson plan for the observation and debriefing of this example is Sample Lesson 1, included in Resource A.

Figure 6.2   Sample Debriefing Notes

Use of the Chart

There was broad agreement among both students and observers that the Chemical Test Results Chart is an essential tool to help students identify chemicals based on evidence.

Related to this, many students also found the Observations and Deductions Lab Sheet helpful in sorting out their observations and deducing what the chemicals could or couldn't be. Although there were observations of students struggling with the amount of writing involved. Some ideas were offered on how to accommodate students.

When I did the lesson, I did not notice how much writing was involved.

Mary and Theresa—Theresa did most of the talking. The new lab sheet was very helpful—They went through a process of elimination near the end. They seemed comfortable going back and forth among the chart, test results, and lab sheet.

Vocabulary

The thought emerged that we need to honor the language that students use—but connect this language to one of the scientific vocabulary words melting, dissolving, mixture, or properties. The words transparent, translucent, and opaque came up in the context of an observer who was surprised that students did not use these words, particularly because the minerals unit does use them.

The use of the word characteristics or properties was discussed—The final commentator recommended using the word properties because it is used throughout physical science in later grades.

Is property a word used only for nonliving things? Attributes is another word that comes up that is confusing. Attributes is also used in math.

Accommodations

For the students with learning challenges: How can we design this lesson to make them more successful?

Some students with IEPs or other challenges often do well in this kind of lesson. The following comments support this idea:

Laura was right in there. At different levels we were able to bring students along.

Becky was quite engaged, she seemed to be on task. Margaret was using the materials. Their responses seemed to be correct.

Some ideas for accommodations to reduce the amount of writing came up:

Is it possible for there to be one recording (lab sheet) and switch off reporting results and recording? It's not always the same person doing the same job.

Maybe each had a job that was color-coded—three or four jobs (reporter, materials person, recorder). Every person in the group has to do one of these jobs. They know they have to be there to perform for the group if they have to do all of the jobs; it also gets them doing things outside of what they are most comfortable with.

Each team member may want to review all of the collected data. Another option is for the team to sort the data, with each member responsible for reviewing a specific piece and reporting findings to the team. There are several ways to sort the data. Individuals or pairs might look at

- A specific section of the lesson plan (Introduction, Explore, Summary, etc.)
- Individual goals of the lesson
- One of the points of evaluation
- One type of data (debriefing notes, reflection logs, observations, student work, etc.)

Figure 6.3 reviews the step of gathering and reviewing the data.

Figure 6.3 Step 1: Gather and Review the Data

Guiding Questions	Description
What evidence do we need to authentically inform the team's learning?	Teams go over the artifacts they have collected throughout their lesson study process. For the revision of the lesson, teams may want to include the following: ○ Student work ○ Photos of the blackboard ○ Videotape of lesson ○ Notes from the debriefing on participants' and team members' observations ○ Post-debriefing individual reflection logs
Example	

Our team gathered the following items:
- ○ *Research notes that were taken during the planning that focused on content, student understanding, and pedagogy*
- ○ *The lesson plan*
- ○ *Carole's notes from the debriefing*
- ○ *Team members' individual reflection logs*
- ○ *Student work*
- ○ *Photos of the blackboard*

STEP 2: ANALYZE THE DATA

As team members review the data, they are looking for evidence of student learning and identifying where students did and did not meet the goals of the lesson. If the team members completed the Post-debriefing Log (see Forms 5.3 and 5.4 in Chapter 5), the team will have a head start on Step 2 (Figure 6.4). The following questions from the log are useful to guide the data analysis process and to organize the discussion.

- What are the observations around student learning? Include details of what students said, did, and wrote or produced.
- Were there any unanticipated student responses? Explain.
- To what extent were the goals of the lesson achieved? Provide supporting evidence.
- In what ways were the goals not met? Provide supporting evidence.

As team members share ideas around these questions, one person can serve as a recorder, organizing the ideas around the goals, student learning, and instruction into two charts: Evidence of Students Meeting Goals and Evidence of Students Not Meeting Goals. The points of evaluation and the sections of the lesson plan can also serve as an organizer—a lesson might have Introduction, Explore, and Summary sections.

In addition to using charts, it may be helpful to provide team members with a tool for recording their reflections and ideas as they analyze the data. Form 6.1 is a sample revising log. Teams can expand on this template and adapt it to meet their needs. (Please note that the recording areas have been compressed to save space.) Like the charts, the revising log can be structured around the points of evaluation or the organization of the lesson plan.

Figure 6.4   Step 2: Analyze the Data

Guiding Questions	Description
What do the data reveal about student understanding and learning? To what extent were the goals of the lesson achieved? What aspects of the lesson contributed to student learning? Which goals are the students still struggling with?	As teams examine the artifacts, they identify evidence of student learning. In addition, teams begin identifying areas where students were still struggling with developing understanding of the goals.
Example	

The goal of our lesson is for students to be able to effectively communicate their own and each other's strategies for solving the problem. During the "Explore" portion of the lesson, observers divided themselves among the groups. Three observers took notes on Kylie's group. They noted that when the students were working together at their table, they had drawn an elegant diagram along with the written explanation of their solution. However, when the teacher asked them to transfer their solution onto an overhead transparency, they did not have sufficient time and space to replicate the diagram with the written explanation.

During the "Summary" portion of the lesson, observers focused and took notes on all the groups of students that were presenting in front of the classroom. Observers indicated that after Kylie's group finished sharing, the other students replied they did not understand the solution strategy that the group presented. The group spoke in a clear manner, but because they left out the diagram in their explanation, it was more difficult for the other students to understand.

Form 6.1 Revising Log—General Observations and Comments

Record evidence of unanticipated student responses. Identify any possible changes to the lesson.

Unanticipated Response:	
Evidence:	Possible changes:
Unanticipated Response:	
Evidence:	Possible changes:

Record evidence that the goals of the lesson were met. Identify elements of the lesson that contributed to students' success.

Goal:	
Evidence:	Successful elements:
Goal:	
Evidence:	Successful elements:

Record evidence that the goals of the lesson were not met. Identify any possible changes to the lesson.

Goal:	
Evidence:	Possible changes:
Goal:	
Evidence:	Possible changes:

STEP 3: IDENTIFY NEEDED CHANGES

After analyzing the data, the team discusses how to restructure the lesson and make it more effective. The teachers connect student learning with the instructional activities in the lesson. They determine which parts of the lesson support student learning and which parts might be revised to more successfully help students meet the goals.

Using the charts and the revising logs generated in Step 2, the team may find it helpful to group similar observations together and identify themes. It will be easier to discuss and resolve contradictory evidence if observations are grouped together. Several visual tools may help sort the themes:

- Use different colored highlighters to circle themes on the chart.
- Cut the chart across the rows and reorganize the ideas.
- Create a new list of themes.

Teams might review their research notes from planning for ideas about content, instruction, and student learning to inform the types of changes that could be made. The teachers may want to conduct additional research on instructional materials to inform their revisions.

Whether or not the lesson will be taught immediately to a particular class should be taken into consideration. Differences in classroom environment may have an impact on the lesson design. If there is a class in mind, the team will need to reconsider the students' prior knowledge and experiences and any additional misconceptions and reactions they may have. This means that the team will need to think about additional anticipated student responses or student misconceptions that the class may have and how this should be factored into the revised lesson. Questions to facilitate the team's discussion include the following:

- Based on our evidence, what aspects of our lesson plan should we change?
- How might this instructional change affect students' responses?
- Why do we think this change would improve the lesson?
- Is there information from our earlier research that may be relevant to these changes?

The team may want to make a list of the issues identified and post it where it remains visible. Additional items can be added to the list over the course of the revision process, and items can also be crossed off as they are addressed. This may help keep the team on track when ideas are flowing quickly or the discussion begins to wander. If there is limited time for revising, the team may need to prioritize the list to ensure that the most crucial changes are made first.

When the list of issues to address is complete and priorities have been established, the team can begin identifying changes to the lesson plan. The attention to detail involved in the process will vary depending on the time available and the preferences of the team members. Sometimes the teachers may want to decide on a general solution to the problem and leave the details to the teacher (or teachers) who will be making the revisions to the lesson plan. In other cases, the team may want to spend time getting the details exactly right—for example, the wording of a key question.

Figure 6.5 provides some examples of problems that might have occurred during the first observation and revisions that might be used to address them. Example 1 is from a language arts research lesson, and Example 2 is from a mathematics research lesson.

Figure 6.5 Sample Revisions

Example 1

Goal

Students will be able to define and use strategies for comprehending text.

Evidence of Students Not Meeting the Goal

When we asked students to describe the strategies they used, it seemed as if many students were randomly selecting a strategy merely because we asked them to. Observers noticed that many students filled out the strategies section after they completed the questions.

When revisiting the goals of the lesson, we realized that the questions we gave students were not complex enough. They did not need to plan their comprehension strategies because the questions were easily completed.

Suggestions for Instruction

○ Select a longer and more challenging passage of text.
○ Revise the questions to require higher-order thinking processes.
○ Have students complete the strategies section before giving them the text and questions.

Example 2

Goal

Students will analyze various strategies for adding fractions with unlike denominators and devise "algorithms" that are efficient and will always work.

Evidence of Students Not Meeting the Goal

Observers noted that about three-fourths of the students were able to understand the numeric models for representing strategies for adding fractions with unlike denominators. However, they noted that Chloe, Audrey, Florence, Max, and Brandon had a difficult time understanding the numeric models.

Suggestions for Instruction

○ The teacher will note groups that use visual models and ask them to share first. Have students using numeric models make connections with the visual models.
○ Slow down the "Summary" part of the lesson and have small groups "ponder" the strategy that the group just shared. Ask them explicitly to draw a visual model of the numeric model before going on to the next group's strategy.

FROM THE FIELD

Karen Daily, Mary Holmberg, and Merle Hom are a team of sixth-grade teachers at Meadows Elementary School in Lacey, Washington. They were working on revising their mathematics lesson. The goal of the research lesson is "Students will develop fluency in adding fractions," and the team's long-term goal is for students to develop their abilities to communicate effectively.

The "Introduction" of the lesson prompts students to recall their prior knowledge of adding fractions with unlike denominators. Next, students work in groups of four to solve three addition problems. Finally, the lesson includes a 20-minute "math congress" to enable students to share strategies for adding fractions and then to evaluate whether or not they work.

During the teaching of the lesson, the research team observed that many of the students lost interest toward the end of the math congress. They noticed that as groups continued to present their strategies, fewer students showed that they were listening to what was being shared. This was confirmed when the teacher asked the students to compare the strategies of the different groups and to evaluate whether or not they would work—students did not raise their hands. The teacher then chose to review each strategy verbally and make comparisons and evaluations herself.

At the debriefing, observers noted that during the math congress, students were sharing strategies that had already been shared by other groups. "Perhaps that was why they became disengaged," one team member said. In addition, students showed their work on the overhead projector and then removed it when they finished, and that might have contributed to why the students had a difficult time comparing and evaluating the different strategies.

The team revised several aspects of the lesson. First, while the students are working in groups, the teacher will identify the students and groups that she would like to have share their strategies during the math congress. This will ensure that all strategies are presented in an order that makes sense, and that the class will not waste time listening to strategies that have already been shared. Second, the team decided to have students record their work on poster paper that will remain on the whiteboard, replacing the use of the overhead projector. This will help students to compare and evaluate the different strategies.

Figure 6.6   Step 3: Identify Needed Changes

Guiding Questions	Description
What do the analyses of the data on student learning tell us about the impact of our instructional decisions?	Teams connect student learning with the instructional decisions in the lesson. They determine which parts of the lesson support student learning and which parts might be revised to be more effective. Teams might review their research notes from planning for ideas about content, instruction, and student learning to inform the types of changes that could be made.
How can we change the lesson plan to help students more effectively reach the goals?	
Example	

In our discussion, team members came up with the following list of suggestions for changes:

  o *Give students chart paper at the beginning of the group work and have them record directly onto that so that it can be shared during the summary of the lesson.*
  o *Borrow a document camera and projector so that students can share their original papers.*
  o *Give students overhead transparencies at the beginning of the group work and have them work directly on those.*

STEP 4: REVISE THE LESSON PLAN

After the changes are identified, it is time to revise the lesson plan (Figure 6.7). Often, one of the teachers will be responsible for making the changes and distributing the revised plan to the rest of the team.

It is very important to keep a copy of the original plan, both to refer back to and to include in the report. It also may be helpful to identify the changes in the new plan with highlighting, italics, boxes, or different fonts.

If possible, the team should get back together to discuss the lesson plan and to identify any further changes that need to be made. This can be done electronically if there is not enough time to hold a meeting and the teachers take responsibility for sharing their comments with each other.

Sample Lesson 3 is an example of a revised lesson included in Resource A. Additions or changes have been underlined and deletions have been crossed out. The original lesson plan is Sample Lesson 1, which is also included in Resource A. Note that the lesson study team has decided that the research lesson will take three days instead of just one as they originally planned. The sample debriefing notes from Figure 6.1 are among the data that the team used to identify their revisions.

Figure 6.7   Step 4: Revise the Lesson Plan

Guiding Questions	Description
How do we document the changes to the lesson plan?	It is important for teams to retain a copy of the original lesson plan for the reflecting and sharing stage of lesson study. With this in mind, be sure to create a new file in your computer where you will save the revised version of the lesson. It can be beneficial to indicate how the revised lesson plan is different from the original lesson plan. Some groups highlight changes with text boxes or by using a different font. Teams then make enough copies for members and all observers to use during the reteaching of the lesson.
Example	
Tim volunteered to record the changes to our lesson plan. He saved version one of the lesson in a separate file and renamed this lesson by adding "revised" to the end. He made copies for all the team members and observers for the reteaching.	

CHALLENGES OF THE REVISION PROCESS

There are several challenges that are unique to the process of revising the lesson.

Dilemma: We want to start over—our lesson was a disaster.

Sometimes the research lesson does not go as well as planned. Although the lesson looked beautiful on paper, the teachers may have miscalculated how well the students had mastered prerequisite skills. Or perhaps the context and task that the team had so carefully constructed failed to spark students' interest. When problems like this arise, the team may feel deflated and their initial response may be to abandon the lesson altogether.

Another Perspective

This is a situation in which one of the mantras of lesson study is very apt: The purpose of lesson study is not to produce the perfect lesson. The success of lesson study depends on what the teachers learn, not on how well the lesson goes. A research lesson that goes disastrously but that results in many new insights into student learning is actually more successful than a "perfect" lesson that teachers can learn nothing from.

When things do not go as planned, the team's first instinct may be to put the problems behind them and move ahead. Yet it makes more sense to build on the existing lesson to move forward with more purpose and better understanding. Perhaps the revised lesson will be a radical departure from its first incarnation. If the teachers fail to investigate what went wrong, they will fail to take advantage of the hard work and careful planning that they have already completed.

Questions to Consider

- What does the evidence indicate about the extent to which students met the goals of the lesson?
- To what can we attribute students not meeting the goals?
- What can we change about the lesson to support students in meeting these goals?

> **Dilemma:** We need to change the goals of the lesson.

Lesson study teams are sometimes tempted to change the goals of the lesson after they observe students. This may happen because the teachers believe that they overestimated students' abilities to meet the goals; conversely, they may feel that the goal is not challenging enough for their students. Sometimes teams find that the evidence they have collected does not address the goals of the lesson or that the goal is poorly worded and therefore unclear.

Another Perspective

Changing the lesson goal is sometimes a reasonable option. For example, rewording the goal so that it is more specific and measurable will usually improve both the research lesson and teacher learning.

In other cases, it will be better to stick with the initial goal. For example, if the teachers determine that the assessment they developed does not provide evidence of whether or not the goal was met, it may seem easier to change the goal to match the assessment rather than modifying the tool. Nevertheless, going this route will bypass an opportunity to gain insights that will enable teachers to more effectively monitor student learning throughout all of their lessons.

Questions to Consider

- In what ways are the goals measurable? How do we know the extent to which all students met the goals of the lesson? Did we provide sufficient opportunities for students to reveal their thinking?
- Did observers diligently and accurately record student thinking?
- How do the goals of the lesson connect to the goals of the unit?

> **Dilemma:** The students were not successful, so the lesson must be too difficult.

If students struggled during the lesson, teachers' first reaction may be to make the lesson easier. For example, in a lesson about area and perimeter, students had difficulty making accurate measurements. As a result, they were not able to get through the activity as quickly as planned. The teachers decided to revise the lesson by providing the measurements for the students. During the second teaching, students were able to complete the activity quickly, but it became mostly a fill-in-the-blank exercise with little opportunity for thinking and problem solving.

Another Perspective

It is natural for teachers to want their students to be successful, especially when they have an audience. Yet when students are successful because their work is not challenging enough, they are ultimately shortchanged because no learning is taking place. Rather than making a lesson less difficult, think about ways to support students in meeting the challenge. Sometimes a brief discussion at the opening of the lesson is all students need to connect with their prior knowledge. Rather than doing their work for them, the teachers might provide more time for students to make their measurements or design a brief pre-lesson activity that would enable the students to practice their skills and the teacher to assess their abilities.

Questions to Consider

- What are the important and enduring concepts that we wanted students to understand?
- Did we provide enough supports during the "Introduction" so that all students could begin working on the problem?
- Were there any manipulatives, visuals, or organizers that might have helped students?

> **Dilemma:** The lesson was perfect. We don't need to revise it.

When teachers put so much effort into planning a lesson, it may be very difficult for them to remain open to feedback and suggestions. They may be reluctant to look at the evidence of student learning. Or they may seek rationale for ignoring the evidence and the suggestions from the debriefing.

Teams have been known to focus on student engagement rather than student learning, making a leap from the observations of students enjoying themselves and working hard to assuming that therefore students were achieving the goals of the lesson. If some of the students were successful, but others were not, the team may focus on the groups who did demonstrate that they understood the content. And when a lesson is very successful, revision may seem pointless to the teachers.

Another Perspective

Remember that no matter how well a lesson went, there is always more to be learned. If the team really has created the perfect lesson, will it be equally perfect for all students? Will it be accessible for students with special learning needs? Will it work as well with another class? It may be helpful for the teachers to identify changes that will extend the investigation of their questions and theories about student learning.

This type of situation highlights both the importance of an effective debriefing and the contributions that outside observers and knowledgeable others can make to a team's thinking. When teachers cannot identify areas for improvement, they should be able to build on the suggestions that the observers shared at the debriefing.

If the team is ultimately not able to identify any changes, then it is probably best to move on. It may be helpful to move ahead to the reteaching, testing the initial lesson plan with a new group of students. If teachers are reluctant to conduct the second teaching, it may be best to move on to the report. At this point, the team should identify ways to create a better learning opportunity for themselves with the next cycle.

Questions to Consider

- Was the lesson equally effective for all students?
- What changes might make the lesson more challenging?
- Are there other approaches that we can test against the results from the first teaching?

RETEACHING AND FOCUSING THE DEBRIEFING

After the team has finished revising, the lesson is presented again to a different group of students. Usually, a different team member teaches the revised version, but the same person may teach the lesson a second time to a different group of students. Sometimes more observers are invited to the teaching of the revised lesson.

The team will explore differences between the evidence of student learning from the two versions of the research lesson. During the debriefing, they may discuss the possible causes behind these differences.

Pre-observation Meeting

If any invited guests will be observing the reteaching of the lesson, the lesson study team will hold a pre-observation meeting. The team clarifies the underlying concepts being addressed in the lesson and what the team would like the students to know and be able to do by the end of the lesson. When introducing a revised lesson, the team briefly summarizes the evidence that was collected during the first teaching and explains the changes they made to address the evidence. It may be helpful to distribute copies of the original lesson plan, especially if some of the observers were not present during the first round. Finally, the team outlines the evaluation questions for observers to focus on during the teaching.

Debriefing

The debriefing session for the revised lesson follows the same format as the first. It may be helpful to review the strategies and suggestions provided in Chapter 5. There are some additional questions that teams should consider.

- How were the observations about student understanding from the first lesson different from those of the revised lesson? What may have been the causes for these differences?
- Did the changes to the lesson bring about desired changes in student learning?
- Keeping the goals in mind, did the changes to the lesson result in a more effective lesson?

FROM THE FIELD

A lesson study team from Anchorage, Alaska—Deb Benedict, Joy Curry, Julia Gibeault, Amy Lyman, and Linda Michele—was working on a fourth-grade research lesson. The lesson had four goals:

1. Research theme: Create confident, lifelong problem solvers.
2. Process goal: Broaden students' problem-solving abilities in geometry through vocabulary development.
3. Content goal: Classify, identify, and describe properties of polygons using verbal clues.
4. Lesson goal: Demonstrate understanding of attributes of polygons by giving directions to draw two-dimensional figures.

In the first version of the lesson, students brainstormed a list of polygons. Each student then had the name of a polygon taped to his back. Other students had to list attributes of the shape, while the student had to guess which shape was on his back. Many students had trouble remembering what the written shape on the back of each person actually looked like. In addition, they had trouble recalling the terminology of each physical attribute (e.g., parallel lines, obtuse or acute angles, equal length, etc.). Students could easily say how many sides a shape had, "Your shape has four sides. It's not a square." They could have been talking about a rhombus, rectangle, parallelogram, trapezoid, and others. It appeared that they did not have access to the vocabulary to further define the characteristics.

In the second iteration of the lesson, the teacher asked the students to brainstorm a list of polygons, but also had them describe some attributes of each shape. She recorded the terminology for these characteristics on the board. When it came time to give students the shapes to tape on their backs, she included several pictures of each shape in addition to the written name of the shape. So for a rhombus, it said "rhombus" and had three drawings of different rhombi. When other students had to describe the characteristics of the shape to the student with the rhombi on his back, they had access to the terminology on the board and could see the examples of the shape on his back.

On reflection, the teachers felt good about the second teaching of the lesson.

The brainstorming session in the "Introduction" did take longer, but that was needed given the level of this group of children. We did notice that adding the picture of the shape to the cards on students' backs seemed to help some children. There were a few students who traced over the shape with their finger before they gave attribute clues to their partner. It was a nice visual piece to give support to those students that needed it.

REFLECTING AND ASSESSING PROGRESS

It is important for teams to reflect on the revising process, as well as the entire lesson study cycle to date. Team members should think about and discuss not only what they learned about students, content, and instruction around this specific research lesson, but also what is transferable to other lessons. Teachers should consider how the subtle and not-so-subtle changes made to the activities and instruction had an impact on student outcomes and any implications this might have for other lessons.

It is also important to reflect on the team's work and their progress in developing their lesson study practice. The following questions may be helpful in guiding the team's reflections on the core elements of lesson study (see Figure 6.8). The teachers may want to devote a lesson study meeting to sharing their responses. If time together is hard to come by, it may be more efficient to conduct the discussion via e-mail.

Lesson Study Process

- Was the revising process effective?
- What would we do differently next time and why?
- Did we have adequate evidence from the observation and debriefing to inform the revisions?
- How useful were the observation notes? What about the debriefing notes?
- How could the data be improved?

Figure 6.8   Core Elements of Lesson Study

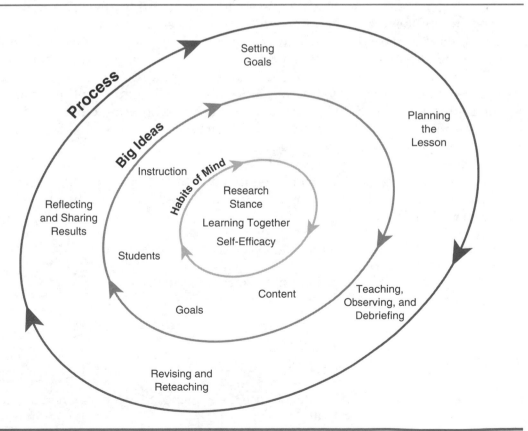

Big Ideas

- What have we learned about each of the following areas:
  o Goals
  o Content
  o Student learning
  o Instruction
- Beyond the research lesson, what are the implications of what we have learned?

Habits of Mind

- Were we able to look at our lesson plan with a critical eye?
- Were we open to critiques from observers?
- Did we maintain a focus on evidence?
- Are there any areas for improvement in our interactions with each other? How can we address them?
- What were my contributions to the revising and reteaching process?

MOVING ON TO THE NEXT PHASE

After the reteaching and debriefing of the revised lesson, the lesson study team will decide how they want to complete the research lesson. One option is to make additional revisions to the lesson plan. An alternative is to capture the evidence from the reteaching and possible revisions in the lesson study report.

Sometimes teams find that they want to pursue a third teaching and observation. The teachers may identify significant changes that they want to test with students, or the revised lesson may not have led to adequate improvements in student outcomes. Going through a third iteration is not unheard of, but it is not usually a productive adaptation of the lesson study model. The research lesson can be finished even if it is not yet perfect, and this should not prevent the team from moving forward. Instead, the teachers can concentrate on using what they learned, as well as any new questions or ideas that they want to pursue, to inform the next research lesson and future lesson study cycles.

The next endeavor in the lesson study process is to create the lesson study report. In this final stage, the teachers will bring together the artifacts and experiences that they have collected. The following revising and reteaching documents should be added to the collection:

- Notes and logs from the revising process
- Revised lesson plan
- Observation and debriefing notes from the reteaching
- Student work
- Post-debriefing reflection logs

KEY IDEAS

- Teachers look closely at data and use the evidence they have gathered to make changes to the lesson plan.

- Revising the research lesson allows teachers to apply what they have learned during the observation and debriefing.
- Reteaching the lesson provides more information about student learning and extends teacher learning as a result.

From Our Team to Yours

Anticipating Student Responses

Planning and revising research lessons have changed the way that the members of the Detroit Lesson Study Group—Brandon Graham, Byron Timms, Vicki Vorus, Elana Webster, and Jason White—approach their work. A significant change that the teachers describe is anticipating student responses. This is a skill that they have developed and that they use on a continuous basis.

Brandon: "A lot of times we as teachers think too much about what we're going to say and we don't think about what impact we're going to have on the students or what they're going to give back to us. Anticipating student responses is a powerful tool. Even when I plan my own lessons I ask myself, 'If I present it this way, what are the students going to get from this? What are they going to say? How is it going to impact their thinking?' So I think that the whole lesson study process really retrains or reconditions your thinking process as a teacher in the classroom."

Jason: "If the students aren't receiving the message, then the teacher is not really teaching. You may say, 'I taught that lesson great!' but then you look at the data, you see maybe they didn't do well. You've got to take some ownership for that. If you're going to take ownership when students shine, you've got to take it when they don't do so well."

Vicki: "Lesson study has helped me to look at teaching a totally different way—considering my students, what they know and what they don't know. These were things that I had never done before when planning a lesson. I just opened my curriculum guide, and when it said do it this way, I did it that way. I can remember times when I would ask questions and there would be this deadly silence in the room. Now I have other questions and other things that I'm ready for just in case my initial question doesn't work. So I'm just a different teacher."

7

Reflecting and Sharing Results

The final phase of the lesson study cycle is developing a report about the research lesson. The team reflects on both the lesson and their lesson study practice. By creating a report, the teachers document their work and have a means of sharing their professional knowledge.

The end of the cycle is also a time for the team to consider how they can evaluate their efforts. An evaluation can be used to improve lesson study practice and to validate its effectiveness. The team's reflections, the lesson study report, and the evaluation findings can be used to plan the next cycle of lesson study.

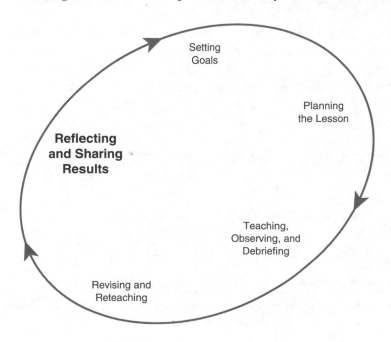

We strongly suggest that lesson study groups produce reports about their lesson study work, as Japanese teachers do. The purpose of these reports is to provide a reflective record of the work that a group engaged in, so that it can be shared with others and can serve as a future reference tool. The lesson plan alone will not do justice to your group's thinking and learning process.

~Fernandez & Chokshi (2002, p. 133)

IMPORTANCE OF REFLECTION

Reflection is a key component of theories about effective teaching and adult learning (Brookfield, 1986; Regan, Case, & Brubacher, 2000). Reflection enables teachers to extract knowledge from their experiences, frame questions about the assumptions that influence their teaching, and form new hypotheses (Briscoe, 1991; Hiller, 1995).

The process of reflecting is a key step in ensuring that experiences lead to learning and change (Boud, Keogh, & Walker, 1985; Jarvis, 1987). It helps learners to identify and examine beliefs and values from different perspectives, often by engaging in dialogue (Brookfield, 1986). Reflection helps learners understand how their beliefs and assumptions shape their experiences and the meaning they create from their experiences (Merriam & Caffarella, 1999). This leads to a sharper and broader perspective, which learners use to guide future decisions and actions.

Reflection is an essential part of the entire lesson study cycle. As they begin their work, teachers reflect on their goals for their students. They think about challenging academic or affective student goals to identify a worthwhile lesson. Reflection enables teachers to learn from the process of planning a lesson and examining its impact on students. It also contributes to the team members' ability to apply the knowledge they gain to their practice beyond the research lesson.

Each member of the lesson study team is responsible for fostering and supporting reflection during the lesson study process. Creating an emotionally safe space with positive verbal reinforcement will provide an environment that supports deep reflection. Modeling self-reflection encourages others to take an active part in this contemplative process.

Reflection is especially important at the end of a lesson study cycle, when teachers can reflect on the process itself. If teams do not reflect on their lesson study practice, they are in danger of going through the motions of lesson study without reaching the potential for deep learning and significant changes in instruction. It is helpful for the team to consider both what went well and what changes need to be made to improve the next cycle (Lewis, 2002b).

FROM THE FIELD

A group of facilitators met at the end of the school year in Traverse City, Michigan, to share their experiences with guiding separate lesson study groups. They set the agenda of this meeting to reflect on lessons learned. Their guiding questions included the following:

Successes: What worked? What helped produce positive outcomes?

Challenges: What didn't work? What would we have changed?

Next Steps: Should we continue lesson study? If so, what support is needed?

First, each person identified the main goals of their group. Eric, a science content coordinator, had facilitated a group of teachers who developed a fifth-grade science lesson on barometric pressure. Mary, a mathematics consultant, worked with a group of elementary teachers who created a lesson on value versus quantity of coins. She relayed that the teachers began their process by sharing past observations of student misconceptions. Tom, a science consultant, worked with a small group of high school biology teachers, all from different districts. His lesson study team chose to focus their lesson on photosynthesis and respiration.

Successes: This meeting was a natural way to revisit what worked because it was held at the end of the school year. The facilitators shared the positive experiences of their teams. Mary indicated that the focus on creating the lesson plan especially helped her group. Specifically, this process contributed to anticipating student responses, which changed the lesson in a positive way. Eric and Tom both relayed the sentiments of the teachers from their teams—being involved in professional development that relates to their own instruction was a huge motivator for teacher participation.

Challenges: The facilitators also took turns sharing the problems that their groups faced with lesson study. Tom identified his team's anxiousness to move on to other content areas. Mary said that for elementary teachers who have multiple subjects and content areas, it is hard for them to give up the guided lesson from the textbook. She attributed that challenge to both tradition and time.

Next Steps: The facilitators ended the meeting with a discussion about where their teams left off and in what direction they saw future work going. For example, Eric reported that as other educators saw the benefits of lesson study in their schools, they were urging him to include more teachers. Consequently, the facilitators planned a half-day session for fifth-grade teachers to introduce more people to the process.

Tools for Reflection

Prior experience with practicing reflection is not a prerequisite for lesson study. Therefore, it may be helpful for teachers to gain practice by reflecting individually and writing their thoughts in a journal before sharing with the group. Probing questions and activities that foster reflection among group members help to further everyone's lesson study experience.

The previous chapters of this book include a section on "Reflecting and Assessing Progress." The questions are designed to help teams reflect on their lesson study practice and their learning during each phase of the cycle. Another set of reflective tools are the logs for team members focused on the planning phase (Form 4.3), the debriefing (Form 5.3), and the revising phase (Form 6.1). These forms are designed to help the team members capture their learning and their reflections.

Two additional tools to encourage and facilitate reflection are included here. Form 7.1 is a 3–2–1 Reflection Activity, which aids in capturing ideas learned, points to ponder, and actions to take (North Central Regional Educational Laboratory, 2000). This tool can be used by teams at the end of a lesson study cycle to reflect on the knowledge they have gained. During a final meeting, team members write down what they have learned and what they still want to know. The tool can also be used to reflect on and capture learning around the big ideas of lesson study: content, goals, student learning, and instruction. The answers garnered may help to set the agenda for the next cycle. Figure 7.1 provides some sample responses that might be generated from this activity.

Figure 7.1   Sample Responses—3-2-1 Reflection

Big Ideas

Student learning and misconceptions go hand in hand.

The questions we developed helped us to get students involved in their own learning.

Our lesson reflected the group's thinking rather than the thinking of any one teacher.

Points to Ponder

How do we refine unit goals and the sequence of the lesson we created?

What are strategies for creating more time to examine student work?

Actions

Compare lesson study process with Teaching for Understanding group process.

Thoughts from the Big Ideas section can help to identify key areas of learning. Responses from the Points to Ponder section may uncover what team members are still confused about or what areas need improvement. The Actions section can be used to start the conversation about the next cycle of lesson study.

Form 7.2 is a Read and Reflect Activity, which facilitates participants' individual metacognition and group discussions (North Central Regional Educational Laboratory, 2000). At the end of a lesson study cycle, the team can use this thinking log to identify and discuss lessons learned from the process. The tool is designed to be used with an article or excerpt from a book that will help the team to reflect on their lesson study process. For example, the teachers may find it helpful to compare their experiences to those of another lesson study team. Such comparisons can generate ideas about things they would like to do differently in their work.

The questions can be adapted to the selected text and the purpose of the activity. After reading and reflecting individually, the team members share what they have learned with each other. The object is for reflection to promote critical thinking and problem solving to improve the lesson study process.

Form 7.1 3-2-1 Reflection Activity: Lesson Study

3-2-1 Reflection Activity: Lesson Study

What are **3 big ideas** that you have taken away from this cycle of lesson study?

What are **2 points** that you will continue to ponder?

What is **1 action** that you will take immediately?

Form 7.2 Read and Reflect Activity: Lesson Study

Read and Reflect Activity: Lesson Study

This Thinking Log is designed to be an individual metacognitive tool and to facilitate rich group discussion. Please answer the following questions thoughtfully, using specific examples whenever possible.

Before you read:

- What do you already "**K**now" about the topic and the content of the text?

- What assumptions and/or biases do you have related to this content?

- What more do you "**W**ant to know" about this content?

After you read:

- What are some of the ideas or strategies you have "**L**earned" from the reading that you consider to be significant?

- What of your previous knowledge has been extended or modified by reading this text?

- In what ways might you apply these learnings in your own context? (Please give specific examples of your own ideas and/or adaptations or extensions of ideas presented in the readings.)

- What do you still "**W**ant to Learn" about this topic?

SOURCE: © 2000 by the North Central Regional Educational Laboratory.

FROM THE FIELD

A middle school team has just completed its first cycle of lesson study. The teachers gather for a final meeting and decide to use a "Read and Reflect" activity to guide their discussion. They choose the article "A Lesson Is Like a Swiftly Flowing River" by Catherine Lewis and Ineko Tsuchida (1998) to reflect on their lesson study experience. The team's facilitator modifies the activity to fit the article and the team's experiences. First, the team members individually answer the questions in the "Before you read" section to record their current knowledge of lesson study:

Before you read:

- What do you already know about the unique features, supporting conditions, and potential impact of research lessons?
- What assumptions or biases do you have related to the implementation of research lessons in the United States?
- What more do you want to know about research lessons?

The teachers read the short article individually and write their responses to the questions in the "After you read" section:

After you read:

- What are some of the ideas or strategies you have learned from the article that you did not experience during your own involvement in lesson study?
- What previous knowledge has been extended or modified by reading the article?
- In what ways can you apply the content from this article to your future lesson study cycle?
- What do you still want to learn about research lessons?

The team shares their responses to the questions. Each person talks about how their ideas or opinions have changed and how the article has contributed to their understanding of their own practice. The team uses their reflections to plan their next lesson study cycle.

Reflection not only guides the process of planning, teaching, observing, refining, and reteaching a single lesson, it also helps teachers develop a lesson study report. The two activities are intertwined, because the report can, in turn, serve as a means for teachers to reflect on their learning.

LESSON STUDY REPORTS

In Japan, lesson study teams produce reports about their research lessons. For school-based groups, copies of the reports are kept at the school and are available for other teachers to use. Some reports are also published and sold at bookstores (Fernandez & Yoshida, 2004). The report serves as a means for teachers to reflect on their learning from lesson study, as well as to capture and share their knowledge.

The research lesson is a valuable product of the lesson study cycle. Yet the lesson alone cannot capture the intensive planning and thinking that went into its development. It does not reflect the results of the observation and debriefing or the evidence collected to inform the revision.

The lesson also fails to record the teachers' learning and therefore cannot communicate the professional knowledge they have developed. A beneficial outcome of developing a report is the opportunity it provides for teachers to reflect on and solidify their learning from lesson study.

In spite of the strong rationale for lesson study reports, many teams do not complete this phase of the cycle. The idea of writing what may be perceived as a long document can be a significant barrier for many. Teachers are faced with time constraints and paperwork overload, so it is not surprising that preparing a report may seem like an unnecessary burden. Nevertheless, there are several strategies that can help the lesson study team develop the report quickly and easily.

- **Embed report-writing in the cycle.** Planning and revising the lesson are not the only tasks that the team should work on together. Meetings should also be scheduled to work on the report as a group. Plan for this time at the beginning of the lesson study cycle when the schedule is being developed.
- **Identify multiple uses.** Teachers are often asked to fill out paperwork and reports that are never used. Make sure to identify who will have access to the report when it is finished. Consider how the team and other teachers can use the report to inform their work.
- **Find an audience.** Share the report with administrators and school board members who have expressed interest in lesson study. The report can also be used to stimulate interest among other teachers.

Perhaps the most important strategy is to plan for the report from the beginning of the cycle. When the team members gather the documents and other artifacts from each phase of lesson study on an ongoing basis, a large portion of the report development is already complete. If the team members have the report in mind throughout the lesson study process, they are more likely to preserve these artifacts—accurately piecing together the process as an afterthought will be much more difficult.

Contents of the Report

There is not a set format for a lesson study report. The organization and content of the report should allow the team to document and reflect on the different stages in the process of lesson study. The Lesson Study Research Group at Teachers College recommends that teams use the structure in Figure 7.2 to organize their reports. The guidelines were developed by Sonal Chokshi, Makoto Yoshida, and Clea Fernandez and they are available at the Group's Web site (see the Additional Resources section).

Figure 7.2   Lesson Study Report Contents—Option 1

Goal selection	Describes the goals and the process used to develop them
Planning I	Documents the planning process
Lesson I	Describes the implementation of the lesson and includes the research lesson
Debriefing I	Provides an overview of the evidence discussed and summarizes the comments
Planning II	Documents the revising process
Lesson II	Describes the second implementation of the lesson and includes the revised research lesson
Debriefing II	Provides an overview of the evidence discussed and summarizes the comments
Group Reflections	Describes the challenges that the team faced and the learning that resulted from the lesson study cycle
Individual Reflections	Includes the impressions of the individual team members about the research lesson and about lesson study in general
Appendices	Includes lesson plans, student work, and other artifacts

SOURCE: Lesson Study Report Guidelines. Sonal Chokshi, Makoto Yoshida, & Clea Fernandez. ©2001, Lesson Study Research Group. www.tc.columbia.edu/lessonstudy/tools.html

As an alternative, the teachers might use a structure similar to a more traditional research report (Figure 7.3).

Figure 7.3   Lesson Study Report Contents—Option 2

Background Information	Describes the goals, the research that informed the research lesson, and the planning process
Lesson I	Describes the lesson and its implementation
Results	Documents the evidence discussed during the debriefing and summarizes the revisions made to the lesson
Lesson II	Describes the revised lesson and its implementation
Results	Documents the evidence discussed during the debriefing and summarizes the final revisions made to the lesson
Conclusions	Describes the professional knowledge acquired by the team and the implications of this knowledge for practice

Artifacts are a crucial component of the report. The previous chapters provided suggestions for collecting artifacts from all phases of the lesson study cycle. At this point, the team will have gathered the documents outlined in Figure 7.4.

Figure 7.4   Lesson Study Artifacts

Setting Goals

- Group charter or set of group norms
- Documentation of the development of the research theme
- Research Theme Statement
- Roles/Responsibilities and Schedule for the lesson study action plan

Planning the Research Lesson

- Agendas, notes, and minutes from the planning meetings
- Teacher and facilitator logs
- Records of the background research that the team conducted
- Documents related to the process of mapping the unit and developing the goals
- Drafts of the research lesson
- The final version of the research lesson

Teaching, Observing, and Debriefing

- Observation notes
- Student work
- Photos of the blackboard
- Notes from the debriefing on participants' and team members' observations
- Post-debriefing individual reflection log

Revising and Reteaching

- Notes and logs from the revising process
- Revised lesson plan
- Observation and debriefing notes from the reteaching
- Student work
- Post-debriefing reflection log

PROCESS FOR DEVELOPING THE REPORT

The following process is designed to help a lesson study team use the artifacts they have collected to create a report. It is not meant to prescribe a process or product for all teams. The method can be broken down into the following steps:

1. Gather artifacts.
2. Create a frame.
3. Describe and reflect on the cycle.
4. Write a narrative.

The process can be customized to the needs of the team and the time and resources available for the development of the report. If there is little time, a team can develop a simple report using Steps 1 and 2. If the team decides to create a more elaborate final product, they can proceed through Steps 3 and 4. As they develop the report, it may be helpful for the team members to consider what they would want another teacher to know about the research lesson.

Step 1: Gather Artifacts

Collect the artifacts into a notebook or folder. The idea is to create a collection of the team's work similar to a student portfolio. The list from the previous section identifies the possible pieces that can be included.

It may be helpful to organize the documents around the phases of the lesson study cycle. The team should also consider creating a list of the pieces included, with short descriptions if necessary. This list can help readers from outside the team to get a sense of what is included in the collection and its purpose.

Guiding Questions

- What artifacts do we have of the lesson study cycle?
- Are the pieces self-explanatory, or do they need a short description of their purpose?

Step 2: Create a Frame

The next step is to develop an introduction and a conclusion for the collection of artifacts. This will provide a frame that puts the pieces into context. It will help those outside of the team to interpret the artifacts and gain meaning from them.

The introduction will describe the team members and their backgrounds. The narrative will give an overview of the team's lesson study process and the goals that guided their work. It will also describe the research lesson and the planning that went into it. If the team conducted a pre-observation meeting, that presentation can be adapted and used here.

The conclusion will provide an overview of the revisions made to the research lesson, describing the evidence used to make the changes. The team members will reflect on the impact of lesson study, and they will identify areas for improvement to inform the next cycle.

The team can develop the content for the introduction and conclusion collaboratively with a brainstorming session. This will require one or two teachers who are willing to type up the first draft and make revisions. The team members can also divide up the writing to work on it individually. They will share drafts of the sections and then pull together a final draft.

Guiding Questions

- How can we describe our work?
- What goals guided the development of the research lesson?
- What do we want others to know about the research lesson?
- What has been the impact of lesson study on our practice? Has there been an impact beyond the team?
- How can we improve our work in the next lesson study cycle?

Step 3: Describe and Reflect on the Cycle

If the teachers are able to continue beyond Step 2, they will develop reflective pieces for each phase of the cycle. These narratives will describe the artifacts and summarize significant learning from each tool. Completing this step will help others who read the report to understand the team's process and the outcomes of their work.

Guiding Questions

- How can we describe the work that each artifact represents?
- How did each tool contribute to the lesson study process?
- What professional knowledge resulted from each phase of the cycle?
- What would we do differently next time?

Step 4: Write a Narrative

The final step in developing a report is to bring together the pieces from the previous steps into a continuous narrative. Taking the report to this stage will result in a stand-alone final product that is less like a portfolio. Instead of descriptive pieces that accompany a collection of artifacts, the team will select examples from the collection that can be embedded in the narrative.

If the pieces developed so far are detailed and descriptive, there may be very little additional work involved in Step 4. A structure and transitions may be all that are needed, or the existing pieces may need to be expanded or embellished. It may be helpful to use a format such as Figure 7.2 or Figure 7.3.

If some of the team members enjoy writing, they may want to approach this step as an opportunity to tell the team's story. This type of narrative can be more creative, going beyond the somewhat rigid structure presented here. Writing is an effective means of reflecting on and synthesizing the teachers' professional knowledge.

Guiding Questions

- How can we tell our story?
- What additional information do we need to make this a stand-alone report?
- What are the best artifacts to illustrate the lesson study process and our work?

It is worth repeating that this process is not required to produce a useful report. Some teams develop a final version of the research lesson, based on the second observation and debriefing. For their report, they present the three iterations of the research lesson. Including the debriefing notes as well helps readers to understand the changes that were made.

Some lesson study teams may find the four-step process too cumbersome, or the artifacts may not be available to guide the development of a report. If so, the Lesson Study Report Guidelines included in Form 7.3 can help the team to reflect on the lesson study cycle and create a report. The resulting product can be as simple or as detailed as the team is willing or able to make it.

Form 7.3   Lesson Study Report Guidelines

Priority questions

What did you learn through this cycle of lesson study that can be applied to other areas of your work? What learning can be generalized to other situations?

Student Learning

Pedagogy

Lesson Study Process

In what ways can you improve your lesson study work?

What questions would you like to explore in your next cycle of lesson study?

FROM THE FIELD

In the San Mateo–Foster City School District in California, lesson study got off the ground in 2000. Since that initial year, the program has grown to encompass multiple teams from different schools, content areas, and grade levels.

The teams usually conduct two lesson study cycles over the course of a school year. At the end of the year, the teachers submit a copy of their research lesson, samples of student work, minutes from team meetings, and a conclusion about what they have learned.

The district also holds a meeting in the spring where the lesson study teams are invited to share their work and their experiences. "We use this meeting to hear from groups about what they have learned in their lesson study cycle," says Jackie Hurd, the district's lesson study coordinator. "We also reflect on how our lesson study practice is going and what improvements we could make."

At Highlands Elementary School, where lesson study is a schoolwide practice, the teachers conduct an additional culminating activity. At staff meetings held toward the end of the year, the teams share their work with each other. The teachers talk about the implications of what they have learned for the school overall and begin planning their work for the following year.

ALTERNATIVES TO A REPORT

There are additional ways for lesson study teams to record and share their work with others. One way of doing this is to prepare and conduct a presentation about lesson study. The teachers might report on their work at a district or school board meeting. They could share what they have done with other teachers in the school or the district. An additional advantage of these presentations is that they will potentially generate more interest in lesson study and spark new lesson study groups.

Taking a wider and perhaps more ambitious approach, the lesson study team can submit a presentation for a regional or national conference. Growing interest in lesson study suggests that there may be demand for these types of presentations. Another option, which is much closer to the actual report, is for the teachers to prepare an article about their lesson study cycle for a local or state newsletter, or even for professional journals.

A final option is to hold a meeting at the end of the cycle for the team to reflect on what they have accomplished and what they have learned. If there are multiple teams involved in the project, this can be a time for them to share their work with one another. This type of meeting can also benefit a team working on their own because it gives them an opportunity to celebrate and process their learning and to begin thinking about their next lesson study cycle.

EVALUATING LESSON STUDY

The teachers create the lesson study report, which revolves around sharing their professional knowledge. An evaluation of lesson study will measure the impact of the process and ensure that it is effective. Facilitators or outside consultants are usually responsible for conducting evaluations.

Other possible uses of an evaluation are similar to those of the teacher-driven lesson study report. It can support further funding of lesson study by providing evidence of impact to administrators, school board members, and other stakeholders. An evaluation also may be useful for recruiting additional teachers to join lesson study. The lesson study report may potentially serve as a starting point for an evaluation that will be supplemented with additional information.

Evaluating Professional Development

Thomas Guskey, a professor of educational policy studies and evaluation at the University of Kentucky, has developed a model of the Critical Levels of Professional Development Evaluation (Guskey, 2000). The five levels in his model provide a useful framework for designing evaluations.

1. Participants' reactions

2. Participants' learning

3. Organization support and change

4. Participants' use of new knowledge and skills

5. Student learning outcomes

In the first level—participants' reactions—data are used to reveal whether participants liked the professional development experience and found it to be valuable. Often, this information is gathered through a questionnaire. The second level focuses on knowledge, skills, and attitudes gained from the professional development. Participants' learning can also be captured in a questionnaire, but a more rigorous evaluation will include an assessment rather than relying solely on self-report.

The first two levels of the model are often captured in evaluation efforts, but the other levels of evaluation are less commonly assessed. The middle level of organization support and change is often left unexamined. Document analyses and interviews can be used to measure the effects of professional development at the organizational level.

Change in participants' practices and knowledge is the fourth critical level for evaluation. If teachers do not implement the new knowledge and skills they gain through professional development, improvement efforts will fail. Observing classroom teaching and analyzing lesson plans before and after professional development takes place are ways to measure teachers' use of knowledge and skills.

The final level is the most important—and yet the most difficult—to measure: improvements in student learning outcomes. Student work samples and test scores are rich data sources for measuring student learning outcomes. Student learning can also be affective or social. Student interviews or questionnaires can be used to capture this type of learning.

A single chapter does not provide enough space to address the complexities of designing and conducting an evaluation. This section outlines some of the issues involved in evaluating lesson study. The resources listed in Figure 7.5 provide more detailed guidance and support.

It is helpful to consider two kinds of evaluation: formative and summative. Each type may be used for different purposes in evaluating lesson study.

Formative Evaluation

The purpose of a formative evaluation is to provide procedural knowledge that can help guide the lesson study process. This involves collecting and analyzing data

Figure 7.5   Evaluation Resources

Cook, C. J., & Fine, C. S. (1997). *Critical issue: Evaluating professional growth and development.* Naperville, IL: North Central Regional Educational Laboratory. Available online at www.ncrel.org/sdrs/areas/issues/educatrs/profdevl/pd500.htm

Frechtling, J. (2002). *The 2002 user-friendly handbook for project evaluation.* Arlington, VA: National Science Foundation. Available online at www.nsf.gov/pubs/2002/nsf02057/start.htm

Frechtling, J., & Sharp, L. (Eds.). (1997). *User-friendly handbook for mixed method evaluations.* Arlington, VA: National Science Foundation. Available online at www.ehr.nsf.gov/EHR/REC/pubs/NSF97-153/START.HTM

Guskey, T. R. (2000). *Evaluating professional development.* Thousand Oaks, CA: Corwin Press. (See especially Chapter 3: "Practical Guidelines for Evaluating Professional Development")

Killion, J. (2002). *Assessing impact: Evaluating staff development.* Oxford, OH: National Staff Development Council.

---

about the cycle as it unfolds. Ongoing feedback and improvement loops are a key component of formative evaluation. Unlike summative evaluation, it is not concerned with generalizability and replicability.

Many of the tools from the previous chapters can be used as formative evaluation tools. The following are some suggestions for using the artifacts as evidence for an evaluation.

Teacher logs (Planning—Form 4.3, Debriefing—Form 5.3, Revising—Form 6.1). These logs record what happened during the lesson study process. They are meant to be completed by each teacher involved in the lesson study group. The information can be used to cross-check with the facilitator's logs and to provide information about interactions. The logs document both the content and duration of the cycle, as well as results of the group activities.

Facilitator logs (Planning—Form 4.4). The log is designed for a lesson study facilitator to fill out at the end of each meeting or event. They allow for a running record of how much time is spent on lesson study, who is involved, and the purpose and outcomes of the meetings. When the logs are used formatively, they serve as a continuous measure of the team's lesson study practice and the results of their work. The facilitator also makes note of the challenges or barriers that the team faces. With this knowledge, the teachers can focus on what is working and create solutions for what is not as successful. Without such a tool, it is easy to go through the process without realizing that key components of lesson study may be missing.

3–2–1 Reflections (Form 7.1). The results of this reflection activity can be used to assess how the individuals and the team as a whole have progressed in their understanding of lesson study. Identifying unanswered questions and action items that have not been addressed will help the team identify areas of need to address in their future work.

Lesson documents. The lesson plan and revised lesson plan can help participants to see where the research lesson began and what progress has been made. Reviewing these documents can help the team identify key learnings and areas for further development.

Student work. This is possibly the most important formative evaluation tool. Student work from the research lesson will help the lesson study team gauge student understanding. Team members should analyze student work and look for evidence that students made progress toward the learning goals.

Observation and debriefing notes. These notes can serve as data for determining whether the objectives of the research lesson were met. Looking at the quality of the notes and thinking about their usefulness in assessing and refining the research lesson is also helpful. The team may identify this as an area in need of improvement for their lesson study practice.

Reflections. These may be informal, personal accounts of the lesson study process. If the team reviews the reflections on an ongoing basis, they may gain perspective that can help improve the interactions and work of the group before the end of the cycle.

Once the data and artifacts are collected, a qualitative analysis approach can be used to reveal themes. The analysis should solidify or discount previous claims about the effectiveness and impact of lesson study. The beauty of formative evaluation is its continuous nature. Once data are analyzed, the results can be used right away—unanswered questions or future implications can be immediately addressed.

Summative Evaluation

The purpose of summative evaluation is to gauge the value of lesson study. Summative evaluation is focused on outcomes. It will assess the lesson study team's success in fulfilling its purpose and producing positive results. One of the distinctions between formative and summative evaluation is that the former takes place during the lesson study process, whereas the latter is completed after a cycle has ended.

Conducting a credible summative evaluation requires criteria that will be used to make judgments about lesson study. The criteria must be established before the data are collected and analyzed. It may be helpful for lesson study teams to agree on learning goals for themselves to identify the criteria and evidence necessary to evaluate their lesson study efforts. In addition, the school mission and goals may be used, especially as they relate to the research theme.

Another source of criteria or indicators for a summative evaluation of lesson study is a list of potential areas of impact. Chapter 1 described the initial outcomes of lesson study that have emerged from research studies and evaluations. They include improvements in the following areas:

- Collaboration
- Knowledge of subject matter
- Instructional knowledge
- Researcher stance
- Attention to student learning
- Lesson planning

In her research on lesson study in the United States and Japan, Catherine Lewis has identified a set of key pathways through which teachers improve instruction (Lewis, 2005). These pathways are listed in Figure 7.6.

Figure 7.6   Lesson Study—Key Learning Pathways

- Increased knowledge of subject matter

- Increased knowledge of instruction

- Increased ability to observe students

- Stronger collegial networks

- Stronger connection of daily practice to long-term goals

- Stronger motivation and sense of efficacy

- Improved quality of available lesson plans

SOURCE: Lewis, C. (2005). How do teachers learn during lesson study? In P. Wang-Iverson & M. Yoshida (Eds.), *Building our understanding of lesson study* (pp. 77–84). Philadelphia: Research for Better Schools.

Form 7.4 is a sample evidence log based on Lewis's key pathways. The log can be used to monitor and track the team's lesson study practice throughout the cycle. By documenting the aspects of lesson study that were put into practice, the evaluation can provide an accurate picture of implementation and avoid measuring outcomes for something that never actually took place. This is a common weakness of program evaluation: measuring the alleged effects of a "treatment" that never happened.

The tools and artifacts described in the formative evaluation section can also be used for a summative evaluation. For example, the teacher and facilitator logs can be analyzed to identify changes in teachers' lesson study practice or knowledge of content and instruction. Analyzing the original lesson plan, each revision, and the final version may provide evidence of curricular improvement. The research lessons can also be analyzed with a rubric to determine how well they reflect the characteristics of high-quality learning experiences. This documentation can be supplemented with teacher interviews and questionnaires.

Form 7.4   Evidence Log—Key Learning Pathways

1. Increased knowledge of subject matter
Evidence:
Barriers:
2. Increased knowledge of instruction
Evidence:
Barriers:
3. Increased ability to observe students
Evidence:
Barriers:
4. Stronger collegial networks
Evidence:
Barriers:
5. Stronger connection of daily practice to long-term goals
Evidence:
Barriers:
6. Stronger motivation and sense of efficacy
Evidence:
Barriers:
7. Improved quality of available lesson plans
Evidence:
Barriers:

FROM THE FIELD

In the Pawtucket School District, we started doing lesson study in 2002. My colleagues and I always knew we should be evaluating the program. But as is often the case with people who aren't evaluating, it was a matter of resources and staff. We barely had time to do lesson study—there weren't any resources for evaluation.

So evaluation was something that we had to build up to. The evaluation that we did in 2004 came about because I was in a doctoral program, and it was a way for me to combine my work with a project for school. That project made it possible for me to dedicate the extra time and effort to an evaluation.

There's no question that we need to evaluate to make sure that our efforts are being productive. I had two additional reasons that I wanted to evaluate lesson study. First, I wanted to demonstrate to the district that they had supported a worthwhile effort and that it was making a difference. Second, I wanted the people who were participating in lesson study to have a mirror to see what they were doing. Lesson study takes commitment and effort on the part of teachers, who have lots of challenges and lots of other things on their agendas. So one of my major motivations for doing the evaluation was for the teachers to see the results of their work. It needed to be more that just us saying, "Oh, it's working. It's successful, and you're learning so much." I wanted them to see evidence.

The evaluation also helped us to identify some things that we need to do differently. One of the big issues we uncovered was that the teachers wanted lesson study to spread, and they saw themselves in the pilot role. That came through very clearly, that there needed to be more opportunities for them to bring in their colleagues and widen participation.

To be able to conduct evaluations of lesson study, districts need accessible tools, as well as some guidance on how to use them. The other thing that helps to keep lesson study going, in general, is someone in a facilitator role. My experience is that teachers are just too busy to be the apparatus and the structure. So if a school or a district has people who are facilitating lesson study, evaluation could be included in their responsibilities.

~Andre Audette, Regents Fellow, Rhode Island
Department of Elementary and Secondary Education,
(former standards coordinator for the Pawtucket School District)

NOTE: The instrument used to evaluate lesson study at Pawtucket is included in Form 7.5.

A credible evaluation will validate both positive and negative outcomes that result from the lesson study process. As the team members learn to trust each other to provide constructive criticism regarding the lesson, so too must the evaluation concentrate on honest assessments of the lesson study process. This can be challenging, especially when the results may determine whether future lesson study activities are possible.

The stakes make be high, but the findings should describe areas for improvement and further investigation rather than focusing exclusively on positive outcomes. Lesson study is intended to be a long-term effort of continuous improvement. Summative evaluations must reflect this long-term perspective. Rather than determining success or failure after one or two years of lesson study, the evaluation should examine and document growth over time.

Form 7.5   Pawtucket Lesson Study Questionnaire

Part 1: Lesson Study Workshops	Disagree				Agree
1. I understood the goals and process of lesson study (LS) prior to starting a LS cycle.	1	2	3	4	5
2. The materials provided were helpful to develop my understanding of LS.	1	2	3	4	5
3. The introductory activities were helpful to develop my understanding of LS.	1	2	3	4	5
4. I found the time to collaborate with my LS group members helpful to develop my understanding of LS.	1	2	3	4	5
5. The facilitation helped me to develop my understanding of LS.	1	2	3	4	5
6. The workshops provided me enough time to develop my understanding of LS.	1	2	3	4	5
7. The workshops were held at convenient times for me.	1	2	3	4	5
8. The workshops were valuable.	1	2	3	4	5

Part 2: The Lesson Study Cycle	Disagree				Agree
9. Meetings during the LS cycle were held at convenient times.	1	2	3	4	5
10. I was able to attend all of the meetings during the LS cycle.	1	2	3	4	5
11. My LS team collaborated effectively to plan a research lesson.	1	2	3	4	5
12. The research lesson matched our overarching goal.	1	2	3	4	5
13. My LS group used textbooks, research, or other outside information to help plan the research lesson.	1	2	3	4	5
14. We had an opportunity during the LS cycle to do the problem of the research lesson to help anticipate student understanding.	1	2	3	4	5
15. Developing the research lesson allowed me to think deeply about issues in my content or teaching.	1	2	3	4	5
16. Developing the research lesson allowed me to increase my content knowledge.	1	2	3	4	5
17. Developing the research lesson allowed me to better understand student thinking and/or challenges in my content.	1	2	3	4	5

(Continued)

Form 7.5 (Continued)

		Disagree			Agree	
18.	Observing student learning and thinking during the teaching of the research lesson was an important learning opportunity.	1	2	3	4	5
19.	I feel our research lesson was successful.	1	2	3	4	5
20.	Participating in a LS cycle was a valuable professional development activity.	1	2	3	4	5

Part 3: Applying and Learning From Lesson Study	**Disagree**			**Agree**	
21. I gained specific new understandings about my content and teaching from LS.	1	2	3	4	5
22. I have been able to apply these new understandings to my teaching.	1	2	3	4	5
23. I think about lesson planning and my teaching differently as a result of participating in LS.	1	2	3	4	5
24. I more carefully select instructional materials and questions as a result of LS.	1	2	3	4	5
25. I anticipate and plan for student understanding in my lessons as a result of LS.	1	2	3	4	5
26. Lesson Study has helped me to be a better teacher.	1	2	3	4	5

What do you think are the strengths of lesson study?

What are your concerns about lesson study?

What suggestions do you have that would help us better implement lesson study?

Useful summative evaluations will also address a number of different audiences. The findings can be used to demonstrate the outcomes of lesson study to a variety of stakeholders, including teachers, administrators, funding sources, school boards, and parents. The conclusions from the Northern Michigan Lesson Study Initiative are included in the following vignette. The findings from this case study were also developed into a poster format—see Figure 7.7. Using this medium to present the findings at stakeholder meetings can help ensure that the summative evaluation data reach a broad audience.

Figure 7.7   Evaluation Findings—Poster Format

Case Study: Northern Michigan Lesson Study Initiative

Description	Methodology

4 Lesson Study Groups
 	
• Multidistrict Group
 	
   – 3 high school biology teachers
   – Focused on photosynthesis and respiration
 	
• Traverse City Public Schools
 	
   – 7 elementary school teachers
   – Focused on 5th grade science lesson on weather, specifically barometric pressure
 	
• Pine River Area Schools
 	
   – 4 middle and 2 elementary school teachers
   – Focused on science lesson about inherited traits
 	
• Suttons Bay Elementary School
 	
   – 4 elementary school teachers
   – Focused on mathematics lesson on value vs. quantity of coins
 	
Professional Development
 	
• Each group received technical assistance, including initial training, content expertise, classroom observations, and group discussion support from an outside facilitator and "knowledgeable other."
	Data Collection Tools
	
	• Facilitator Activity Log
	
	   – Activity Information (# hours, # participants)
	   – Description of activity
	
	• Teacher Activity Log
	
	   – Activity Information (# hours, # participants)
	   – Description of activity
	
	• 7 Key Experiences Evidence Log
	
	   – Evidence and Barriers for each experience
	
	• Videotaped Interviews
	
	• 3-2-1 Reflections
	
	• Lesson Revision Documents
	
	Analyses
	
	• Qualitative analysis of logs, interviews, reflections, and lesson revision documents.
	• Theoretical lens of "Professional Development 'In' Work" (Bredeson, 2003).

Outcomes

Implementation & Results

• **Evidence of 7 Key Experiences of Lesson Study (Lewis, 2001)**

  1. Think Carefully About the Goals of a Particular Content Area, Unit, and Lesson:
     Redesigned lesson when included too many concepts. Focused on one goal per lesson.

(Continued)

Figure 7.7 (Continued)

2. Think Deeply About Long-Term Goals for Students:
   Weak evidence for this experience is shown.

3. Study the Best Available Lessons:
   Reviewed numerous materials that taught similar concepts.

4. Learn Subject Matter:
   Appeared to have improved, though gaps in understanding still remain. Needed to focus more on content of lesson before trying to create a lesson plan.

5. Develop Instructional Knowledge:
   Spent a large amount of time addressing how to get students involved in their learning.

6. Build Capacity for Collegial Learning:
   Strong relationships formed among group members as they planned and discussed in a positive and encouraging manner. The focus was on the whole group's lesson.

7. Develop "The Eyes to See Students":
   Planned what to look for during the observation of the lesson, such as students' conceptual understanding and engagement.

- **Barriers**
  Time, poor content knowledge, commitment to traditional teaching strategies, reliance on textbooks, dependence on curriculum of previous and following grades, short-term thinking

Conclusions

- **Facilitator Effect**
  Helped the group think about the lesson in new ways, kept the group focused on the lesson, and recorded the group's process.

- **"Knowledgeable Other" Effect**
  Brought valuable pedagogical content knowledge to the group, provided additional lens for classroom observation of the lesson.

- **Teacher Change**
  Teachers report lesson study has made a difference in how they approach a lesson and how they view student learning.

FROM THE FIELD

The structure of the Northern Michigan Lesson Study Initiative professionally supported the participating teachers' practice more effectively than their previous individual approaches and informal collegial activities. The facilitators of each lesson study group helped the participants think about the lesson in new ways, kept the team focused on the lesson, and recorded the group's process. The "knowledgeable other" brought valuable pedagogical content knowledge to the group, and provided an additional lens for classroom observation of the lesson.

Most important, teachers reported that lesson study has made a difference in how they approach a lesson and how they view student learning. At the beginning of the lesson study process, participants were drawn to the ideas of collaboration, quality teaching and best practices, process, student learning, and reflection. They were concerned about the time it would take and how to build support in their schools for this initiative. Teachers vowed to focus more on student learning and to find allies among their colleagues for lesson study.

This case study has implications for further research. On a general level, there are several questions that remain unanswered: How can the "knowledgeable other" effectively build teachers' content knowledge in the beginning stages of lesson study? What is a reasonable time line for a lesson study group to implement all elements of the designing, teaching, redesigning, and reteaching process? In other environments, how have teachers successfully focused on long-term goals for students? Though there are many questions still to answer, the results from this case study provide valuable insight into the challenges and advantages of implementing the lesson study process.

TYING REFLECTION AND EVALUATION TO A NEW CYCLE OF LESSON STUDY

Reflection and evaluation support the continuous nature of lesson study. As they begin a new cycle, the lesson study team will build on the results of their work so far. A celebration is in order—both to look back at the team's successes and to anticipate the work ahead.

The next cycle will build on the teachers' learning and their progress toward their goals. The team will also consider the changes they want to make in their future lesson study practice (Lewis, 2002b).

KEY IDEAS

- Reflection is an essential part of learning how to engage in the core elements of lesson study and of gaining knowledge from the process.
- The lesson study report is a means for teachers to reflect on their learning, to capture what they have learned, and to share their professional knowledge with others.
- Conducting an evaluation of lesson study will help the team to identify areas for improvement.
- An evaluation can also contribute by helping to determine lesson study's impact and effectiveness.

8

Growing and Sustaining Lesson Study

T he challenges associated with completing even one cycle of lesson study are significant. Once a cycle is complete—whether it is the first or the fifteenth—the team should take time to celebrate their hard work and accomplishments. Nevertheless, lesson study is not a series of independent cycles, but a continual effort to accumulate professional knowledge. Sustaining teachers' efforts and creating a long-term, ongoing approach is crucial to its success. It is important to look to the future and plan the next steps.

MAINTAINING MOMENTUM

Schools in the United States tend to have a short attention span when it comes to trying new things. Often administrators and teachers will find something new they want to try that has promise to help improve teaching and learning. When the results are slow to appear, an innovation is often abandoned and the search resumed for the next new thing. The danger with lesson study, in particular, is that the team may give up before they have really learned how to do lesson study well.

After completing one or two lesson study cycles, teachers sometimes lose their initial enthusiasm for lesson study. This may occur because the novelty of collaboration wears off. Some of the team members may run out of steam, tiring from such demanding work. Other changes—such as a new curriculum or district initiative—may shift teachers' priorities away from lesson study.

Taking time to celebrate and recognize the team's accomplishments can help to create energy for the next lesson study cycle. This can take many different forms. Plan an event to mark the completion of the research lesson, such as an afterschool

153

party sponsored by the school or a dinner that the team members organize themselves. Provide recognition for the team with an announcement about their work in a district newsletter or on the school Web site. Even a short letter from an administrator thanking the teachers for their efforts can be a powerful gesture.

Maintaining realistic expectations will also help the team continue to move forward. First, do not try to do too much. It may be possible to fit two or three lesson study cycles into a school year, but it is not necessary to do so. It may be tempting to squeeze in as much as possible to increase the number of research lessons that are developed. This is not likely to result in more *learning* if the teachers are rushing through the process. In Japan, a school may have up to five or six research lessons in the span of one year because there are multiple teams, but an individual team usually completes only one or two cycles (Fernandez & Yoshida, 2004).

It will also be helpful to take steps to prevent the teachers from burning out. The team members should rotate responsibilities rather than always looking to the same people to coordinate logistics, lead meetings, or teach lessons.

The ideas in the rest of this chapter will also contribute to maintaining momentum. By hosting an open house, the lesson study team will gain energy from sharing their work with a broader audience and receiving positive feedback. Opportunities for teachers who have gained experience to serve as facilitators for beginning teams contribute new challenges and often help teachers sustain their enthusiasm.

DEALING WITH TURNOVER

Although changes in membership can contribute to a team's loss of momentum, turnover is usually unavoidable. Teachers' mobility is common in most schools and districts. Turnover is also common in Japan, where teachers change their assignments and rotate through different grade levels frequently at the elementary level (Stevenson & Stigler, 1992). The system is organized this way so that teachers will broaden their knowledge by teaching different grade levels.

As a result, the membership of school-based Japanese lesson study teams changes frequently. This turnover is viewed as an asset. It allows cross-pollination, with new members contributing the knowledge they developed with their previous team. Japanese teachers have an advantage that makes it possible for them to take this perspective—they have frequent experiences with lesson study, and it is a regular part of their professional lives (Fernandez, 2002). Teachers in the United States do not yet have this opportunity.

Outreach efforts can help to ease the transition by increasing these opportunities. Extending invitations to other teachers when a research lesson is taught and observed is a good way for them to experience lesson study. Team members can share what they are doing with their colleagues, both informally and formally.

To sustain lesson study over the long term, facilitators and teams will need to carefully consider how to bring in new members. Begin by sharing the team's charter or the list of group norms. The beginning of each lesson study cycle is a good time to reflect on the list and make any needed changes. Asking new members for their own additions or suggestions can be very easily worked into the update process. New members can also get up to speed by reading the research lessons and reports that the team has created.

The facilitator or the leader of each meeting should ensure that new team members are participating in the planning of the lesson, rather than remaining on the periphery of the group. Unless new members feel otherwise, it may be helpful to hold off on asking them to teach a lesson. This will allow them to participate in a cycle, becoming more familiar with the process and more comfortable with the team.

ADDING TEAMS AND SITES

Issues of scale are often thought of only in terms of increasing the number of teachers or schools involved in an innovation. Equally important—especially considering complex efforts such as lesson study—are issues around maintaining the depth and integrity of the program. More sophisticated models look into other dimensions of scale in addition to breadth—depth, sustainability, and shifting ownership to teachers (Coburn, 2003).

The issue of breadth or spread is not just a matter of increasing the numbers of teachers or schools involved. The norms of participation must become embedded in the policies and practices of the district and schools. That is why effective professional development addresses more than just teacher learning. It also focuses on increasing school capacity to support improved instruction by creating a professional community and developing a coherent approach that is sustained over time (Carpenter et al., 2004; King & Newmann, 2000).

Because of the challenges in creating and maintaining depth and sustainability, it is usually best to aim for gradual growth rather than a quick push for widespread participation. This allows for a more natural progression, with teachers joining in as their interest grows. It also makes it possible for school and district leaders to make the necessary changes in policy, which tend to move at a very slow pace. Creating the conditions that support professional learning communities—which are highlighted in Chapter 2—are prerequisites for a growing and sustainable lesson study program:

- Common Goals
- Mutual Trust and Respect
- Collective Inquiry
- Reflective Dialogue
- Supportive and Shared Leadership
- Continuous Learning Opportunities

Recruiting teachers for additional lesson study teams will call for some of the same strategies that were used to recruit teachers to the first team—reviewing that section of Chapter 2 may prove helpful. The advantage is that now teachers will not have to look outside the school or district to experience lesson study firsthand. It may also be helpful for the original team to recommend people who they think will be interested in participating. Some of the strategies for recruiting teachers include

- Writing invitational letters
- Conducting informational meetings
- Inviting potential new members to attend an observation and debriefing

The pioneering lesson study team, or teams, is a key part of any effort to generate more interest. Teams can help by making short presentations at staff meetings or holding a general informational meeting dedicated to lesson study. The team members can share their work, what they learned, and what they find most valuable about lesson study.

A crucial strategy for scaling up innovative approaches to teacher learning is to make sure that new groups are connected in some way to the original group

(Carpenter et al., 2004). To create these links, teachers from the first team or teams can work with new teams as facilitators. This is often ideal because the local facilitators benefit from both an understanding of lesson study and knowledge of the local needs and issues that teachers face.

The original team will not serve as a model that can simply be replicated with new people in new settings (Hargreaves & Fink, 2000). Every group will be different. Teachers will need to modify the structural and procedural aspects to meet their needs, while also maintaining the substance and spirit of lesson study.

> *I often think of the Fibonacci sequence (1, 2, 3, 5, 8 . . .). I think that you have to experience lesson study the first time just as a participant. And then later you'll experience as a participant but yet you are also thinking as a facilitator. And then you become a facilitator. And more groups spawn. I think that lesson study is going to grow, but it's a plant of slow growth and it has to be sturdy and that makes it even stronger.*
>
> ~Dr. Joanne Caniglia, professor of
> mathematics, Eastern Michigan University

FROM THE FIELD

When the lesson study process first began emerging in the professional literature five to eight years ago, we were intrigued by it. But we did not believe that we had the capacity to do lesson study on our own. So gathering external resources—which was primarily people trained in this process who had experienced it and had worked with other districts—was our big challenge. When we brought those folks in, we moved along with amazing rapidity.

Lesson study helped us and allowed us a very specific process to improve our work with teachers. We actually have to turn people away. That's a great problem to have, but it's a capacity issue. How do you scale this up in such a way to maintain the quality of the lesson study process and still accommodate all the people who want to participate?

One of the questions we've asked ourselves is do we want to triage people? For example, we have some people who have participated in lesson study for three years. They have developed high capability with this, and they are probably ready to be group leaders themselves. We have other senior staff who are interested in it and would like to participate. We also have some junior staff who have not had such opportunities and we'd like to be able to bring them along. So we are trying to identify the entry-level skills in terms of participating in lesson study in a meaningful way. How do we help teachers learn to use this process more or less on their own?

~Eric Dreier, science coordinator

Lesson study has been a critical part of my learning. So my one desire is to see lesson study continue. It would be great to spread lesson study throughout the district. My hope would be to continue the process next year so that it's an integral part of everybody's teaching. I think it's great professional development.

So I'm wondering, where do we go from here? I'd love to keep this team together and go on to a new lesson next year. Or would it be better to try to bring in new teachers, share what we've done? I see the value in both. I would love to help the other teachers and be more of a facilitator. But, boy, I don't want to give up the opportunity for myself too. I really have learned a lot from it.

~Linda Egeler, teacher

EMBEDDING LESSON STUDY

Lesson study is not intended to be a stand-alone effort. It is not likely to be sustainable—or to reach optimal effectiveness—if it is not tightly connected to a coherent professional development program. Lesson study should be one aspect of a school culture devoted to professional learning.

When lesson study begins with a single team of teachers and a school or district begins to look for ways to expand the number of teachers involved, efforts should be made to embed lesson study in other professional development and school improvement efforts. When lesson study has a place in the broader professional development system, it will be more likely to be sustained as the needs and priorities of the school change.

Ideally, the research theme will serve as a common goal for all professional development. A school might decide that an area of need is differentiated instruction. Lesson study teams will conduct their work to gain knowledge of this topic. But teachers and administrators will also use differentiated instruction as the focus for other learning experiences such as attending conferences, visiting other schools, taking classes, and conducting study groups.

Similarly, lesson study can serve as a follow-up activity for summer institutes or workshops. For example, a school might identify a specific content area as a focus, based on student achievement and other sources of data. Teachers might begin their work with a weeklong institute during the summer focused on that content area. They could then conduct one or two cycles of lesson study to develop research lessons in the content area, applying what they have learned to their classrooms.

HOSTING AN OPEN HOUSE

A lesson study open house is a one-day event in which a school or district invites people to participate in observing and discussing research lessons. Such events usually take place at sites with multiple lesson study teams. On a smaller scale, even a single team can open up their lesson to other teachers in the district or the region.

A lesson study open house is *not* a showcase, but a learning experience. Teachers in the United States need more opportunities to participate in lesson study, both those who are new to the idea and experienced teams. Open houses help to broaden the lesson study community. Holding an open house is an excellent way to kick off an effort to scale up lesson study.

When lesson study teams present their research lessons at an open house, they gain additional insight into their work. The guests bring fresh eyes to the lesson. Open houses are also a means for spreading professional knowledge. The teachers share what they have learned with colleagues outside the team. Open houses can help to build a network of teachers and other educators to support lesson study. The team has an opportunity to discuss the benefits and challenges of doing lesson study with other experienced practitioners.

Attending research lessons presented by other teams contributes to teachers' professional growth and their knowledge of conducting lesson study. Participating as a member of a team is only one way that teachers improve their lesson study practice. Attending an open house is an opportunity to practice skills for observing students, reflecting on an episode of teaching, and contributing to the debriefing.

Planning and holding an open house will require some additional effort. The Open House Action Plan in Form 8.1 helps illustrate the decisions that are involved in planning an open house, but it should not be considered an exhaustive list of all the tasks involved.

FROM THE FIELD

At Meadows Elementary School in Lacey, Washington, three teams culminated their first year of lesson study with an open house. At the beginning of the year, several of the teachers were somewhat reluctant to begin lesson study. But as they went on to plan, teach, observe, and debrief their first research lessons, they saw the contributions that lesson study made to their professional growth. "A personal 'ah-ha' is the realization that it is not the amount of time I spend with my students, but the quality of my instruction getting at the heart of their understanding," says Heather Rader, a fifth-grade teacher.

As the teams began their second cycle, they were presented with an opportunity to hold an open house at their school. As part of a larger lesson study event, the open house would draw about 70 observers from around the country to participate in the observation and debriefing of their research lessons. One teacher's initial response was one of disbelief: "We can't fit 25 observers in the room! Where will we put them?" Another expressed with great concern, "I've just gotten over teaching in front of my colleagues. How could I possibly teach with 25 strangers in my room?"

When the teachers considered the benefits of holding an open house, both to themselves and to the educational community, they overcame their initial reluctance. With support from their principal, the teams decided to tackle this challenge and prepare for the open house.

Several months later and after much logistical coordination and planning, the open house began with a pre-observation meeting. Each team shared the underlying concepts that the lesson was designed to address and discussed the decisions that had informed their planning. About 20 observers crowded into each of the three classrooms to observe the lesson and collect data on student learning. At the debriefing, the Meadows team members were very excited to have the opportunity to share their work but, more important, to engage in valuable conversations about student learning, content, and instruction. In addition, there were many positive responses from the invited guests:

- "Today has moved my thinking to lesson study as a long-range process as opposed to an experience."
- "Lesson study is a huge change that is needed in our thinking as educators—it is how to create thinkers—what real learning is all about."
- "Today I saw the value of the post-lesson discussion in supporting teacher learning. Asking good questions helped to push the teachers more to reflect on how they met their goal."

In spite of their initial hesitancy about holding an open house at their school and the hard work it required, the Meadows teachers were enthusiastic about the knowledge and momentum that they gained. "Having the lesson study open house at Meadows was stressful," said first-grade teacher Anna McCourt. "But it was very valuable because it gave us many eyes to observe our students and some useful feedback."

Form 8.1   Lesson Study Open House Action Plan

Initial planning

1. Schedule the event—Determine when the lesson will be taught. Lesson study teams usually present the revised lesson rather than the first teaching. Create a tentative agenda for the event.

2. Determine the target number of attendees that can be accommodated—How many teams are available to teach lessons? How many extra people will fit in the classrooms?

3. Identify locations—Where will the pre-observation, the teaching, and the debriefing be held? If there will be one research lesson and more people than can be accommodated in a classroom, the lesson can be held in a larger room, such as the cafeteria or the gym.

4. Invite participants—Draw up a list of people to invite and develop a registration process. If the site can accommodate a larger number of people, the team might want to post an announcement about the event.

5. Invite others—Identify knowledgeable others and final commentators and invite them to participate.

At least one month before the event

6. Students—If the event will be held during school hours, teachers' classes will need to be covered. If not, arrangements will need to be made to bring students to the school for the lesson.

7. Refreshments—Will the school be providing food and drinks for participants? Will participants be on-site during lunch?

At least one week before the event

8. Create materials—Gather resources for participants. The packets will include the agenda for the day, a map of the school, a copy of the research lesson, and any other helpful materials.

The day before

9. Put up signs—Each classroom should be clearly marked. Arrows that direct participants on how to get between rooms and to the restrooms will also be helpful.

GOALS FOR TEACHER LEARNING

To ensure that the lesson study team continues their professional growth, it may be helpful to identify individual goals or a team goal that is focused on teacher learning. The idea is to make lesson study more intentional and to emphasize the learning that is the primary outcome of the process.

Teacher learning goals are not a standard part of the lesson study model. Yet without purposeful attention, teams may take part in the process without ever advancing their lesson study practice or their professional knowledge. The goals are intended to help teachers grow in their ability to conduct lesson study. They will help team members identify and reflect on the learning that they gain. The goals can also be used to connect teacher learning with goals for students.

As the needs of the team change over time, the focus of the goals is also likely to change. A group of teachers beginning their first lesson study cycle may want to concentrate on improving their knowledge of the lesson study process. Just getting a sense of what lesson study looks like and feels like is a very significant first step. Other appropriate goals might involve building rapport among team members or overcoming isolation.

After this, building skills in some of the specific lesson study practices may be helpful—for example, writing rich and meaningful goals or gaining better understanding of the curriculum. A goal might involve additional effort outside of the lesson study cycle. Teachers may want to build their observation skills to collect better data during the lesson and contribute to a more substantive debriefing. They might spend time observing students in other teachers' classrooms. Other possible goals of this type include improving the connection between goals and the lesson or developing better research hypotheses.

Another strategy for identifying goals is to start with the Core Elements of Lesson Study (Figure 1.2) or Catherine Lewis's (2005) Key Learning Pathways (Figure 7.6). Which of the core elements have received less emphasis in the work so far? Are there learning pathways that the team has not experienced?

The goals for teacher learning can also contribute to an evaluation of lesson study. When the teachers are working toward specific goals, it is easier to identify criteria and outcomes for assessing their efforts. The goals will also inform the type of data to be collected and thus the instruments and methods to be used in the evaluation.

FINAL THOUGHTS

The purpose of this book is to lay out a concrete and systematic approach to engaging in lesson study. Whenever possible, both ideal and somewhat more realistic paths have been set. Reaching the ideal approach to lesson study will not be possible in many situations. Nevertheless, it can be helpful to keep these ideals in mind as something to strive for over time. The following are some of the things that contribute to a sustainable program in which teachers will continually improve their lesson study practice.

- Dedicated time during the school day for teachers to work together on at least a weekly basis
- Support from building and district administrators

- A coherent professional development program
- Site-based facilitators and a coordinator to manage logistics and other details
- Access to knowledgeable others and other outside resources
- High-quality curricula that are coherent and standards based
- Opportunities for teachers to participate in lesson study beyond their work as a team
- Time for teams to reflect on their work, complete reports, and share their knowledge
- Information from formative and summative evaluations to inform program improvements and justify lesson study as a valid professional development model

These features may be the ideal, but they are not prerequisites for conducting lesson study. Moreover, they will not ensure that lesson study teams will have meaningful experiences in which they generate professional knowledge. Teachers are the driving force behind the power of lesson study. They help to ensure its success by adopting a reflective and thoughtful perspective on their participation. This means looking beyond just the surface features—research lessons, observations, debriefings, and reports. Doing lesson study by the book is not as important as embracing its substance and its spirit.

- Are the goals guiding the lesson plan?
- Are teachers studying teaching materials?
- Are teachers gaining new ideas?
- Are teachers gaining knowledge about how students learn?
- Are teachers developing new understanding of content and how to teach it?
- Are teachers pushing themselves and trying new things?
- Are teachers reflecting on their work and their learning?

Resource A

Sample Research Lessons

SAMPLE LESSON 1

Fourth-Grade Science Research Lesson

School: Traverse City Area Elementary Schools, Betha Voss, Cherry Knoll, Norris, Oak Park, and Westwood

Date: 2005

Instructor: Robin Brister

Team Members: Robin Brister, Linda Egeler, Mary Jeffrey, Kathy Johnston, Abby Leppien, Karen Nelson, and Kristen Sak

1. Title of the Lesson: Modeling for Student Observations and Deductive Thinking

2. Lesson Study Goals

   Students will learn to do the following:

   a. Apply previously learned knowledge and skills to identify unknown chemicals.
   b. Work collaboratively to solve problems.
   c. Make careful observations of both positive and negative results.
   d. Use deductive reasoning based on evidence to narrow choices.

3. Relationship between this lesson and Michigan's Science Curriculum Framework

Constructing New Scientific Knowledge
  a. Generate questions about the world based on observation.
  b. Develop solutions to problems through reasoning, observation, and investigation.
  c. Construct charts and graphs and prepare summaries of observations.

Reflecting on Scientific Knowledge
  a. Develop an awareness of the need for evidence in making decisions scientifically.

Physical Science: Matter and Energy
  a. Classify common objects and substances according to observable attributes/properties.

Physical Science: Changes in Matter
  a. Describe common physical changes in matter (e.g., dissolving).
  b. Prepare mixtures and separate them into their component parts.

ABOUT THIS LESSON

Why did we choose this topic for lesson study?

In this unit, "Chemical Tests," students investigate unknown solids (sugar, alum, talc, baking soda, and cornstarch). They explore physical properties of these solids, including water mixtures. Students then move on to testing these unknown solids with three different chemical liquids: vinegar, iodine, and red cabbage juice. Heat is the next test that is applied to the unknown solids.

Through careful testing, observing, and recording data on reactions that occur, students summarize their test results. There were several factors that led us to design this particular lesson for lesson study.

- Students tend to focus on positive results when trying to identify an unknown solid rather than making deductions based on both positive and negative results.
- Students tend to jump to conclusions about the identity of an unknown.

Why is it important to have this lesson at this particular time in students' learning?

This lesson draws on the prior knowledge that students have about physical and chemical properties of solids based on experimentation and evidence gathering.

Making careful observations of both positive and negative results and drawing conclusions based on evidence is a cornerstone of inquiry science. These process skills are invaluable, both within this unit and virtually every science unit they will experience after Grade 4.

Why did you choose the main activities?

We chose the main activities in the lesson because we wanted students to apply what they know about mixtures and about the tests they could perform to figure out the two chemicals. The lab sheet was designed to help students focus on both positive and negative results and to make deductions about what the solids could and could not be.

What are the key instructional strategies that are needed for this lesson?

This lesson engages students through an initial activity that poses a problem or question; teacher models a heat test; and students work collaboratively using different tests to try to figure out the identity of the two chemicals. Students are engaged in observations, recording data on lab sheets, using their prior knowledge (results chart), and making deductions based on evidence.

4. Unit Plan

See Figure 4.4 in Chapter 4.

5. Lesson Process

Steps of the Lesson: Learning Activities and Key Questions	Expected Student Reactions or Responses	Teacher's Response to Student Reactions/Things to Remember	Assessment
Think-Puzzle-Explore (prior knowledge—difference between physical and chemical properties)			Check for understanding as they go along. Are there common responses to the question?
Launch (5–10 min.) Use mixture B from Lesson 14B (alum and sugar). I have two chemicals and they got mixed together. How can we figure out what's in there? I need your help to figure out what's in there.	Students may say, *We could do the heat test . . . baking soda and vinegar* *You're mixing two things.*	What am I doing? What are you thinking that makes you think I'm mixing? How do you know it's two?	
Talk in pairs. I will check in with you in a few minutes and then we will share ideas in small groups.			Informal assessment of prior knowledge; gather evidence of student misconceptions
What tests could we perform to figure out these chemicals?	*We could look at our charts.* *We could see how it feels.* *They may suggest tests like vinegar, iodine, etc.*		

Steps of the Lesson: Learning Activities and Key Questions	Expected Student Reactions or Responses	Teacher's Response to Student Reactions/Things to Remember	Assessment
Explore (25–50 min.)			
Teacher models heat test (5–10 min.)		What evidence would the heat test give us to prove it's a chemical?	Do students bring up both physical and chemical tests?
Performing the heat test and modeling how to fill in the lab sheet		What could we learn from the heat test?	
Why do you do the test and what evidence are you looking for?	It's melting. It's boiling. It smells like it's burning.	Because it didn't react, what does that tell us? How could we prove that with a chemical test?	
Move to groups prior to whole-group activity (teacher discretion)	Students will probably turn to their results chart.	**Note:** Black paper under the wax paper enables kids to see. Use the small spoons from the kit.	
1. Whole-group activity 2. Vinegar (Day 1) 3. Water (Day 1) 4. Cabbage juice (Day 2) 5. Iodine (Day 2)		**Materials** Poster of the Results Chart LCD projector (to project mixture-reaction) Overhead projector	Are students talking about evidence from the test to make deductions?
After each test—whole group completes observation-deduction lab sheet (14A)		Confusion may occur between mixture and solutions—refer to the Teacher Manuals. Look for observation prompts: color, sound, dissolve-clumping, clear-white, cloudy-white	Are students talking about what they see as well as things they might not see?

(Continued)

5. Lesson Process (Continued)

Steps of the Lesson: Learning Activities and Key Questions	Expected Student Reactions or Responses	Teacher's Response to Student Reactions/Things to Remember	Assessment
What are the two chemicals?			Look at the student work—have students completed the lab sheet for the fourth and fifth tests?
Observations and Deductions Concluding Statement (see revised sheet)			
What was hard for you and what was easy for you? How did the lab sheets help you? How did the evidence from the results chart help you?	It helped . . . . I was confused . . . . It didn't help me.	**Lab Sheets** Can you give me some real examples? Can you show me where it was confusing or not helpful?	Look at the lab sheets to see if they are including both reactions they did see and things they did not see. Did students use the chart and did it help them?
Student Reflection Prompts: What did we do? What did you learn? Which group were you in? Any surprises? Anything you still wonder about? What did you like best? Anything else?	I already knew that.	What could be done to make it better? So what's your evidence?	Can students name the two chemicals and support their claim with evidence?

6. Evaluation

    a. Do students attend to both positive and negative results as they make deductions and narrow their choices as to the chemicals in the mixture?

    b. Do students work collaboratively to problem solve?

    c. Do students use vocabulary and descriptive words appropriately and consistently?

    d. Do students utilize previously learned knowledge and skills to identify unknown chemicals?

Name: _____

Chemical Tests: Observations and Deductions Lab Sheets

Test	Observation From Test	Deduction From Observation and Supporting Evidence
	It did:	Therefore it could be: _____ because _____ _____
	It didn't:	Therefore it can't be: _____ because _____ _____
		What are you wondering about? _____ _____
Test	Observation From Test	Deduction From Observation and Supporting Evidence
	It did:	Therefore it could be: _____ because _____ _____
	It didn't:	Therefore it can't be: _____ because _____ _____
		What are you wondering about? _____ _____

Concluding Statement

I think the two unknown chemicals are _____ and _____ .

What's your evidence?

I think it's _____ because the _____ test shows _____ .

I think the other unknown is _____ because the _____

test shows _____ .

Name:

Chemicals Test Results Chart

Chemical Tests

	First Observation	Water	Water Mixture & Filtration	Vinegar	Iodine	Red Cabbage	Heat
Red							
Yellow							
Green							
Blue							
Orange							

Chemicals

SAMPLE LESSON 2

Third-Grade Language Arts Research Lesson

School: Greenwood Elementary School Kalamazoo Public Schools

Date: January 5, 2005

Instructor: Dawn Thompson

Team members: Kathy Edlefson, Nancy Lechota

1. Background Information
   a. Background Goals of the Lesson Study Group:
      - Work cooperatively.
      - Build community.
      - All students will be accomplished readers, writers, speakers, and listeners.
      - All students will be able to identify and utilize text features to construct meaning when reading nonfiction.

   b. Narrative Overview of the Background Information

As evidenced by our low MEAP (Michigan Educational Assessment Program) scores, Greenwood students struggle with reading and understanding expository text. Our ITBS (Iowa Test of Basic Skills) results indicate a large number of third-grade students are not performing at grade level in reading comprehension.

Nonfiction text allows students to draw on their prior knowledge and experience to construct meaning. Using nonfiction text enables the students to broaden their world experiences and increase their conceptual knowledge and vocabulary. Our students need more experience reading and constructing meaning with nonfiction.

The third-grade students have some prior knowledge of narrative and expository text. It is important for the students to be able to identify and utilize nonfiction text features to assist in determining the importance of text and gaining meaning.

2. Unit Information
   a. This unit on Reading Comprehension will focus on learning how to read and comprehend nonfiction text. The goal is for the students to be able to identify text features and compare the differences between nonfiction and fiction genres. The students will use the knowledge of nonfiction text features to assist in determining what is important to learn, understand, and remember.
   b. This lesson is part of a full-year unit and instruction on Reading Comprehension Strategies.
   c. This unit relates to Standards 3.1, 3.2, and 3.3 of the Michigan English/ Language Arts Framework.
   d. This unit teaches comprehension strategies to support student achievement on the following assessments: Ed Performance, ITBS, and MEAP.

3. Lesson Information
   a. Name of the Lesson: Identifying and Utilizing Text Features in Determining the Importance Within Nonfiction Text
   b. Goals of the Lesson:
      - Activate prior knowledge.
      - Compare narrative and nonfiction text.
      - Identify nonfiction text features that signal importance.
      - Utilize nonfiction text features to gain new knowledge.
   c. How this lesson is related to the Lesson Study Goal:
      - Students will work in cooperative pairs and in whole group.
      - While students are engaged in reading nonfiction text, they will have the opportunity to support one another's learning through partner work.
      - Students will identify and utilize text features to help them determine what is important and to gain new knowledge.

d. Process of the Lesson

Steps of the Lesson: Learning Activities and Key Questions	Expected Student Reactions or Responses	Teacher's Response to Student Reactions/Things to Remember	Assessment
INTRODUCTION 1. Discriminating Between Narrative and Nonfiction Text Features			
WHOLE GROUP A. Teacher performs Picture-Walks. "Let's explore the two texts we have on display." "As we move slowly through the pages of these texts, think to yourself: 'What do I see that is the same about the texts? What do I see that is different?'" (about 5 min.: anticipatory set)	• Active independent participation: nonverbally identify similarities and differences between the two texts • Eye contact with the text and teacher	• Check nonverbal behaviors of students actively participating (eye contact). • Use two big books on weather: one a narrative and one nonfiction. • Redirect attention when necessary.	• Active independent participation of all students during the Picture-Walks
PARTNER B. Think-Pair-Share Teacher models a Think-Pair-Share. Students engage in a Think-Pair-Share: "Turn to your partner and share what you have noticed." (about 2 min.)	• Understand the format on how to Think-Pair-Share. • Attend and participate in a Think-Pair-Share discussion by engaging in substantive conversation regarding the two text selections.	• Model how to Think-Pair-Share. • Visually check for active participation from each partner. • Redirect attention when necessary.	• Evidence of prior knowledge as they think-pair-share (listen in on sharing) • How much do they help/support each other during their sharing time? • Are students engaged in purposeful dialogue about the concept?

174

Steps of the Lesson: Learning Activities and Key Questions	Expected Student Reactions or Responses	Teacher's Response to Student Reactions/Things to Remember	Assessment
WHOLE GROUP C. Think-Pair-Share Feedback Teacher may need to prompt with questions specific to the different genre: "What do we know about how narratives or stories are written?" "How we can we tell the difference between a narrative and a nonfiction book?" Teacher scaffolds student learning of text features (Vocabulary Chart and overhead transparencies) based on the students' current knowledge and what they have yet to learn. (about 12 min.)	• Recall prior knowledge of narrative and nonfiction text • State text features of each genre. Examples: Narrative (story, characters, problem, setting, plot, etc.) Nonfiction (table of contents, index, glossary, headings, illustrations, etc.) • Notice that both texts are about weather. • High engagement or distractions in identifying similarities and/or differences due to current weather conditions in the world (hurricanes and tsunamis). • Attend and participate with whole-group discussion. • May ask clarifying questions. • Students may be subdued at first, due to demo situation.	• Support comfort level and risk taking of group. • Before providing new information to students, the teacher will check comprehension through questioning what students already know. • Teacher will provide new vocabulary words (text features) and definitions. • Teacher will provide a Vocabulary Chart of Text Features (definitions). • Teacher will provide overhead transparencies to teach each new text feature in isolation. • Redirect attention when necessary.	• Do students understand the differences between fiction (narrative) and nonfiction text? • Do students notice the similarity in topics? • Can students identify and discriminate between text features using specific vocabulary?

(Continued)

d. Process of the Lesson (Continued)

Steps of the Lesson: Learning Activities and Key Questions	Expected Student Reactions or Responses	Teacher's Response to Student Reactions/Things to Remember	Assessment
INTRODUCTION *2. Using a Venn Diagram to Compare and Contrast Narrative and Nonfiction Text*			
WHOLE GROUP A. "How have you used a Venn Diagram?" "Why do we use them?" (about 2 min.)	• Students state past experiences with using this graphic organizer (Venn Diagram). • Active independent participation: Eye contact with the Venn Diagram and teacher.	• After initial student responses, provide support by using a Checklist Chart (Characteristics of the Venn Diagram). • Scaffold previous student responses with the Checklist Chart by circling previous responses from the chart. • Teach any characteristics not identified by student responses. • Redirect attention when necessary.	• Do students understand the primary purpose of using a Venn Diagram? (comparison: similarities and differences)
WHOLE GROUP B. Share as a group differences and similarities between the two texts. "Let's put what we know into a Venn Diagram. We will have one circle for narrative text and one for nonfiction." "What did you discover about the texts? What characteristics can we list, and where would we put them on our Venn Diagram?" (about 4 min.)	• Students will share characteristics they already know about these two types of genres. • Students may only share a limited number of characteristics.	• May need to scaffold with questions to focus attention to text characteristics. • Only some of the students may have prior vocabulary knowledge of both genres. • Call attention back to the big books to encourage student responses. • Noting each individual's skill level and knowledge base will determine the structure of the next part of this lesson. • Redirect attention when necessary.	• Are the students able to recall and label the characteristics of both genres (Narrative, Nonfiction) on the Venn Diagram accurately?

Steps of the Lesson: Learning Activities and Key Questions	Expected Student Reactions or Responses	Teacher's Response to Student Reactions/Things to Remember	Assessment
LESSON STUDY FOCUS *3. Identifying Text Features in Nonfiction*			
WHOLE GROUP A. Text Mapping: Teacher will choose two students to model Partner Roles and Duties of the lesson. Student #1: Clipboard Reporter Student #2: Features Detective (about 3 min.)	• Active independent participation from class: Eye contact with students who are Partner Modeling and the Teacher. • Expect clarifying questions.	• Assist with Partner Modeling. • Clipboard Reporter: 1. Select the colored Post-It note that coincides with the text feature on the checklist and hand it to the Detective. 2. Read the definition to the Detective. 3. Check off with pencil the text feature on list if you believe the correct item was found; otherwise, help partner find the correct text feature. • Detective: 1. Find the text feature by referring to your partner for help using the clipboard. Place the Post-It next to the place in the text where the text feature is found. • Check for understanding before beginning the activity. • Redirect attention when necessary.	• Answer any clarifying questions. • Ask questions to students regarding the lesson format, roles, and duties.

(Continued)

d. Process of the Lesson (Continued)

Steps of the Lesson: Learning Activities and Key Questions	Expected Student Reactions or Responses	Teacher's Response to Student Reactions/Things to Remember	Assessment
PARTNER B. Text Mapping: • Students will work in pairs on a nonfiction textbook formatted onto a laminated scroll. • The scroll will have a red line signifying the bottom of the page. • The students will take turns using a checklist or scroll to identify and label text features. • The students will use different colored markers to label the six text features: diagram, caption, illustration, map, heading, bolded text. (about 15 min.)	• Students may ask questions or need assistance "manipulating" the scroll. • Students will be highly engaged when using Post-Its, which could cause some distraction. • Students may not be able to identify/find the text features and may ask for help. • Text Mapping will make it easier for the student to find text features because the whole text is laid out and in view (eliminates constant page turning). • Text Mapping brings a physical element into comprehension work that will help "active" students stay engaged. • Students may need to be reminded to reference the clipboard sheets for examples of text features and their definitions.	• The scroll will have a red line signifying the bottom of the page. Instruct students this is to prevent them from viewing the text upside-down. • Check that students are alternating turns: Clipboard Reporter and Features Detective. • Reinforce how to use the clipboard, scroll, and markers with students who may be having difficulty. • Model (thinking out loud) how to determine that something is important. • Circulate, monitor, and listen to student/group thinking—ask Why, How, What, Where questions. • Redirect attention when necessary.	• Are students able to identify and label the text features accurately? • Do students understand the assignment given? • What teaching could further add to their learning in future lessons? • What instruction could be adapted to improve this lesson?

Steps of the Lesson: Learning Activities and Key Questions	Expected Student Reactions or Responses	Teacher's Response to Student Reactions/Things to Remember	Assessment
LESSON STUDY FOCUS 4. Utilizing Text Features in Nonfiction			
WHOLE GROUP A. Teacher instructs students that they will be sharing some text features that they have learned with the class. • "Each partner group will be given a paper to fill out to present to the class." "This paper will help you to teach the class about your text features." • "Work with your partner to fill out your paper and practice teaching what you will say with your partner about the text feature that you draw (sticks)." • Teacher models one text feature for the students to see the format of the presentation. • Teacher asks for clarifying questions and hands out sticks. (about 3 min.)	• Students will have clarifying questions regarding the use of the cloze text. • Active independent participation from class. • Random sample by using popsicle sticks to draw will provide unbiased environment.	• Check for active listening • Instruct students on how to fill out the cloze text form. • Model for students the presentation format. • Check for understanding before beginning the activity. • Redirect attention when necessary.	• Answer any clarifying questions. • Ask questions to students regarding the partner work activity.

(Continued)

d. Process of the Lesson (Continued)

Steps of the Lesson: Learning Activities and Key Questions	Expected Student Reactions or Responses	Teacher's Response to Student Reactions/Things to Remember	Assessment
PARTNER B. Partners work on cloze text activity. Partners practice presentation. (about 4 min.)	• Students may need extra support filling out the cloze text or practicing the presentation.	• Circulate through groups and provide support for students who need help with the cloze text or the presentation. • Redirect attention when necessary.	• Are partner groups able to fill out the cloze text and format the presentation correctly? • Are students on task?
WHOLE GROUP C. Student Presentations: • Students will come back together as a group to share/discuss their learning. • "Using your clipboard information, you (each partner group) will have a turn in text mapping a feature on the scroll on the wall. After mapping the feature, you will tell the class how your text feature helps you to determine what is important in your book." • "How can your text feature that you mapped help us to read nonfiction books?" (about 10 min.)	• Students will take turns independently teaching the class about a text feature. • Some students may be reluctant to share in front of whole group. • Some students may not have identified the correct text feature.	• Provide motivational support for students presenting to the class. • Provide instructional assistance with scaffolding any information not shared by the student about their text feature. • Redirect attention when necessary.	• Did the students identify what was important in the text and could they tell why and how they determined the importance? • Did the text feature examples provided adequately assist students in their presentation? • Could the students tell how they knew the text feature was important?

SAMPLE LESSON 3

Fourth-Grade Science Research Lesson

School: Traverse City Area Elementary Schools, Betha Voss, Cherry Knoll, Norris, Oak Park, and Westwood

Date: 2005

Instructor: Linda Egeler

Team Members: Robin Brister, Linda Egeler, Mary Jeffrey, Kathy Johnston, Abby Leppien, Karen Nelson, and Kristen Sak

1. Title of the Lesson: Modeling for Student Observations and Deductive Thinking

2. Lesson Study Goals

   Students will learn to do the following:

   a. Apply previously learned knowledge and skills to identify unknown chemicals.
   b. Work collaboratively to solve problems.
   c. Make careful observations of both positive and negative results.
   d. Use deductive reasoning based on evidence to narrow choices.

See Sample Lesson 1 for the complete background information.

---

5. Lesson Process Final Version: (Three Class Sessions)

Steps of the Lesson: Learning Activities and Key Questions	Expected Student Reactions or Responses	Teacher's Response to Student Reactions/Things to Remember	Assessment
Day 1: Model Teacher Think-Aloud for Tests 1 and 2		<u>Teacher models deductive thinking—All information recorded on the sheet comes from the teacher.</u>	Check for understanding as they go along.
Launch (5–10 min.) Use mixture B from Lesson 14 (alum and sugar)		(This is a demonstration for how to fill in the chart.)	
I have two chemicals and they got mixed together. How can we figure out what's in there? I need your help to figure out what's in there.	Students may say, *We could do the heat test . . . etc.* *baking soda and vinegar*		Are there common responses to the question?
	You're mixing two things.	*What am I doing?* *What are you thinking that makes you think I'm mixing?* *How do you know it's two?*	
Talk in pairs. I will check in with you in a few minutes and then we will share ideas in small groups.	*We could look at our charts.* *We could see how it feels.* *They may suggest tests like vinegar, iodine, etc.*		Informal assessment of prior knowledge; gather evidence of student misconceptions
What tests could we perform to figure out these chemicals?			

Steps of the Lesson: Learning Activities and Key Questions	Expected Student Reactions or Responses	Teacher's Response to Student Reactions/Things to Remember	Assessment
Explore (25–50 min.)		What evidence would the heat test give us to prove it's a chemical?	
Teacher performs the heat test and models how to fill in the lab sheet. (5–10 min.)		What could we learn from the heat test?	
Why do you do the test and what evidence are you looking for?	Students may say: *It's melting.* *It's boiling.* *It smells like it's burning.*	Because it didn't react, what does that tell us? How could we prove that with a chemical test?	Do students bring up both physical and chemical tests?
Move to groups prior to whole-group activity (teacher discretion).	*Students will probably turn to their results chart.*	**Note:** Black paper under the wax paper enables kids to see. Use the small spoons from the kit.	Are students talking about evidence from the test to make deductions?
Whole-group activity 2. Water (Day 1) ~~3. Vinegar (day one)~~ ~~4. Iodine (day two)~~ ~~5. Cabbage juice (day two)~~		Teacher guides student thinking, continues to model deductive thinking.	Are students talking about what they see as well as things they might not see?

(Continued)

5. Lesson Process Final Version: (Three Class Sessions) (Continued)

Steps of the Lesson: Learning Activities and Key Questions	Expected Student Reactions or Responses	Teacher's Response to Student Reactions/Things to Remember	Assessment
Day 2: 14b. Guided Think Aloud: Modeling Lesson (Vinegar, Iodine, and Red Cabbage Juice)			
Materials Poster of the Results Chart LCD projector (to project mixture-reaction) Overhead projector		Confusion may occur between mixture and solutions—refer to the Teacher Manuals.	Look at the student work—have students completed the lab sheet for the fourth and fifth tests?
Review yesterday and share evidence about the reactions from the heat and light tests.		Be aware that within a small group, students play different roles: recorder, materials manager, reporter of results; these roles can shift to different students during the lessons.	Look at the lab sheets to see if they are including both reactions they did see and things they did not see. Do students use the chart and did it help them?
After each test—whole group completes observation-deduction lab sheet (14A).		Look for observation prompts: color, sound, dissolve-clumping, clear-white, cloudy-white	Do students navigate easily among the chart, chemical test, and board work?
Accommodations: Shifting roles within groups Grouping strategies Groups stop and reflect on results, one person writes. Use chart paper/whiteboard, not overhead.		Link the words "transparent" and "translucent" with the minerals testing unit or light unit.	Do students refer to chemicals by color, or by their names, or do they bounce back and forth? Can students name the two chemicals and support their claim with evidence?

Steps of the Lesson: Learning Activities and Key Questions	Expected Student Reactions or Responses	Teacher's Response to Student Reactions/Things to Remember	Assessment
What are the two chemicals?			
Observations and Deductions Concluding Statement (see revised sheet)			
What was hard for you and what was easy for you?	It helped. . . .	Lab Sheets Can you give me some real examples?	
How did the lab sheets help you?	I was confused . . .		
How did the evidence from the results chart help you?	It didn't help me.	Can you show me where it was confusing or not helpful?	
	I already knew that.	What could be done to make it better?	
~~Student Reflection Prompts:~~		So what's your evidence?	
~~What did we do?~~			
~~What did you learn?~~			
~~Which group were you in?~~			
~~Any surprises?~~			
~~Anything you still wonder about?~~			
~~What did you like best?~~			
~~Anything else?~~			

(Continued)

5. Lesson Process Final Version: (Three Class Sessions) (Continued)

Steps of the Lesson: Learning Activities and Key Questions	Expected Student Reactions or Responses	Teacher's Response to Student Reactions/Things to Remember	Assessment
Day 3: 14c. Science Partners Complete Experiments: **Independently Complete Observation Lab Sheet** (no teacher modeling) Mixture A or C Follow "Chemical Tests" Lesson 14.			

Resource B

Frequently Asked Questions

Planning the Research Lesson

CHALLENGES OF LAYING THE GROUNDWORK

> **Dilemma:** How do we know the right amount of time
> to spend on planning the lesson?

Planning a research lesson may seem tedious to some teachers, or they may feel pressed for time because of all the other work that needs their attention. School culture in the United States generally doesn't support the kind of extended discussion and research that is devoted to research lesson planning.

Another Perspective

Lesson study, to become sustainable, requires protected time in which teachers can collaboratively research and plan lessons. It may be helpful to look at examples of research lessons and read the background information that is provided for the lesson. A classroom is a complex environment, and it takes time to examine and assemble the individual pieces that contribute to the realization of the research lesson goals. A teacher who is an experienced lesson study practitioner is often effective in communicating the importance of taking time to think deeply about a lesson.

Questions to Consider

- Is there time during the school day in which the team can plan without interruption?

- Are there models of effective research lessons that can be examined to get a sense of the level of detail required?

> **Dilemma:** Is it necessary to use the research lesson template?

This may represent a concern about a perceived or real lack of time or a misunderstanding about the purpose of using the template. The research lesson template is significantly different from the typical lesson plans that teachers develop. It may seem to be overly complicated or detailed. For some, this template may be another reminder that the way they have always planned lessons is under scrutiny.

Another Perspective

The lesson template forces people to think differently about the design of the lesson. Most teachers find that anticipating student responses is the most unfamiliar activity, and the most rewarding. Remember that the template serves several different purposes—it is a planning tool, it is used to communicate the team's ideas, and observers will use it to collect data. It is relatively easy to walk through the steps of lesson study, but to do lesson study well represents a complex, culture-changing approach to improving both teacher and student learning. Although teachers will gain ideas that can help them in their day-to-day planning, the research lesson is not a model for all lesson plans.

Questions to Consider

- What is the purpose of the template?
- Does the team need to exhaust all of the anticipated student responses?
- Is there a research lesson near our school that we could observe and see how the template facilitates lesson study?

> **Dilemma:** What if the whole unit needs work? Should we still spend time on one lesson?

One of the realities of education is that significant topics are taught from the curriculum in a superficial way. Some curricula used by lesson study teams are not research based and do not support challenging learning experiences for students. There is a sense that the unit remains the same even after a lesson study cycle.

Another Perspective

It is essential to understand the unit in which the research lesson is placed. The research lesson format should include some narrative about the unit and how the lesson will foster greater student understanding. Often, a strong research lesson will expand into more than one lesson. The team can also use what they learn to improve the other lessons in the unit.

Questions to Consider

- How can we plan a lesson or lessons that lead to the greatest possible impact on the unit?
- Could we map out the unit to see where the greatest leverage is in terms of a lesson or lessons?
- How can we use what we learned from the research lesson to improve the unit?

> **Dilemma:** We are having trouble coming to consensus about some parts of the lesson. What should we do?

Disagreements about design of the instruction within a research lesson are not unusual. The team members may have different philosophies about teaching and learning. It can be difficult to move away from familiar ways of teaching a lesson when an alternative way is proposed.

Another Perspective

Disagreements are a natural part of the process in lesson study. Competing ideas about how to teach the lesson can offer occasions for generating new knowledge among the group. One approach to resolving disagreements is to go back to the research theme and goals and to come to consensus about the design that will best support the goals of the lesson.

Sometimes, both approaches seem equally valid. The team can incorporate the different ideas into their research questions, with the lesson taught one way for the first teaching and another way for the second teaching.

Questions to Consider

- How can we encourage diverse perspectives regarding the research lesson without becoming mired in competing views?
- Do disagreements reflect deeply held views on how to teach this content, or do they relate to surface features of the lesson?
- Is there evidence or research that supports one approach over another?

> **Dilemma:** What if the research lesson is not very challenging?

Teams who are new to lesson study may not have experience conducting research on topics and investigating materials and curricula. The teachers may feel safer by tackling a topic or skill that is familiar and that seems easier to develop a research lesson around. It is also natural for team members to be tempted to develop a lesson that they know will lead to student success.

Another Perspective

Lesson study is about teachers researching how students learn challenging concepts and how best to teach all students. An "easy" lesson may provide good feelings afterward—for example, the students had fun—but it will not provide insights that advance an understanding of teaching and learning. Research lessons that are challenging to plan and teach will require more time for the team to investigate other materials and research on teaching. The benefits include professional learning that will improve instruction—not just for this lesson but also for other lessons—and habits of minds that support teachers as researchers.

Questions to Consider

- How can the planning process support the selection of a topic that is challenging to teach, difficult for students to understand, or both?
- What do we want to accomplish through our lesson study work?

> **Dilemma:** Why is the research lesson so scripted?

Because of the detailed nature of the plan, research lessons often appear to be scripted. Written teacher questions and anticipated student responses appear to support a more regimented approach to teaching and learning. Many teachers are uncomfortable with the idea of following a prescribed routine.

Another Perspective

Research lessons are noted for their detail, including written teacher questions and anticipated student responses. This enables observers to understand the team's rationale for the lesson plan and reveals the thoughtful nature of the design. A well-planned research lesson is, in fact, very different from a script. The anticipated student responses and teacher supports should provide for the different ways that the lesson may play out in the classroom.

The detailed lesson plan is the result of all the research and discussions conducted by the team. It is this work that results in the impact that lesson study has on instruction as a whole, not just on the research lesson.

Questions to Consider

- How does the written plan contribute to the investigation of student learning?
- How does the written plan contribute to evaluating the effectiveness of the lesson?

Resource C

Additional Resources

BOOKS

Fernandez, C., & Yoshida, M. (2004). *Lesson study: A Japanese approach to improving mathematics teaching and learning.* **Mahwah, NJ: Erlbaum.**

This book looks at lesson study in Japan and describes, in detail, a lesson study cycle conducted by elementary teachers in mathematics. Readers see the planning of a mathematics lesson, including the knowledge that teachers draw on to make instructional decisions. They observe students' problem-solving strategies and learn how Japanese teachers prepare themselves to identify those strategies and facilitate the students' discussion.

Lewis, C. (2002). *Lesson study: A handbook of teacher-led instructional change.* **Philadelphia: Research for Better Schools.**

This handbook describes both the key ideas underlying lesson study and the practical support needed to make it succeed in any subject area. Topics addressed include the basic steps of lesson study, supports, misconceptions, and system impact. The handbook provides practical resources including schedules, data collection examples, protocols for lesson discussion and observation, and instructional plans.

Stigler, J., W. & Hiebert, J. (1999). *The teaching gap: Best ideas from the world's teachers for improving education in the classroom.* **New York: Free Press.**

Based on the TIMSS video study that compared the teaching of eighth-grade mathematics in Germany, Japan, and the United States, this highly readable book shows the extent to which teaching is a cultural activity. The descriptions of Japanese lesson study provide insight into this system for developing professional knowledge and giving teachers the opportunity to learn about teaching.

Wang-Iverson, P., & Yoshida, M. (Eds.). (2005). *Building our understanding of lesson study.* Philadelphia: Research for Better Schools.

This publication offers insights from a range of perspectives: teachers, facilitators, principals, and knowledgeable others. The essays in the book are based on presentations at two Research for Better Schools lesson study conferences. Experienced Japanese practitioners share their many years of experience. Individual schools offer their own perspectives and advice on how to overcome common obstacles and other strategies for success when implementing the practice in U.S. schools.

WEB SITES

Global Education Resources

http://www.globaledresources.com

Global Education Resources (GER) offers professional development and consulting in implementing lesson study. GER was founded by Makoto Yoshida, who is joined by Bill Jackson from Paterson School No. 2, Akihiko Takahashi, and Tad Watanabe.

Lesson Study Communities Project in Secondary Mathematics

http://www2.edc.org/lessonstudy/

This Educational Development Center project supports teams of secondary mathematics teachers in the eastern Massachusetts region in implementing lesson study. Along with providing general information about lesson study, this site provides tools such as sample lessons, workshop materials, and team meeting materials.

Lesson Study Group at Mills College

http://www.lessonresearch.net

This Web site is hosted by Mills College Education Department in Oakland, California, and features the work of Catherine Lewis and her colleagues. The site provides articles, papers, and other publications on lesson study, including a bibliography. Video clips of lesson study from Japanese classrooms are available, and videotapes and DVDs are available for purchase. News of events and funding opportunities related to lesson study and links to additional resources are also available.

Lesson Study Research Group at Teachers College/Columbia University in New York

http://www.tc.edu/centers/lessonstudy

This site provides links to articles and tools that support the work of lesson study teams. Teachers will also find information about how to join the group's lesson study

Listserv and databases that collect information on lesson study teams, research projects, and consultants from across the United States.

Northwest Teacher, Northwest Regional Educational Laboratory Mathematics and Science Education Center

http://www.nwrel.org/msec/lessonstudy/msec.pubs.html

Northwest Teacher is a publication of the Northwest Eisenhower Regional Consortium about mathematics and science teaching and learning. The journal had two issues devoted to lesson study. The title of the spring 2001 issue (Vol. 2, No. 2) is "Lesson Study: Teachers Learning Together." The title of the spring 2003 issue (Vol. 4, No. 3) is "Lesson Study: Crafting Learning Together."

Research for Better Schools

http://www.rbs.org/lesson_study/

This site provides a number of resources, including presentation papers and newsletter articles, a list of frequently asked questions about lesson study, and a lesson study glossary. Visitors will also find a useful list of additional Web sites and resources.

VIDEO

Gahala, J., O'Brien, R., & Schuch, L. (Eds.). (2002). *Teacher to teacher: Reshaping instruction through lesson study* [Multimedia kit]. Naperville, IL: North Central Regional Educational Laboratory.

http://www2.learningpt.org/msec/lessonstudy/msec.pubs.html

This multimedia kit is designed for teacher facilitators and professional developers to support the implementation of lesson study. The facilitator's guide includes activities, handouts, transparencies, facilitator notes, tools, and articles. The video includes an introduction to lesson study and two segments highlighting schools and teachers involved in lesson study.

Yoshida, M. (with Fernandez, C.). (2002). *Lesson study: An introduction* [CD-ROM]. Madison, NJ: Global Education Resources.

http://www.globaledresources.com/products/dvd/lesson_study_intro.php

This CD-ROM presents a general overview of the lesson study process and answers questions frequently asked by American audiences when they hear about lesson study for the first time. Makoto Yoshida created this resource in collaboration with Clea Fernandez of the Lesson Study Research Group/Teachers College, Columbia University.

Lesson Study Research Group at Mills College

http://www.lessonresearch.net/res.html

Catherine Lewis and her colleagues have developed a number of videotapes and DVDs that depict lesson study in both Japan and the United States.

The following titles are a sample of the resources available:

Can You Find the Area?—A series of three lessons (abridged) taught by Dr. Akihiko Takahashi to fourth graders in the San Mateo–Foster City School District, California.

Can You Lift 100 kg? (220 pounds)—The planning, teaching, and debriefing of a science research lesson in a Japanese school.

How Many Seats?—Excerpts from a lesson study cycle conducted by U.S. teachers during a 10-day summer workshop on lesson study and algebra.

To Open a Cube—A public research lesson taught by Dr. Akihiko Takahashi to fifth graders in the San Mateo–Foster City School District, California.

Glossary

Debriefing	the discussion that takes place after the teaching and observation of the research lesson.
Debriefing protocol	the structure that guides the debriefing, which focuses on who will speak and in what order.
Facilitator	usually a person from outside the lesson study team who helps coordinate logistics and other details, helps the team access resources, and monitors lesson study practice.
Final commentator	the individual, usually a knowledgeable other, who summarizes and closes the debriefing.
Invited guests	people from outside the lesson study team who are invited to observe a research lesson.
Knowledgeable other	an individual who works with the lesson study team, providing expertise in content knowledge, pedagogy, lesson study practice, or other relevant areas. (Also known as an **outside expert** or **outside advisor**.)
Konaikenshu	a Japanese term for school-based professional development, of which lesson study is one component. Literal translation: in-school teacher education (Yoshida, 1999).
Kyozaikenkyu	a Japanese term for the practice of studying teaching materials, including textbooks, curriculum scope and sequence, standards, teacher manuals, research, and research lesson reports. Literal translation: investigation of instructional materials (Takahashi et al., 2005).
Lesson study	a professional development practice in which teachers collaborate to develop a lesson plan, teach and observe the lesson to collect data on student learning, and use their observations to refine the lesson.
Lesson study cycle	the complete series of steps in the lesson study process.
Lesson study process	the steps involved in conducting lesson study.
Long-term goal	see "Research theme."

Moderator	the person who leads the debriefing, who can be a team member or an outside facilitator.
Observation guidelines	the list of guidelines and suggestions that serve as a structure for the observation of the research lesson.
Open house	an event in which a school or a district invites guests to participate in observing and discussing research lessons.
Outside advisor	see "Knowledgeable other."
Outside expert	see "Knowledgeable other."
Report	the final product of the lesson study cycle, in which the team captures and shares the research lesson and the professional knowledge they have gained.
Research focus	see "Research theme."
Research hypothesis	the question or theory that guides the selection of goals, the planning of the research lesson, and the evaluation of its effectiveness. It defines what the teachers hope to learn from the lesson study cycle.
Research lesson	the lesson that the team plans and investigates during the lesson study cycle.
Research lesson template	the format and structure for the research lesson.
Research theme	a broad, long-term goal that is focused on students and that guides the lesson study team's work. (Also known as the **research focus** or the **long-term goal**.)

References

American Association for the Advancement of Science. (2001). *Atlas of science literacy.* Washington, DC: Author.

Ancess, J. (2000). The reciprocal influence of teacher learning, teaching practice, school restructuring, and student learning outcomes. *Teachers College Record, 102*(3), 590–619.

Ball, D. L., & Cohen, D. K. (1996). Reform by the book: What is—or might be—the role of curriculum materials in teacher learning and instructional reform? *Educational Researcher, 25*(9), 6–11.

Ball, D. L., & Cohen, D. K. (1999). Developing practice, developing practitioners: Toward a practice-based theory of professional education. In L. Darling-Hammond & G. Sykes (Eds.), *Teaching as the learning profession: Handbook of policy and practice* (pp. 3–32). San Francisco: Jossey-Bass.

Bierema, L. L. (1999). The process of the learning organization: Making sense of change. *NASSP Bulletin, 83*(604), 46–56.

Black, S. (1997). Creating community. Research report. *American School Board Journal, 184*(6), 32–35.

Borasi, R., & Fonzi, J. (2002). *Foundations: Professional development that supports school mathematics reform* (Vol. 3). Arlington, VA: National Science Foundation.

Boud, D., Keogh, R., & Walker, D. (1985). *Reflection: Turning experience into learning.* New York: Kogan Page.

Bray, J. N., Lee, J., Smith, L. L., & Yorks, L. (2000). *Collaborative inquiry in practice: Action, reflection, and making meaning.* Thousand Oaks, CA: Sage.

Briscoe, C. (1991). The dynamic interactions among beliefs, role metaphors, and teaching practices: A case study of teacher change. *Science Education, 75*(2), 185–199.

Brookfield, S. D. (1986). *Understanding and facilitating adult learning.* San Francisco: Jossey-Bass.

Bryk, A. S., & Schneider, B. (2002). *Trust in schools: A core resource for improvement.* New York: Russell Sage Foundation.

Byrum, J. L., Jarrell, R., & Munoz, M. (2002). *The perceptions of teachers and administrators on the impact of the lesson study initiative.* Louisville, KY: Jefferson County Public Schools. (ERIC Document Reproduction Service No. ED467761)

Carpenter, T. P., Blanton, M. L., Cobb, P., Franke, M. L., Kaput, J., & McClain, K. (2004). *Scaling up innovative practices in mathematics and science.* Madison: Wisconsin Center for Education Research.

Chokshi, S., & Fernandez, C. (2004). Challenges to importing Japanese lesson study: Concerns, misconceptions, and nuances. *Phi Delta Kappan, 85*(7), 520–525.

Clarke, D. (1994). Ten key principles from research for the professional development of mathematics teachers. In D. B. Aichele & A. F. Coxford (Eds.), *Professional development for teachers of mathematics: 1994 yearbook* (pp. 37–48). Reston, VA: National Council of Teachers of Mathematics.

Coburn, C. E. (2003). Rethinking scale: Moving beyond numbers to deep and lasting change. *Educational Researcher, 32*(6), 3–12.

Cohen, D. K., & Hill, H. C. (1998). *Instructional policy and classroom performance: The mathematics reform in California* (CPRE Research Rep. No. RR–39). Philadelphia: Consortium for Policy Research in Education.

Collay, M., Dunlap, D., Enloe, W., & Gagnon, G. W., Jr. (1998). *Learning circles: Creating conditions for professional development.* Thousand Oaks, CA: Corwin Press.

Corcoran, T. B. (1995). *Helping teachers teach well: Transforming professional development* (CPRE Policy Brief No. RB–16). Philadelphia: Consortium for Policy Research in Education.

Darling-Hammond, L. (1997). *The right to learn.* San Francisco: Jossey-Bass.

Darling-Hammond, L., & McLaughlin, M. W. (1995). Policies the support professional development in an era of reform. *Phi Delta Kappan, 76*(8), 597–604.

Davis, E. A., & Krajcik, J. S. (2005). Designing educative curriculum materials to promote teacher learning. *Educational Researcher, 34*(3), 3–14.

Donovan, M. S., & Bransford, J. D. (Eds.). (2005). *How students learn: History, mathematics, and science in the classroom.* Washington, DC: National Research Council, National Academies Press.

Driver, R., Squires, A., Rushworth, P., & Wood-Robinson, V. (Eds.). (2003). *Making sense of secondary science: Research into children's ideas.* New York: Routledge.

Dufour, R. P. (1999). Help wanted: Principals who can lead professional learning communities. *NASSP Bulletin, 83*(604), 12–17.

Dufour, R., & Eaker, R. (1998). *Professional learning communities at work: Best practices for enhancing student achievement.* Bloomington, IN: National Educational Service.

Elmore, R. (2002). *Bridging the gap between standards and achievement: The imperative for professional development in education.* Washington, DC: Albert Shanker Institute.

Fernandez, C. (2002). Learning from Japanese approaches to professional development: The case of lesson study. *Journal of Teacher Education, 53*(5), 393–405.

Fernandez, C., Cannon, J., & Chokshi, S. (2003). A U.S.-Japan lesson study collaboration reveals critical lenses for examining practice. *Teaching and Teacher Education, 19*(2), 171–185.

Fernandez, C., & Chokshi, S. (2002). A practical guide to translating lesson study for a U.S. setting. *Phi Delta Kappan, 84*(2), 128–134.

Fernandez, C., & Yoshida, M. (2000). Lesson study as a model for improving teaching: Insights, challenges and a vision for the future. In A. Poliakoff & T. D. Schwartzbeck (Eds.), *Eye of the storm: Promising practices for improving instruction* (pp. 32–40). Washington, DC: Council for Basic Education.

Fernandez, C., & Yoshida, M. (2004). *Lesson study: A Japanese approach to improving mathematics teaching and learning.* Mahwah, NJ: Lawrence Erlbaum.

Fraser, B. J., Giddings, G. L., & McRobbie, C. J. (1995). Evolution and validation of a personal form of an instrument for assessing science laboratory classroom environments. *Journal of Research on Science Teaching, 32*(4), 399–422.

Garet, M. S., Porter, A. C., Desimone, L., Birman, P. F., & Yoon, K. S. (2001). What makes professional development effective? Results from a national sample of teachers. *American Educational Research Journal, 38*(4), 915–945.

Gill, A. (2005). For knowledgeable others: AFT's experience in Volusia county. In P. Wang-Iverson & M. Yoshida (Eds.), *Building our understanding of lesson study* (pp. 53–62). Philadelphia: Research for Better Schools.

Greene, M. (1995). *Releasing the imagination: Essays on education, the arts, and social change.* San Francisco: Jossey-Bass.

Guskey, T. R. (2000). *Evaluating professional development.* Thousand Oaks, CA: Corwin Press.

Hargreaves, A., & Fink, D. (2000). The three dimensions of reform. *Educational Leadership, 57*(7), 30–34.

Hawley, W. D., & Valli, L. (1999). The essentials of effective professional development: A new consensus. In L. Darling-Hammond & G. Sykes (Eds.), *Teaching as the learning profession: Handbook of policy and practice* (pp. 127–150). San Francisco: Jossey-Bass.

Hiebert, J. (2000). Improving classroom teaching: Enabling the potential of standards-based reform. In A. Poliakoff & T. D. Schwartzbeck (Eds.), *Eye of the storm: Promising practices for improving instruction* (pp. 26–31). Washington, DC: Council for Basic Education.

Hiebert, J., Gallimore, R., & Stigler, J. W. (2002). A knowledge base for the teaching profession: What would it look like and how can we get one? *Educational Researcher, 31*(5), 3–15.

Hill, H. C., Rowan, B., & Ball, D. L. (2005). Effect of teachers' mathematical knowledge for teaching on student achievement. *American Educational Research Journal 42*(2): 371–406.

Hiller, N. A. (1995). The battle to reform science education: Notes from the trenches. *Theory into Practice, 34*(1), 60–65.

Hord, S. M. (1997). *Professional learning communities: Communities of continuous inquiry and improvement.* Austin, TX: Southwest Educational Development Laboratory.

Jackson, B. (2005). For facilitators: Experiences from Paterson School No. 2. In P. Wang-Iverson & M. Yoshida (Eds.), *Building our understanding of lesson study* (pp. 45–51). Philadelphia: Research for Better Schools.

Jarvis, P. (1987). *Adult learning in the social context.* London: Croom Helm.

Kennedy, M. (1998). *Form and substance in inservice teacher education.* Madison, WI: National Institute for Science Education.

King, M. B., & Newmann, F. M. (2000). Will teacher learning advance school goals? *Phi Delta Kappan, 81*(8), 576–580.

Langer, J. A. (2000). Excellence in English in middle school and high school: How teachers' professional lives support student achievement. *American Educational Research Journal, 37*(2), 397–439.

Lewis, C. (1995). *Educating hearts and minds: Reflections on Japanese preschool and elementary education.* Cambridge, England: Cambridge University Press.

Lewis, C. (2000, April). *Lesson study: The core of Japanese professional development.* Paper presented at the annual meeting of the American Educational Research Association, New Orleans, LA.

Lewis, C. (2002a). Everywhere I looked—levers and pendulums. *Journal of Staff Development, 23*(3), 59–65.

Lewis, C. (2002b). *Lesson study: A handbook of teacher-led instructional change.* Philadelphia: Research for Better Schools.

Lewis, C. (2005). How do teachers learn during lesson study? In P. Wang-Iverson & M. Yoshida (Eds.), *Building our understanding of lesson study* (pp. 77–84). Philadelphia: Research for Better Schools.

Lewis, C., Perry, R., & Murata, A. (2003, April). *Lesson study and teachers' knowledge development: Collaborative critique of a research model and methods.* Paper presented at the annual meeting of the American Educational Research Association, Chicago, IL.

Lewis, C., Perry, R., & Murata, A. (2006). How should research contribute to instructional improvement? The case of lesson study. *Educational Researcher, 35*(3), 3–13.

Lewis, C., & Tsuchida, I. (1997). Planned educational change in Japan: The shift to student-centered elementary science. *Journal of Educational Policy, 29*(3), 4–14.

Lewis, C., & Tsuchida, I. (1998). A lesson is like a swiftly flowing river. *American Educator, 22*(4), 12–17, 50–52.

Lieberman, A., & Miller, L. (1999). *Teachers: Transforming their world and their work.* New York: Teachers College Press.

Linn, M., Lewis, C., Tsuchida, I., & Songer, N. (2000). Beyond fourth-grade science: Why do U.S. and Japanese students diverge? *Educational Researcher, 29*(3), 4–14.

Lipsey, M. W., & Wilson, D. B. (1993). The efficacy of psychological, educational, and behavioral treatment: Confirmation from meta analysis. *American Psychologist, 48*(12), 1181–1209.

Liptak, L. (2005). For principals: Critical elements. In P. Wang-Iverson & M. Yoshida (Eds.), *Building our understanding of lesson study* (pp. 39–44). Philadelphia: Research for Better Schools.

Little, J. W. (1990). The persistence of privacy: Autonomy and initiative in teachers' professional relations. *Teachers College Record, 91*(4), 509–536.

Little, J. W. (1999). Organizing schools for teacher learning. In L. Darling-Hammond & G. Sykes (Eds.), *Teaching as the learning profession: Handbook of policy and practice* (pp. 233–262). San Francisco: Jossey-Bass.

Loucks-Horsley, S., Hewson, P. S., Love, N., & Stiles, K. E. (1998). *Designing professional development for teachers of science and mathematics.* Thousand Oaks, CA: Corwin Press.

McCombs, B. L., & Whisler, J. S. (1997). *The learner-centered classroom and school: Strategies for increasing student motivation and achievement.* San Francisco: Jossey-Bass.

McLaughlin, M. W. (with Zarrow, J.). (2001). Teachers engaged in evidence-based reform: Trajectories of teacher's inquiry, analysis, and action. In A. Lieberman & L. Miller (Eds.), *Teachers caught in the action: Professional development that matters* (pp. 79–101). New York: Teachers College Press.

Merriam, S. B., & Caffarella, R. S. (1999). *Learning in adulthood: A comprehensive guide* (2nd ed.). San Francisco: Jossey-Bass.

Murata, A., & Takahashi, A. (2002). *Vehicle to connect theory, research, and practice: How teacher thinking changes in district-level lesson study in Japan.* Paper presented at the annual meeting of the North American Chapter of the International Group for the Psychology of Mathematics Education, Athens, GA.

Murphy, C. (1997). Finding time for faculties to study together. *Journal of Staff Development, 18*(3), 29–32.

National Council of Teachers of Mathematics. (2000). *Principles and standards for school mathematics.* Reston, VA: Author.

National Reading Panel. (2000). *Report of the National Reading Panel: Teaching children to read.* Washington, DC: National Institute for Literacy.

National Science Resource Center. (2002). *STC: Chemical tests.* Washington, DC: National Academy of Sciences.

Newmann, F. M., & Wehlage, G. G. (1995). *Successful school restructuring: A report to the public and educators.* Madison: University of Wisconsin, Center for Organization and Restructuring of Schools.

North Central Regional Educational Laboratory. (2000). *Blueprints: A practical toolkit for designing and facilitating professional development.* Oak Brook, IL: Author.

Office of Educational Research and Improvement. (1999). *National awards program for model professional development.* Washington, DC: U.S. Department of Education.

Pardini, P. (1999). Making time for adult learning. *Journal of Staff Development, 20*(2), 37–41.

Perry, R., Lewis, C., & Akiba, M. (2002, April). *Lesson study in the San Mateo–Foster City School District.* Paper presented at the annual meeting of the American Educational Research Association, New Orleans, LA.

Petrescu, C. A. (2005). *Linking teacher knowledge with student learning: A network of partnerships.* Final evaluation report. Ypsilanti: Eastern Michigan University.

Pierce, C. (1994). Importance of classroom climate for at-risk students. *Journal of Educational Research, 88*(1), 37–42.

Preskill, H., & Torres, R. T. (1999). *Evaluative inquiry for learning in organizations.* New York: Doubleday.

Regan, T. G., Case, C. W., & Brubacher, J. W. (2000). *Becoming a reflective educator* (2nd ed.). Thousand Oaks, CA: Corwin Press.

Routman, R. (1996). *Literacy at the crossroads: Crucial talk about reading, writing, and other teaching dilemmas.* Portsmouth, NH: Heinemann.

Saul, M. (2001). It all fits together: Notes on a visit to Japan. *Notices of the American Mathematical Society, 48*(11), 1333–1337.

Shimizu, Y. (2002). Lesson study: What, why, and how? In H. Bass, Z. P. Usiskin, & G. Burrill (Eds.), *Studying classroom teaching as a medium for professional development: Proceedings of a U.S.-Japan workshop* (pp. 53–64). Washington, DC: National Academy Press.

Stevenson, H. W., & Stigler, J. W. (1992). *The learning gap: Why our schools are failing and what we can learn from Japanese and Chinese education.* New York: Touchstone.

Stewart, R. A., & Brendefur, J. L. (2005). Fusing lesson study and authentic achievement: A model for teacher collaboration. *Phi Delta Kappan, 86*(9), 681–687.

Stigler, J. W., Gonzales, P., Kawanaka, T., Knoll, S., & Serrano, A. (1999). *The TIMSS videotape classroom study: Methods and findings from an exploratory research project on eighth-grade mathematics instruction in Germany, Japan, and the United States.* Washington: DC: National Center for Educational Statistics.

Stigler, J. W., & Hiebert, J. (1999). *The teaching gap: Best ideas from the world's teachers for improving education in the classroom.* New York: Free Press.

Supovitz, J. A., & Christman, J. B. (2003). *Developing communities of instructional practice: Lessons from Cincinnati and Philadelphia* (CPRE Policy Brief No. RB–39). Philadelphia: Consortium for Policy Research in Education.

Takahashi, A. (2005, June). *Facilitating the process of lesson study.* Paper presented at the Detroit Lesson Study Conference, Detroit, MI.

Takahashi, A. (2006, March 17). Re: Changing the research lesson during the teaching. Message posted to the Lesson Study Research Group's Lesson Study electronic mailing list, archived at www.tc.columbia.edu/centers/lessonstudy/listservarchives.html

Takahashi, A., & Yoshida, M. (2004). Ideas for establishing lesson-study communities. *Teaching Children Mathematics, 10*(9), 436–443.

Takahashi, A., Yoshida, M., & Watanabe, T. (with Wang-Iverson, P.). (2005). Improving content and pedagogical knowledge through *kyozaikenkyu.* In P. Wang-Iverson & M. Yoshida (Eds.), *Building our understanding of lesson study* (pp. 101–110). Philadelphia: Research for Better Schools.

Thompson, C. L., & Zeuli, J. S. (1999). The frame and the tapestry: Standards-based reform and professional development. In L. Darling-Hammond & G. Sykes (Eds.), *Teaching as the learning profession: Handbook of policy and practice* (pp. 341–375). San Francisco: Jossey-Bass.

Turner, M. A. (2004). *Case study: Northern Michigan Lesson Study Initiative.* Naperville, IL: Learning Point Associates.

Voelkl, K. E. (1994). School warmth, student participation, and achievement. *Journal of Experimental Education, 63*(2), 127–138.

Watanabe, T., & Wang-Iverson, P. (2005). The role of knowledgeable others. In P. Wang-Iverson & M. Yoshida (Eds.), *Building our understanding of lesson study* (pp. 85–91). Philadelphia: Research for Better Schools.

Watkins, K. E., & Marsick, V. J. (1993). *Sculpting the learning organization: Lessons in the art and science of systemic change.* San Francisco: Jossey-Bass.

Weiss, I. R., Pasley, J. D., Smith, P. S., Banilower, E. R., & Heck, D. J. (2003). *Looking inside the classroom: A study of K–12 mathematics and science education in the United States.* Chapel Hill, NC: Horizon Research.

Westheimer, J. (1998). *Among schoolteachers: Community, autonomy, and ideology in teachers' work.* New York: Teachers College Press.

Wiggins, G., & McTighe, J. (1998). *Understanding by design.* Alexandria, VA: Association for Supervision and Curriculum Design.

Wiliam, D. (2006, March 17). Re: Changing the research lesson during the teaching. Message posted to the Lesson Study Research Group's Lesson Study electronic mailing list, archived at www.tc.columbia.edu/centers/lessonstudy/listservarchives.html

Wilms, W. W. (2003). Altering the structure and culture of American public schools. *Phi Delta Kappan, 84*(8), 606–615.

Wilson, S. M., & Berne, J. (1999). Teacher learning and the acquisition of professional knowledge: An examination of research on contemporary professional development. In A. Iran-Nejad & P. D. Pearson (Eds.), *Review of research in education* (pp. 173–209). Washington, DC: American Educational Research Association.

Woolf, V. (1976). A sketch of the past. In J. Schuylkind (Ed.), *Moments of being: Unpublished autobiographical writings.* New York: Harcourt Brace Jovanovich.

Yoshida, M. (1999, April). *Lesson study [jugyokenkyu] in elementary school mathematics in Japan: A case study.* Paper presented at the annual meeting of the American Educational Research Association, Montreal, Canada.

Yoshida, M. (2006, March 17). Re: Changing the research lesson during the teaching. Message posted to the Lesson Study Research Group's Lesson Study electronic mailing list, archived at www.tc.columbia.edu/centers/lessonstudy/listservarchives.html

Zederayko, G. E., & Ward, K. (1999). Schools as learning organizations: How can the work of teachers be both teaching and learning? *NASSP Bulletin, 83*(604), 35–45.

Index

CORWIN PRESS